The Homebuilt Winery

THE HOMEBUILT WINERY

43 PROJECTS *for Building and Using Winemaking Equipment*

Steve Hughes

Foreword by Daniel Pambianchi

Storey Publishing

*The mission of Storey Publishing is to serve our customers by
publishing practical information that encourages
personal independence in harmony with the environment.*

Edited by Margaret Sutherland and Philip Schmidt
Art direction and book design by Jessica Armstrong
Text production by Liseann Karandisecky

Photography by © Lara Ferroni, except for © ihsanyildizli/iStockphoto.com: spine,
   © Sean Boggs/ iStockphoto.com: chapter openers, © Lezh/iStockphoto.com: page v,
   © Hans Slegers/iStockphoto.com: page 55, and © Stephen Hughes: pages 67 and 95.
Project illustrations by © Michael Gellatly
Plan drawings by © Stephen Hughes, modified by Jessica Armstrong

Indexed by Nancy D. Wood

Storey Publishing   4867 1258 7/12
210 MASS MoCA Way
North Adams, MA 01247
www.storey.com

Printed in the United States by Edwards Brothers Malloy
10 9 8 7 6 5 4 3 2 1

LIBRARY OF CONGRESS CATALOGING-IN-PUBLICATION DATA

Hughes, Steve, 1953–
  The homebuilt winery / by Steve Hughes.
    p. cm.
  Includes index.
  ISBN 978-1-60342-990-0 (pbk. : alk. paper)
  1. Wine and wine making—Amateurs' manuals.
  2. Wine and wine making—Equipment and supplies. I. Title.
TP548.2.H84 2012
641.2'2—dc23
                    2012009365

To my wonderful wife, Nancy,
who for decades has been my inspiration,
touchstone, and partner in life and wine.

CONTENTS

ACKNOWLEDGMENTS

To all the folks who have inspired me and helped me develop an obsession for making wine and winemaking equipment and facilities, I am truly grateful and raise a glass in salute:

To my dad, Ken, who, when I was a young boy, furnished me with carpentry tools and scraps of wood to pound, saw, and experiment and play with to my heart's content. He started taking me, at the young age of seven, to work with him building houses and mentored me as I followed in his footsteps, starting my own construction company. His patience, love, and inspiration have been the stuff of stories, legends, and laughter.

To my mom, Therese, who taught me to never say never, that there is no such thing as "can't," and to pursue the things I wanted in life. She is my biggest fan and supporter, and she still works the crusher and bottling lines in our little garage winery.

To my beautiful daughters and dutiful assistants, Adrian and Kelly, for picking tons of grapes with me, working the equipment, and relishing the joy of life and love over a glass of wine with me.

To all my compadres on the home winemakers' web forum Winepress.us, who put up with my questions and comments, and who have helped me immensely to make better wine than I ever could have without them.

To all my dear friends who have sacrificed their time and energy working to help me make (and drink!) wine, including the Neighbors of 171st Street, Blondes with Guns Lane, the wacky Kyle's Krazy Klub, and Adrian and Kelly's many friends who followed them into our wine world to help immeasurably.

And to you, my readers, may this book bring more satisfaction and solutions to your winemaking lives.

Cheers!
— Steve Hughes

FOREWORD

WINEMAKING HOBBYISTS ARE A CRAFTY BUNCH! We are passionate about making wine because we derive immense pride and satisfaction from using raw materials to create something with our own hands. Winemaking allows us to express our artistic talent and proudly share the rewards with our family and friends, and that's why we prefer to build rather than buy. In our pursuit of self-sufficiency, we build all kinds of contraptions — what some call "toys," but we prefer to call "tools of the trade" — to simplify our winemaking or to solve specific problems or needs.

In addition to building a cellar from the ground up (literally, from foundation to framing to wall finishing and installing cooling units), I've been known to build a few contraptions: punch-down tools, barrel racks, and a disgorging freezer. To get extra oak mileage, I've even taken barrels apart for reconditioning. Although I researched my projects extensively, most were created from mental plans developed from all the ideas I had gathered. Many were ill-conceived, and so I've made a few mistakes along the way. I paid dearly in wasted energy and material.

My biggest frustration was the huge void in the literature, and even on the Internet. There have been countless books written on the art of winemaking, but there are no comprehensive books or reliable Internet resources on building projects for winemaking equipment, that is, until now. This book fills that void. As Steve states, "This book is not about making wine, it is about making your winery." And it delivers on his objective "to provide effective solutions for the dilemma of obtaining the necessary equipment and maximizing the use of it." And that's Steve's motto: every problem has a solution, and every solution is the result of thorough, careful consideration of alternatives.

Steve brings his craftsmanship as a talented woodworker and hobbyist together with his passion for winemaking and flair for writing in this practical guide that will help you build 43 of the most useful, tried-and-true projects. From the simple to the more elaborate, from building a crusher-destemmer and press to home wine laboratory equipment, and from bottling equipment to building a cool cellar with racks and bins that would be the envy of any wine enthusiast, you'll find it all here, meticulously detailed with step-by-step instructions, plans, and diagrams.

Even if you are already a craftsperson who has built wine-related projects, you'll find some gems in this book, such as the "topping up" devices for eliminating ullage and the four-spout bottle filler. I know I'll be building and adapting the transfer gun (used with a vacuum pump) for racking wine between barrels, and making my own silicone bungs from all those leftover tubes of silicone caulking. Why had I not thought of that?

Steve has thought of everything for aspiring and advanced winemakers alike — he even tells you how to build a simple yet effective fruit fly trap, guaranteed to come in handy when these pests start invading your fermenting grape juice. If you are a vineyardist, Steve has some handy projects for you too. He shows you how to set up a cutting propagation bed and a vineyard trellis with drip irrigation. And for when you're not making wine, Steve has included some projects, such as the "winedirondack" garden chair and classy winery stool, both built from oak barrel staves to help you relax and enjoy the fruits of your labor.

Steve is a professional building and construction consultant, so you can be sure that his projects are well thought out and cleverly designed for simplicity, usability, efficiency, and durability. How clever are his ideas? Check out the design for the chromatography chamber or rinser-sparger. Rest assured, though, that you need not be a master carpenter or expert craftsperson; you need only basic woodworking skills, a few power tools, materials that are readily available at a good hardware store, and a desire to accomplish fun projects.

If you needed any motivation to dust off those power tools and put them to good use, this book provides the inspiration to energize you and guide you through building exciting wine-related projects. With the high cost of winemaking equipment, you'll save a bundle in the process and quickly realize how smart an investment this book is.

I just wish I had such a resource when I first started building my home winery; it would have saved me a lot of headaches and aggravation, not to mention wasted time, materials, and money. With *The Homebuilt Winery,* I'm now equipped to address old winemaking equipment problems that I never got around to fixing and to build new projects that are sure to simplify my work . . . and impress my friends and family.

— DANIEL PAMBIANCHI
Author, winemaker, and woodworker

INTRODUCTION

MAKING WINE IS A MAGICAL PROCESS. The transformation of grapes to a fine bottle of mouthwatering, teeth-reddening, smile-producing joy is a pastime that is relished by hundreds of thousands of artisan and home winemakers across the globe. These craftspeople, these *garagistes*, often make outstanding wine, in progressive and experimental ways, using rudimentary equipment, in small facilities. They love a challenge and are not afraid to try a new concept for the betterment of their "children." They have a can-do spirit and frequently not only make fine wine but also are creative in many other aspects of their lives.

There are countless good books written by excellent authors that inform and inspire us as winemakers, offering recipes, techniques, formulas, and protocols for making high-quality wines at home or in small wineries, and I encourage my readers to purchase a good number of them to create a wine library of sorts. This book, however, is not about making wine. This is about making your *winery*, whether in a closet, a kitchen, a basement, a garage, or some other special place that serves as your wine production center. In order to make good wine, some very specialized equipment is necessary. And this equipment can be prohibitively expensive and hard to justify for making small batches of wine for the hobbyist. Even if you are able to get a special deal on some of this equipment, much of it is large and space-consuming, while being used only for short periods of time each year.

The goal of this book is to provide very effective solutions for the dilemma of obtaining the necessary equipment and maximizing the use of it. By building much of the equipment needed to make high-quality wines, you not only save thousands of dollars that you can then put into quality raw materials, but you can also have the enjoyment of constructing some fun projects. And with careful analysis of your spaces and facilities, you'll discover a number of ways to efficiently organize and construct your winery, your lab, and your cellar.

You don't need advanced carpentry or metalworking skills to build the winery and winemaking equipment in this book. A basic understanding of some carpentry concepts will be helpful, encompassing simple rules such as "measure twice, cut once"; how to use a saw; how to support your workpiece in such a way that you can stay focused on the tool, rather than maneuvering the workpiece; and so forth. I'll provide some tips for the craftsman/*garagiste* to help make the projects a little bit easier. The tools you should need to build any of the projects are basic to any home workshop (see below for a list of tools for your tool kit).

While keeping in mind that winemaking runs a gamut of methods, materials, and sources, this book discusses the home winery primarily from the standpoint of making wine from scratch using grapes. If you're a kit, juice, or country winemaker, you'll still find valuable information here, as well as lots of great equipment and organizational tips that will enhance your winemaking experience. Winemakers and *garagistes*

from beginner to advanced can use this book to create a fully functional and well-equipped home winery, whether they're building everything from scratch from the plans given here or they're just filling in the missing pieces until the budget allows for upgrading to the big, fancy, shiny (expensive) new tool.

There's a lot of satisfaction in crafting fine wines and successfully building equipment that improves your capabilities. With just some of these pieces of hand-built equipment, you can thrill your friends and expand your winemaking prowess. Be safe, have fun, and enjoy the fruits of your endeavors.

Happy winemaking!

THE WINE BOTTLE RATING SCALE

Some of the projects in this book are more technical than others, and in these cases it's best to have some experience using the suggested tools. I've provided a Wine Bottle difficulty rating for each project on a scale of one to five, with one filled bottle being very easy and five being fairly technical.

BASIC TOOL KIT

Here's a list of some of the basic tools you should have for the projects in this book. In any project, of course, some tools can be substituted for others, so this isn't an exhaustive list, nor are all of the tools required.

- » Square
- » Level
- » Chalk line
- » Hammer
- » Wrenches and pliers
- » Screwdrivers (standard and Phillips)
- » Hacksaw
- » Caulking gun
- » Clamps
- » Vise
- » Painting equipment
- » Sawhorses (I like the plastic folding type)
- » Electric drill with drill and screwdriver bits
- » Jigsaw (saber saw)
- » Circular saw
- » Miter saw/chop saw
- » Table saw
- » Sander
- » Router

A Word about Tool Safety

As someone who has used hand and power tools nearly all of my life, I have a huge respect for the damage that can result from using a tool improperly, pushing a tool beyond its limits, or a split second of distraction. Once when I was just a young boy, working with my dad and uncle in their homebuilding business, I hit my thumb with my little hammer. Uncle Russ saw me do it, and while I was shaking my hand in pain, he gave me my first tool safety lesson: "The best way to keep from hitting your thumb is to hold the hammer with both hands."

I could write a whole book on tool safety, but we want to get to work building your winery. So I'd just like to offer some well-regarded tips to take to heart when working with hand and power tools and with some of the materials used in the projects herein.

1. *Use appropriate personal protection gear* including safety glasses, earplugs, respirators or dust masks, gloves, and attire for working with various materials and tools. Each tool's instruction manual will have specific recommendations.

2. *Use the tools as they were intended.* An employee of my dad's once rigged up a saw blade to an electric motor and used it to cut all the wood to build a cabin by holding onto the motor with his hands. That's *not* what I'm talking about here.

3. *Anticipate.* Consider what could happen if a workpiece jams, jumps, or twists against the tool *before* you perform the task. Be prepared for such eventualities, because it *can* happen at any time, and you need to be ready. If you're using a tool for the first time, practice with it to learn how it responds and performs and understand its limitations.

4. *Keep your body parts well away from the cutting or moving part of the tool.* Again: Anticipate. This may sound obvious, but I've seen folks push a drill through a workpiece and into their hand, slash their thumb when changing a router bit, accidentally grab (and flip) the power switch when a plugged-in router started to tip, slide a tiny piece of wood through a table saw with their fingers within ½ inch of the blade, and shorten their fingers with the blades of a jointer. My stomach wrenches just thinking about it. Please respect the power of the tool and the impact that a careless mistake can have. Give the cutting edges a wide berth.

5. *Read the labels.* Many products are very safe to use *if used properly*. However, if they're used improperly or unsafely, they can cause severe injury or even death. Read the directions and the warnings on the labels so that in the event that, say, you accidentally ingest some acetone ("looked like a martini to me"), you at least have a chance to save your own life.

With all that scary stuff past us, let's get on with building your winery and making some great wines!

CHAPTER ONE

THE HOME WINERY
An Overview

WINEMAKING AT HOME CAN BE A LOT OF FUN and immensely satisfying, and it can be a big mess. If set up well, your winemaking space — your winery — will be efficient and organized, allowing all the functions of winemaking to take place in an environment that is pleasant for you and is the ideal ambience for the wine itself.

Space Requirements

You can make wine in any number of places in your home, including the kitchen, a seldom-used bedroom or bathroom, the laundry room, the basement, the garage, or even a garden shed. The first thing to do is to analyze the spaces in your home and evaluate their potential for accommodating the necessary tasks and storage facilities. You may be spending a fair amount of time in your winery, so be sure your final decision on where to put it also takes into consideration your own personal comfort.

The amount of space you'll need for your winery will depend on how much wine you plan to make. Conversely, the amount of wine you're able to make will be limited by the space available. Efficiency in equipment storage and container management, as well as proximity to a good source of running water and drains, will help optimize the space and increase your winemaking capacity. It's also helpful to have equipment that can perform more than one task.

WINERY WORKFLOW

The tasks that are going to take place in your winery include:

» Crushing, destemming, and pressing

» Fermentation

» Racking wine off the sediment (lees)

» Aging

» Lab analysis

» Bottling

» Cleaning

Crushing and Destemming

If you're making wine from grapes, a crusher-destemmer is a key piece of equipment. After sorting the grapes, you'll put them in the crusher. The crusher breaks open the grapes, releasing a lot of grape juice and crushed skins. There will be spills, splashes, splatters, and little grape berries being squashed under your feet. With the destemmer attached, you'll remove the stems from the crushed grapes and deposit them into another bin destined for the compost heap.

Crushing and destemming is a task best suited for the outdoors, on your *crush pad,* which can be any patch of lawn, patio, driveway, or other area that will clean up easily, or even an open garage with a floor that can be hosed out. Be sure to have an adequate water supply (with a hose and nozzle) and an appropriate power supply to run the crusher-destemmer (unless you're using a fully manual crusher-destemmer).

If your crush pad is paved, it's a good idea to lay down a tarp to protect the concrete from grape juice stains. I've found that a 9 × 12-foot blue tarp works well and is less slippery than the plastic Visqueen-type tarps. However, if you like the idea of an artistic grape-stained patio, consider the tarp an optional piece of equipment.

After crushing, you will transfer the *must* (crushed grapes, skins, and juice that will become wine) into a fermentation container, whether by gravity or other means. The method you use to transfer the must will depend on how much wine you'll be making at a time.

At the high end of the price range are *must pumps;* they are very expensive and overly productive for the relatively small volumes of home winemakers. On the other end of the spectrum, you can simply scoop the crushed grapes into buckets and pour them into your fermenters, though I don't recommend this method. For small batches, crushing directly into the fermenter may also work. A middle-range option is to place a bin below the crusher-destemmer to capture the crushed grapes (a 25-gallon Rubbermaid Roughneck rectangular bin, which I prefer, is large enough for about 125 pounds of crushed grapes. Setting the bin on a homemade dolly would allow for easy transport; you can roll the bin over to a fermenter and scoop out the must. This system equals or beats the speed of must pumps and gives you a workout as well.

Rubbermaid Brute Container (left) and Rubbermaid Roughneck Container (right)

Cold Soaking

Cold soaking is a technique some wine-makers use to improve the color and enhance the fruit forwardness of their wines by crushing the grapes and then cooling down the must to about 40°F for up to a week before adding the yeast culture. If you suspect one of these aspects may be lacking in your fruit, cold soaking may be worth considering. However, it's important to understand that cold soaking can be a risky proposition if temperatures aren't properly maintained. Results can vary, and it is recommended that the winemaker ventures into this process cautiously and diligently. Spoilage organisms, like mold, can quickly take over a fermenter if it's left unprotected.

Fermentation

Fermentation of both red and white wines is best done under monitored temperature control. Whites tend to enjoy long, slow, cool ferments, while reds typically are fermented with warmer temperatures. Your winery must provide the proper ambience for your specific goals. Chapter 2 goes into more detail on controlling temperatures for fermentation. What you need to consider here are the space requirements and procedures performed in your winery to facilitate a good, thorough fermentation.

Your fermentation containers can range from 1-gallon jugs to 4 × 4-foot macro bins to large stainless steel variable-volume tanks. The containers you select will depend on batch sizes and wine types, but be sure they

COLD SOAKING GENERAL GUIDELINES

If you want to try cold soaking, start by educating yourself thoroughly on the process and be mindful of these general guidelines to avoid some of the most common pitfalls:

» Finish the crush of the grapes and place the must in the fermenters along with enough dry ice to cool the must down to refrigerator temperature (about 40°F or lower) to inhibit oxidation and microbial growth.

» Monitor the levels of dry ice carefully, adding more as needed, for the desired duration of cold soaking. Leaving the must at refrigerator temperature extracts water-soluble tannins and additional color from the skins. When the cold soak has yielded the desired result, warm the must rapidly to a temperature suitable for fermentation, and inoculate the must with your selected yeast strain.

» Develop and follow a sulfite regimen to preserve the uninoculated must and enhance the performance of selected yeast strains.

» Consider container management (having the right size and quantity of empty containers available), insulation and coverings for the vats, and sources of dry ice prior to obtaining your grapes. Required equipment may include blankets, a freezer, a fan to blow out carbon dioxide gas, and heavy gloves (dry ice quickly burns skin, so always wear gloves when handling it).

are "food grade" or rated NSF approved. To begin, consider the number of different types of wines you'll make, when you'll start them, and the quantity of must that you'll ferment for each. For grape wines, a rough rule of thumb is that 10 pounds of fruit will make 1 gallon of must. So if you have 100 pounds of grapes to crush, plan on a fermenter that will handle 10 gallons of crushed grapes, skins, and juice. For the container size, I recommend adding 25 to 50 percent capacity over the anticipated must volume. Therefore, 10 gallons of must requires at least a 12½- to 15-gallon fermenter.

For red wines, expect to perform regular punch-downs — pushing down the cap of drying skins that float to the surface as fermentation progresses. You will need room to work around your fermenters with a punch-down tool and a convenient place for cleaning the tool afterward. I like to keep a small bucket near the fermenters with the punch-down tool in it for easy access and transport to the sink or hose for cleaning.

You'll quickly develop a domino routine of punching down one fermenter, removing the cover of the next and placing it on the prior one, punching, moving the cover of the next, and so on. Punching down will be messy. You'll have spatters, skins and berries, and lots and lots of fruit flies around your fermenters. The cleaner you can keep your fermentation area, the better control you'll have over the fruit flies. Wipe up any spills immediately, and cover your fermenters with towels, heavy fabric, or the hard plastic lids that are available with some fermenters to keep the bugs at bay and to allow the escape of carbon dioxide.

> Whites tend to enjoy long, slow, cool ferments, while reds typically are fermented with warmer temperatures.

Red wines are typically fermented at warmer temperatures, above 70°F. If you're making wine in regions that experience cooler fall temperatures, you may need to provide some heat over and above the natural rise in temperature that the yeast provides. You can do this in any number of creative ways, and we'll discuss the issue in more detail in chapter 2. What you need to consider now are the logistics for providing that heating infrastructure, including electricity, thermostats and thermometers, insulating blankets, and even fermentation chambers or closets. Your options should be cost- and space-commensurate with the volume of wine you're expecting to produce.

Controlling temperature for the cool fermentation of white wines requires a totally different approach, and you should keep the reds and whites separate so you can manage the fermentation rate you want for each type. We will discuss a number of methods for controlling cool fermentation in chapter 2, but for starters, you will need room for water baths, chillers, and other cooling devices that will enhance your white wines' progress and prevent stuck fermentation.

Pressing

Pressing the skins is also a messy task, best suited to your crush pad. With both red and white wines, you'll be pouring, pumping, scooping, or shoveling the must into the press and applying a lot of pressure to squeeze all the goodness from the grapes. When the press is in operation, it's common for juice to squirt out the sides of the basket and for the press pans to overflow. A tarp beneath the press is a great help in minimizing the mess and facilitating cleanup. We'll discuss pressing further in chapter 2, including complete instructions for building and operating your own press.

Most commercially available presses take up a lot of space, being about 2 feet or more in diameter and up to 5 feet tall. They are also heavy and awkward to move around. Commercially available presses come in two main types — ratchet and bladder. The ratchet press features a basket with wood staves spaced about ¼" apart to hold the must. A long threaded rod extends up from the press pan through the middle of the basket. A ratcheting lever is threaded onto the rod, over a wood press plate. When the lever is pulled back and forth, it pushes the plate down, squeezing the juice from the grapes. The juice exits via a spout into whatever container you've

Transferring the crushed must to the press can be done by scooping it with a kitchen saucepan.

*Wine that drains through the press before being squeezed from the skins is called **free run**. Free run will make up 50 percent to 75 percent of your total wine volume.*

placed next to the press. The grape skins remaining in the basket are compressed into a disk called the *pomace cake*.

A bladder press (the kind that many home winemakers use) looks similar to a ratchet press, although typically the basket is made of stainless steel mesh. In the center of the basket is an inflatable rubber bladder. As the bladder inflates (being filled with compressed air or water), it presses the skins outward against the basket, rather than down, as with the ratchet press. The advantage of the bladder press is that the skins are pressed against a larger surface area, usually resulting in a thinner pomace cake and greater efficiency (a larger ratio of surface area to volume of pressing). Disadvantages of a bladder press versus a ratchet press are that it is more expensive, it's a little more difficult to remove the pomace, and it requires either a compressor or a hose and spigot nearby. A bladder press is also less able to handle small batches — it needs to be filled to the top of its basket to be effective. (You can process a small batch by inflating the bladder gradually as you fill the basket, but this takes some finesse.) Also, if you use water to inflate the bladder, you have to drain it when you're done, which takes up precious pressing time, and if for some unexpected reason the bladder ruptures, the wine can be ruined.

Another type of press, which is less commercially available, is a hydraulic press. Its basic concept is the same as that of the ratchet and bladder press, except that a hydraulic mechanism is used to exert the pressure rather than a ratchet or bladder. A very effective hydraulic press can be made with commonly available materials and equipment. In chapter 2 we'll discuss how to build a folding, rolling hydraulic press that will easily handle the legal limit of wine that home winemakers are allowed to make.

Carbon Dioxide

Carbon dioxide management should also be a concern for the home winemaker. If you're making wine in a confined space, keep in mind that your desired result is yeast converting sugar into alcohol and carbon dioxide (CO_2). CO_2 is what we exhale as a by-product of our biological functions, and it can become suffocating if the space we're occupying is overwhelmed by it. Make sure you have adequate ventilation for your fermenting functions. A closet of fermenting wine can quickly become full of toxic gas.

Fruit Flies

The nemesis of most wineries is the fruit fly. These little buggers can get almost anywhere and can sniff out fruit and wine within minutes. They can destroy a batch of wine if uncontrolled. There's nothing grosser than finding maggots crawling around in your fermenter. And they are prolific. In her short life span, a female fruit fly can lay 500 to 800 eggs. Needless to say, controlling fruit flies will make your winemaking experience (and that of your friends and family) much more enjoyable.

Fruit fly control begins with keeping your winery and equipment very clean. Wipe up spills, drips, and dribbles promptly with a squirt of 1,000 ppm (parts per million) potassium or sodium metabisulfite solution mixed with citric acid. Once flies begin to proliferate, a fruit fly trap or two is very handy. Sticky flypaper rolls can be effective traps; they'll be even more effective if you leave a small glass of wine next to each roll.

You can also make a simple, effective fruit fly trap from a 2-liter plastic bottle. Drill a small hole in the cap of the bottle, and then cut off the top portion of the bottle, at the shoulder. Fill the bottom with a bit of wine and a couple drops of dish soap, and insert the top, inverted. Tape the cut edges together. You'll have a nice little fruit fly farm in no time!

Sanitation

The primary tool for sanitation in my winery is hot running water. Establishing a convenient setup for rinsing carboys, bottles, hoses, and tubing with hot water is the first step in keeping your equipment clean and long-lasting. A deep sink is a great asset, although a kitchen sink will work just fine. Ideally, a home winery has a stainless, deep, double sink with an adjacent drain board and a wall-mounted faucet that can be connected to a short piece of garden hose, along with a variety of nozzles and sprayers. This sink can serve double duty as a site for soaking and removing labels from bottles scavenged from restaurants, friends, and recycling stations. (We'll talk more about label removal techniques in chapter 7.)

Due to the unavoidable overflow and splashing of the wines in the process of winemaking, the ideal setup also includes a floor drain, especially in a basement winery. A floor drain that is connected to a sewer line or septic system must be installed according to local plumbing codes; improper piping can allow sewer gas to fill

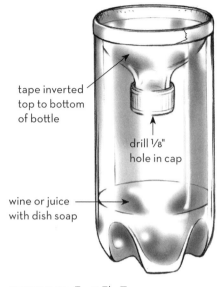

tape inverted top to bottom of bottle

drill ⅛" hole in cap

wine or juice with dish soap

FIGURE 1.01 *Fruit Fly Trap*

the winemaking space with smelly sulfurous gas and flammable methane. In many cases a winery drain may be allowed to discharge into a storm-water drain, which could eliminate costly P-traps, trickle valves, and other plumbing elements. But it should be connected and constructed to keep vermin from using it as a tunnel into the winery. Check with your local health and building authorities for more information on what they will allow.

There are as many opinions about how to clean winery equipment as there are winemakers, but my preference is to thoroughly clean my equipment after each use and then to store it in an enclosed location like a cabinet, drawer, or storage box. Household liquid detergents tend to foam, are difficult to rinse thoroughly, and are frequently scented, so they are not the best choice for cleaning in the winery. I find that unscented sodium percarbonate cleaners (OxiClean is one popular brand name) work very well and are used by many commercial winemakers.

To sanitize equipment before using it, I use solution of potassium metabisulfite (K-meta) and citric acid, made by mixing 8 grams of K-meta and 5 grams of powdered citric acid in ½ gallon of water. I keep a supply in a 16-ounce pump spray bottle. When I'm ready to make wine, I spray some of the solution onto my work surfaces and even into my racking canes and tubing, shake off the excess, and they're ready to use. No rinsing is required. For larger things like carboys, I like to pour about a quart of solution inside, swirl it around to coat all surfaces, and then pour it back into the sanitizer container (use a funnel!). You can reuse this solution several times if you're using it just to give a sanitizing rinse to previously cleaned equipment. Mark your sanitizer container clearly, so you don't accidentally use it to sanitize your wine. I make a label with blue painter's tape, writing on it the name of the solution and the date it was mixed so that I'll know when to toss it out after a few months and mix some new.

You *will* spill wine on tables, counters, racks, and floors, so be sure that these surfaces are easy to clean. While carpeting is nice for cushioning a carboy on the floor, it will get ugly very quickly. Carpet scraps and rubber mats, on the other hand, can be taken outside and hosed down when they get dirty, and they're easy and inexpensive to replace.

Winemaking Log

I highly recommend keeping a very detailed log of each wine you make. A good wine log will allow you to track the daily progress of your wine from vineyard to bottle, and it is a great reference tool for the next time you want to make a similar wine. When, two years after making a great Bordeaux blend, you want to replicate that fantastic vintage, you'll be very happy you kept notes on the simplest details. Which yeast did I use? Did I add malolactic bacteria? Did I adjust the acid? At what temperature did I ferment the wine? And so on.

I have a wine log template that's two pages (see the next page), which I format as a double-sided page (one side on the front and one on the back). I created the template electronically, on my computer, so I can update the form or add information easily. However, I prefer to print out the logs and keep them in my winery in a three-ring binder with a water(wine)proof cover. I wouldn't feel comfortable having my computer near all the activity that goes on in the winery. That said, I wouldn't know what to do without my computer for any number of winemaking tasks, from calculating sulfite additions to making and printing labels.

Each batch or varietal of wine has its own log. The first section deals with the fruit, namely the source of the fruit and any initial data or comments about it. Here I record the conditions under which it was picked or any other information I might want to note. I also like to make note of everyone who helped me with the crush or press, to be sure they get a bottle of this particular wine when it is ready for release.

The next section relates to the fermentation. Here I record the yeast and nutrients

continued on page 16

WINE LOG

Preliminary Name:		Final Name:	
Batch No.:		Label Year:	
		ABV:	

Vineyard/Source		Brix		Price per Lb.	
Address		Date Picked		Total Weight	
CSZ		Date Crushed		Total Cost	
Phone No.		Date Pressed		Cost per Bottle	
Vintage					
Variety(s)					

Comments:

_____

_____

_____

_____

Fermentation

Date	Yeast	Yeast Nutrient 1	Yeast Nutrient 2	MLB	MLB Nutrient 1	MLB Nutrient 2	Oak	Punch Down Avg. x/Day

Analysis	Day	Hydrometer Reading	Temperature	pH	Titratable Acid	SO_2	MLF	Delestage (Date)

Winemaking Notes

Day	Date	Action	Follow-up Action	On (Date)

Adjustments	Date							
	pH							
	Tartaric Acid							
	Calcium Carbonate							
	Sugar							
	Amelioration							
	SO$_2$							
	Other							
	Other							

Bottled	Date			
	Bottle Size			
	Bottle Shape			
	Quantity			
	Corks			

Comments: _____

_____

_____

O   **FERMENTATION CHART**   **X**

°B		°F
27		98
26		96
25		94
24		92
23		90
22		88
21		86
20		84
19		82
18		80
17		78
16		76
15		74
14		72
13		70
12		68
11		66
10		64
9		62
8		60
7		58
6		56
5		54
4		52
3		50
2		48
1		46
0		44
−1		42

°B 1   2   3   4   5   6   7   8   9   10   11   12   13   14   15   16   **°F**

Day

continued from page 13

I used for inoculation and feeding during alcohol fermentation, and the dates I added them. If I use malolactic strains, oak augments, or other additives, I'll note it in this section, along with the date I added them. For red wines or fruit wines, I'll note the average number of times I punched down the cap.

Next is the analysis section, where I record the conditions of the wine from fermentation and bulk aging right up until bottling. It gives a quick picture of the transition of the wine from crush through finish and allows for easy analysis of what might need to be adjusted and when.

Following the analysis section is a notes section where I can track all my actions and adjustments and note what I'll need to do next and when to do it. For example, for one batch I might note, *"October 5th: Inoculated with yeast and nutrient."* My follow-up might be *"Add malolactic bacteria on October 15th."*

Page 2 of the wine log allows me to annotate the various adjustments or additions I make over the course of the batch. Below that I can record the bottle sizes, types, quantity, and closures I used. Then there's room for additional comments that may be important to the wine record.

At the bottom of the log, I like to track the progress of the fermentation in chart form. Each time I check the Brix and temperature of the wine, I'll make a corresponding dot or X on the chart, marking that information for that given day. The lines plotted from the data track the progress of the fermentation and can be helpful in predicting a slow or stuck fermentation.

Equipment Lists

You could purchase a starter equipment kit that will get you on your way to making wine from juice, concentrates, or kits. Typically the equipment kit will have a 6½- to 8-gallon bucket and lid, a carboy, some plastic tubing, a racking cane, and a number of other basic essentials like bottle brushes, a hand corker, and cheap corks. Such an equipment kit is great for someone who isn't sure where to begin, but by educating yourself, being selective, and buying the right equipment for your planned advancement through the winemaking journey, you could save a few bucks and avoid acquiring equipment you'll never use.

The following lists outline the recommended equipment that you'll want to have access to in your winery, organized for beginner, intermediate, and advanced home winemakers. By comparing these lists, and taking into consideration your goals of advancing in the hobby, you can evaluate whether you should skip purchasing some of the basic pieces of equipment in favor of buying an upgraded version or making the equipment yourself. Items listed in bold are those you'll find plans for in this book.

Beginner (up to 30 gallons per year)
EQUIPMENT LIST

- [ ] 8-gallon bucket fermenter
- [ ] Two 5-gallon glass carboys
- [ ] Two 6-gallon glass carboys
- [ ] Airlocks — one per carboy, plus one extra
- [ ] **One-hole bungs (see page 90; variation of silicone bungs)**
- [ ] **Hydrometer (see page 92; triple-scale recommended)**
- [ ] Hydrometer jar
- [ ] 5/16" or 3/8" plastic tubing
- [ ] Potassium metabisulfite
- [ ] **Bottle filler (see page 139; four-spout version recommended for higher production volumes)**
- [ ] Strainer
- [ ] Bottle corker
- [ ] Corks
- [ ] Bottles
- [ ] Bottle brush
- [ ] Long plastic spoon
- [ ] **Bottle tree (see page 125)**
- [ ] Autosiphon or **siphon pump (see page 61)**
- [ ] Pump spray bottle

- [ ] Several sizes of glass jars with lids
- [ ] Measuring spoons
- [ ] ½-gallon plastic bottles
- [ ] Turkey baster
- [ ] Funnel
- [ ] Wine glasses
- [ ] Paper towels
- [ ] Rags
- [ ] Sponge
- [ ] Broom
- [ ] Mop
- [ ] Corkscrew
- [ ] **Log book (see page 14),** pens, and pencils
- [ ] Blue masking tape
- [ ] Felt-tip marker
- [ ] Sink
- [ ] Garden hose and nozzles
- [ ] Scissors
- [ ] Utility knife
- [ ] Steel wool pads
- [ ] Two plastic racking canes

Intermediate (up to 175 gallons per year)
EQUIPMENT LIST

✳ *All of the beginner equipment (see page 17) plus:*

- ☐ Rubbermaid Brute fermenters
- ☐ **Crusher (see page 24)**
- ☐ **Destemmer (see page 30)**
- ☐ **Dolly (see page 56)**
- ☐ **Press (see page 36)**
- ☐ **Punch-down tool (see page 48)**
- ☐ Wine thief
- ☐ Larger hoses
- ☐ A small barrel or two
- ☐ More carboys
- ☐ **Oak augments (see page 193)**
- ☐ **Silicone bungs (see page 89)**
- ☐ More air locks

- ☐ **Lab support stand (see page 97)**
- ☐ 10 ml and 25 ml pipettes
- ☐ Pipette bulb
- ☐ Graduated cylinders
- ☐ Erlenmeyer flasks
- ☐ Beakers
- ☐ Test tubes
- ☐ **Sulfite testing equipment (see page 105)**
- ☐ **Malic acid testing equipment (see page 99)**
- ☐ **Titratable (total) acid testing equipment (see page 96)**
- ☐ pH meter

- ☐ Vacuum pump
- ☐ Inert gas tank and regulator
- ☐ ½" plastic tubing
- ☐ **½" stainless steel racking canes (see page 57)**
- ☐ Chemicals for various tests
- ☐ Double sink with drain board
- ☐ Refrigerator freezer
- ☐ **Rinser-sparger (see page 133)**
- ☐ Bottle cleaner

Advanced and Clubs (175+ gallons per year)
EQUIPMENT LIST

✳ *All of the beginner and intermediate equipment plus:*

- ☐ Stainless steel variable-capacity tanks
- ☐ Power destemmers
- ☐ Must pump
- ☐ Bladder press
- ☐ Larger barrels

- ☐ Stainless steel connectors
- ☐ Laboratory meters
- ☐ Pressure washer
- ☐ Compressor
- ☐ Pallet jack

- ☐ **Wine hoist (see page 70)**
- ☐ Breathable silicone bungs

Wine Storage

A well-organized winery makes for efficient and happy winemaking. "A place for everything and everything in its place" is a good rule to work by. Take a look at the equipment lists on the previous pages, and after deciding what equipment you will need, want, or perhaps grow into, consider where in your winery would be a good place to store it all, keeping in mind that you'll use some pieces, like your crusher, only occasionally, while others, like carboys, lab equipment, and wine bottles, you'll use and move around the winery all year long. Carefully planning how you'll store these items so you can access them easily, without stumbling over other equipment, is key to success.

The majority of the space you'll need for winemaking is for storing the wine, from the first crush to the last sip. You'll need to consider temperature control (protecting the wine from large or rapid temperature swings) as well as access (locating the wine in a place where you can easily test, taste, and monitor it). Home winemakers typically make wine in batches ranging from 1 gallon to 60 gallons. After fermentation, the wine will generally bulk-age in large containers for 6 months to a year or more. These containers can be glass, stainless steel, certain types of plastic, or oak barrels. Anything over 1 gallon can be quite heavy, so plan on developing your storage space to minimize the need to move these containers when they are full. You'll also need unimpeded access to the tops of these containers so that you can insert wine thieves, racking canes and hoses, and additives into them. In considering clearances above your carboys,

Glass and plastic (PET) carboys are preferred and proven containers for aging wines. They're available in 3-, 5-, 6-, 6.5-, and 15-gallon sizes.

Oak barrels are available for the home wine-maker in sizes that range from 1-gallon to full-sized 60-gallon barrels and in different species of oak including American, French, and Hungarian.

keep in mind that airlocks will extend the height required above your carboy, keg, or barrels.

In chapter 3, we'll describe in greater detail the ways in which you can transfer wine from one container to another, as well as devices that you can use to move full containers when it becomes necessary to do so.

Equipment Storage

In addition to storing your wine during bulk aging, you will need a place to store your winemaking equipment. Stored equipment should be easily accessible, so you can get to it when you need it, but it should not intrude upon the winery, your home, or other spaces when it is not in use. Commercially available crushers, destemmers, and presses can take up a lot of space, as can fermenting bins, empty bottles, and containers. In general, do not buy equipment that is larger than what you need to provide efficient processing in the quantities you will be making. For example, sometimes two medium-size presses are better than one really big one.

The Wine Lab

Your wine lab requires a clean counter where you can set up your lab equipment for testing wine samples and store the delicate instruments, glassware, and chemicals. You may want an under-counter refrigerator and closed cabinet storage as well, because some of the chemicals you'll be using have a longer shelf life if kept in a refrigerator, and others keep best if stored away from light. Good organization and identification of the various chemicals and agents are imperative.

The amount of counter space needed ranges from a couple of feet in width to a whole kitchen, depending on your winemaking goals. Chapter 5 has plans for a number of pieces of lab equipment as well as descriptions of the process for each test you'll be performing regularly.

LAB EQUIPMENT

The equipment you might use in your lab includes the following:

» Scale for weighing heavy ingredients like sugar or fruit

» **Gram scale (see page 108)**

» pH meter

» **Lab support stand (see page 97)** with flasks, test tubes, and pipettes

» Aquarium pump

» Magnetic stirrer

» **Chromatography setup (see page 101)**

» Cash still (for very advanced winemakers)

Bottling and Bottle Dressing

Once your wine is ready to bottle, you'll move it to your bottling line. This can be as simple as a hose, tube, and siphon or much more involved, with automatic bottle fillers and corkers, or somewhere in between. In general, the bottling process will involve cleaning and sanitizing bottles, filling them, and inserting the corks. Bottling can be a messy process, so be prepared for overflowing bottles, tubes spraying wine all over, and cleaning carboys or barrels when finished.

I like to combine the total effort of bottling with installing the corks, shrink capsules (or foil caps), and labels all in one operation. Some winemakers don't do that much at once, but with some helpers and proper preparation, it is a fun event and you can get the wine ready to drink just that much faster. We'll describe the bottling line, including how to build and use a bottling machine, labeling jig, and bottle rinser-sparger, in chapter 7.

Cellaring

All the wine is now in the bottle and ready to store. If you use real cork closures, you'll want to store the bottles on their sides. Some winemakers espouse the need to allow the corks to expand for a day or two before laying them down, but with good-quality corks, I have not had one leak in years.

Your cellar should remain at a relatively constant temperature, preferably between 55 and 60°F. The bottles should not be exposed to direct light. And humidity should be kept high enough to avoid cork shrinkage, but low enough to avoid mildew or mold growth on the racks and corks. Air-conditioning usually removes a lot of moisture from the air, so if you're planning to use A/C for cooling your cellar, you'll also need to plan how you will maintain relative humidity around 60 to 65 percent in the cellar.

The size of your cellar will be determined in large part by the type of racking you use. Racks that simply stack bottle on bottle, like a diamond rack, will store more wine than vertical-ladder-style racking. However, when it's time to choose a wine for a special occasion, diamond-style racks don't offer as much versatility as ladder-style racks; you'll have to move bottles around to get down to that perfect bottle.

We'll discuss wine cellars in much more detail in chapter 8, including designs for a number of types of racking arrangements, passive cooling methods, and many other considerations for cellaring wine.

Getting Started

Winemaking is all about process. By evaluating all the tasks you'll need to undertake and planning in advance how and where you'll be doing them, you will have much success in your winemaking endeavors. You'll come to call your winemaking space your "winery," your bottle storage space your "cellar," and the little counter in the laundry room your "laboratory," no matter how small or multifunctional these spaces may be.

So pour yourself a glass of wine, brush the sawdust off your tool belt, and let's get busy building your winery!

CHAPTER TWO

GRAPE & FRUIT PROCESSING

W INEMAKING STARTS WELL IN ADVANCE OF THE FRUIT RIPENING. This is the time to carefully prepare all the equipment, space, and materials you are going to need on that fateful day when your fruit is ready to be converted into wine.

Acquiring Grapes

If you live near a vineyard that will sell grapes to home winemakers, then you are fortunate indeed. Sometimes it takes some schmoozing, begging, and cajoling, but once you make the connection, treat your grower well!

You'll need to pick up your grapes on the day of harvest. (Some growers will crush the grapes for you, relieving you of that step.) Hauling grapes can be awkward, but I have found 25-gallon Rubbermaid Roughneck containers to be helpful in managing the load. Each container holds about 100 pounds of grapes, enough to make about a 6-gallon carboy of wine plus a gallon or so for topping up. I can move the containers in and out of my car more easily than I could larger containers. They have lids that allow them to be stacked, and since they are rectangular in shape, they fit side by side very efficiently. When I'm not using them to haul grapes, I can stack them compactly or use them to store equipment. (I don't, however, use these bins for fermentation, as they are not food grade.)

Upon arrival of your grapes at your crush pad, you're going to sort through the clusters and pull out the MOG (Material Other than Grapes) and then drop or pour the sorted grapes into your crusher, which will gently break open the skins without turning them into a pot of grape mush.

PROCESSING CHECKLIST

These are the items you should have on hand, cleaned and tested to ensure that they are in good working order:

- [ ] Crusher
- [ ] Destemmer
- [ ] Scoops, shovels, or other transfer equipment for moving the fruit from the destemmer to the fermentation containers
- [ ] Press — used at crush for white wines; used when fermentation is nearing completion for red wines
- [ ] Equipment for disposing of the pomace from pressing

- [ ] Fermentation containers and covers
- [ ] Punch-down tool
- [ ] Temperature control setup for the must — cooling for white wines; heating for reds
- [ ] Buckets — food grade
- [ ] Carboys, jugs, and/or barrels
- [ ] Wheeled dollies or hand trucks for moving heavy loaded containers
- [ ] Tarps or other coverings for your crush pad

- [ ] Refractometer and/ or hydrometer
- [ ] Thermometer
- [ ] pH meter
- [ ] Titratable acid testing equipment and reagents
- [ ] Strainer or other sieve for pulling samples of juice from the must
- [ ] Tubing, pumps, and other transfer equipment
- [ ] Rags, towels, sponges, and cleaning agents

In addition to preparing the above items, you'll also want to carefully consider which ingredients or additives you might need to add to your crushed fruit before and during fermentation and make sure they're available:

- [ ] Yeast
- [ ] Yeast starter and nutrients
- [ ] Potassium metabisulfite — both the powdered form and a sanitizing-strength solution combined with citric acid
- [ ] Malolactic bacteria
- [ ] Malolactic starter and nutrients

- [ ] Tartaric acid for increasing titratable acidity or making acidulated water for reducing high sugar levels
- [ ] Calcium or potassium carbonate for reducing titratable acidity
- [ ] Sugar for increasing the °Brix
- [ ] Ice bombs for cooling white wines
- [ ] Dry ice for cold soaking

CRUSHER

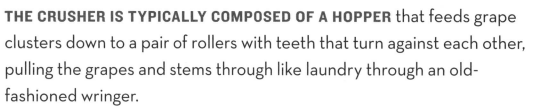

THE CRUSHER IS TYPICALLY COMPOSED OF A HOPPER that feeds grape clusters down to a pair of rollers with teeth that turn against each other, pulling the grapes and stems through like laundry through an old-fashioned wringer.

You can build a crusher with very simple materials available from thrift stores, hardware stores, and lumberyards. The basic mechanism consists of a pair of rolling pins powered by a ½" variable-speed electric drill. This crusher is designed specifically to be paired with a manual destemmer, the plans for which follow this project. Along with the destemmer, my crusher has reliably crushed several hundred pounds of grapes per hour and has run year after year with virtually no problems. Let's get busy.

MATERIALS

- Two 10"-long maple rolling pins with ½" center bore and equal outside diameter (typically 1⅞")
- One 20" length ½" threaded rod
- One 16" length ½" threaded rod
- Four 2" × 2" pieces ⅜"-thick HDPE plastic
- Two 3" × 3" pieces ⅜"-thick HDPE plastic
- Four ½" lock washers

- Twelve ½" flat washers
- Four ½" lock nuts
- Four ½" nuts
- One 4×6-foot sheet plastic laminate (optional)
- One half sheet (4×4-foot) ¾" ACX plywood
- 1 quart contact adhesive (optional; for plastic laminate)
- Twenty 1½" wood screws
- Eight ¾" #3 wood screws

- Sheet metal (untreated steel — not galvanized)
- Four ½" round-head wood screws
- One 2" (+/-) hose clamp

NOTE: *You can obtain HDPE plastic from a plastics supplier, or you can simply use a white plastic cutting board of the appropriate thickness.*

BUILD IT!

1. Cut the pins.

This project gets three filled bottles because of this first step. It takes a lot of concentration, caution, and tool awareness to cut teeth into the rolling pins — so be safe, and keep your fingers away from the saw blades. As you cut these teeth into the pins, the workpiece may want to rotate, so be sure to secure it beforehand. If you have any doubt about your ability to do this, solicit the help of a friend with experience using a table saw. Give him a bottle of wine as a reward (*after* he's done!).

Start by dismantling the rolling pins, unscrewing or pulling off the handles and removing the center rods. Using a nail set or nail, pry out the bushing embedded into the ends of the pins. Verify that the hole through the center of each pin will accommodate the ½" threaded rods, and check to make sure that the holes are relatively centered.

Now let's set up the table saw for cutting the teeth. First, you'll need a carbide-tipped blade in the saw. Then attach a piece of wood to the blade side of the saw fence. Lower the blade below the top of the table. Lock down the fence so that only ³/₃₂" of the blade is situated to the left of the wood fence piece. Mark the edge of the wood fence piece at a point one half the diameter of the rolling pin. Then turn on the saw and raise the blade into the wood fence, cutting up to the mark.

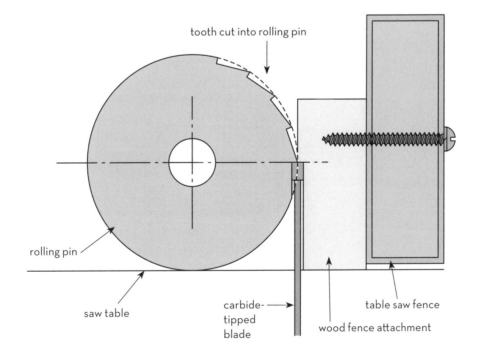

tooth cut into rolling pin

rolling pin

saw table

carbide-tipped blade

wood fence attachment

table saw fence

FIGURE 2.1 *Crusher Roller Table Saw Setup*

Set one of the rolling pins on the saw table, butted up against the wood fence piece. Using push sticks or feather jigs to keep your fingers away from the blade, make the first pass, cutting an L into the side of the pin. (Note: this is when the pin will want to rotate, so be prepared to control it.) This should result in a tooth approximately 3/32" deep and 1/4" in length. Rotate the pin counterclockwise to align the bottom of the vertical cut with the mark on the fence, and make the next cut. Repeat these cuts all the way around the pin. If the last vertical cut is not equal to the others, no worries; the roller will spin just fine.

Repeat the procedure to cut teeth into the second rolling pin. Now you have the hard part behind you, and the fun part can begin.

2. Create the gears.

Shaping the two gear pieces can be a bit tricky, so we've included full-scale templates for making them (see figure 2.2). The templates are based on rolling pins that are 1⅞" in diameter. If yours are larger or smaller, just increase or decrease the size accordingly. Photocopy the template and glue the copies to the 3" × 3" squares of HDPE plastic. Drill the ½" center hole, then cut out the gear teeth with a jigsaw. Clean up the cut edges with a candle flame, singeing the burred edges.

3. Assemble the rollers.

Set the notched rollers side by side on a work surface in front of you, with their teeth oriented to turn toward each other. Insert the 20" threaded rod through the roller on the left and the 16" threaded rod through the roller on the right, pushing the rods through until they extend 2½" out from the far side of the rollers. Then install the HDPE gears on the drive ends (nearer to you) of the threaded rods, and screw the gears into the rolling pins with three 1½" wood screws countersunk into each gear. Install a ½" lock washer on each end of the threaded rods and then a ½" nut. Tighten the nuts well to reduce the chance of the rods spinning while the rollers are stationary. Install two ½" flat washers over the nuts on each end. Now the interior portions of the rollers are done as shown in figure 2.3.

Measure the length of the roller assembly from outer washer to outer washer (rolling pins vary in length); the overall length should be 10⁷⁄₁₆". If necessary, remove the rolling pins and trim them so that the assembly will have this overall length.

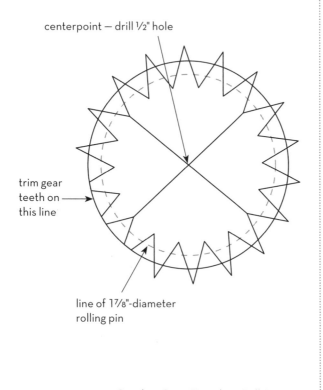

centerpoint — drill ½" hole

trim gear teeth on this line

line of 1⅞"-diameter rolling pin

FIGURE 2.2 *Crusher Gear Template Full Size*

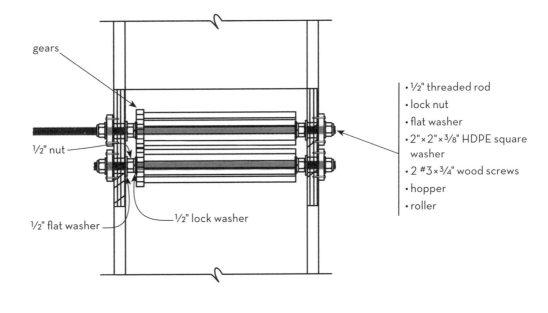

gears

½" nut

½" flat washer

½" lock washer

- ½" threaded rod
- lock nut
- flat washer
- 2" × 2" × ⅜" HDPE square washer
- 2 #3 × ¾" wood screws
- hopper
- roller

FIGURE 2.3 *Crusher Roller Assembly — Top View*

4. Build the hopper.

Now is the time to consider whether you want to line your hopper with plastic laminate (see page 29). While doing so will make cleaning easier, I built mine with just the exposed wood and have had no problems. If you want to laminate the hopper, it's best to laminate the entire half sheet of plywood, on both sides, before making the cuts for the hopper pieces. Using one color on one side and another on the flip side can really add a personal statement to the project! (Note: I do not recommend painting any parts that will be in contact with your grapes. Paint chips in wine are not a good thing.)

Lay out the hopper pieces on the ACX plywood as shown in figure 2.4, then cut them out. Drill the holes (⁹⁄₁₆") for the threaded rod in the two side pieces, as shown. If you'd like to make the spacing of the rollers adjustable, then elongate the hole for the roller with the drive shaft up to ½". (You can do this by drilling two adjacent holes and then just pushing the drill bit sideways while it's spinning, moving it from one hole into the other.)

Drill a ½" center hole in each of the 2" × 2" HDPE squares; these will serve as bushings. Stand one of the side pieces on a table and insert the threaded rods of the rollers through the holes. Install the other side piece at the opposite ends of the roller assemblies. Then put an HDPE bushing over the outside end of each rod, followed by a ½" flat washer and then a ½" lock nut. Keep the lock nuts fairly loose until the rectangular angled end pieces are installed and the bushings are secured in place.

Install the rectangular plywood pieces of the hopper between the angled edges of the side pieces, securing them with 1½" wood screws. If you laminated the hopper, you may want to use some finish washers to make her fancy. Or just countersink the screws so the heads are flush with the laminate.

I've found that for most grapes, the rollers work best when spaced at ⅛", so cut a couple of ⅛" thick spacers and insert them between the rollers. Attach the 2" × 2" HDPE bushing pieces to the hopper with two ¾" countersunk wood screws each. Install a ½" flat washer over the threaded rods outside of the HDPE bushings and then a ½" lock nut, maintaining just enough clearance to ensure free rotation of the rollers.

Cut and bend two pieces of sheet metal as shown in figure 2.5, to form the two gear shrouds. Screw each shroud in place so it covers the gears and nuts of the roller assemblies inside the hopper with a couple of ½" screws.

FIGURE 2.5 *Crusher Gear Shroud*

5. Install the motor.

The motor for this crusher is a ½" variable-speed electric drill. Open the chuck all the way and slip the drill over the long threaded-rod drive shaft. It should seat all the way into the drill with only about ¼" of space between the lock nut and the chuck. If there's more space than this between the chuck and the nut, then shorten the threaded rod as necessary.

To make the drill run constantly at the desired speed (full speed is much too fast) secure the hose clamp over the trigger. You'll probably want to shape the clamp into an oval to better fit the handle of the drill. Tighten the clamp to begin spinning the rollers. When the roller achieves the desired speed, you're ready to start throwing in the grapes! (We'll make a motor mount next as part of the destemmer, so don't turn the drill on just yet or it will spin around.) I've found that one-quarter speed is just about right. I'll describe the process in more detail in the Use It! section of the manual destemmer project (see page 34).

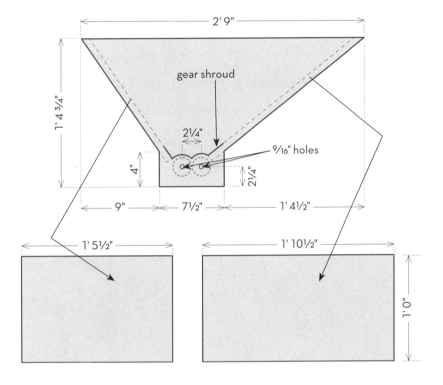

FIGURE 2.4 *Crusher Hopper Assembly — Side View*

APPLYING PLASTIC LAMINATE

Cut out the laminate about ½" larger in each direction than the wood piece to be laminated. Flip the laminate over and apply one thin coat of contact adhesive to both the laminate and the wood surface. Let the adhesive dry until it loses its gloss and is just slightly tacky to the touch. Apply a second light coat of adhesive to both pieces and again allow it to dry until just tacky. Place several thin, clean wood sticks or venetian blind slats in a parallel arrangement across the wood surface. These are temporary spacers that allow you to position the laminate without the two glued surfaces sticking together. Carefully lay the laminate on the sticks so its edges extend ¼" past each edge of the board. Starting at one end, slowly pull out a stick and let the laminate rest gently on the wood. Pull out the next stick, and so on, working toward the other end of the piece. Once all the sticks are out and the laminate is in place, press down the laminate firmly, working outward from the center to eliminate any air bubbles. A final press with a corner of a 2×4 or a laminate roller works well to secure the laminate permanently. Trim the overhanging laminate flush with the board, using a laminate trimmer or a router with a laminate bit. Finally, file the edges of the laminate at a slight bevel, using a fine metal file. This is important to remove razor-sharp edges that result from trimming.

MANUAL DESTEMMER

THE CRUSHER'S COMPANION IS THIS DESTEMMER. As the crushed grapes fall from the crusher into the destemmer, they need to have their stems removed. This can be extremely tedious if you're working by hand, but with this destemmer, you should be able to destem the crushed clusters as fast as your partner sorts and feeds the grapes into the crusher.

MATERIALS

- One 5-foot × 12" sheet 1/8"-thick HDPE plastic
- One 12" × 36" piece 3/4" ACX plywood
- One 8-foot length 1×2 hardwood (oak or maple preferred)
- Ten #6×1" steel wood screws
- One 10½" length 2×10 lumber
- Two 12" × 36" pieces 3/8" ACX plywood
- One 10-foot length 1×4 lumber
- Twenty-six #8×3/4" stainless steel wood screws
- Four 1/4"×2" bolts with nuts and 2 washers each
- One 12" length 2×8 lumber
- One 12" length 2×2 lumber
- One 3-foot length 2×2 lumber

BUILD IT!

1. Prepare the destemmer screen.

Trim the piece of HDPE plastic so that it is ⅛" wider than the crusher and 54¼" long.

On a piece of 8½" × 11" paper, lay out a ¾" × ½" grid centered along the narrow dimension of the paper, with a 1¼" margin on one side. Using a nail set, nail, or center punch, poke holes through the template at alternate grid intersections in each row. Tack the paper to the HDPE with masking tape, 9" in from one end, and transfer the punched hole locations to the plastic with a permanent felt-tip marker. These marks represent the centerpoints of the grid

holes. Move the template down the sheet, aligning the hole alignment points over the last set of holes, marking the centerpoints as you go, until you get to 9" from the other end of the sheet.

Drill a ¾" hole through the plastic at each centerpoint on the HDPE. Now your destemmer screen looks like figure 2.6 and is ready for the screen supports.

2. Build the chute.

The destemmer chute consists of two plywood sides, two plywood screen supports, the screen, and 1×2 screen braces spanning the plywood supports. Cut the screen supports from the ¾" plywood, as shown in figure 2.7. If you're inclined to laminate the sides, do so now (see Applying Plastic

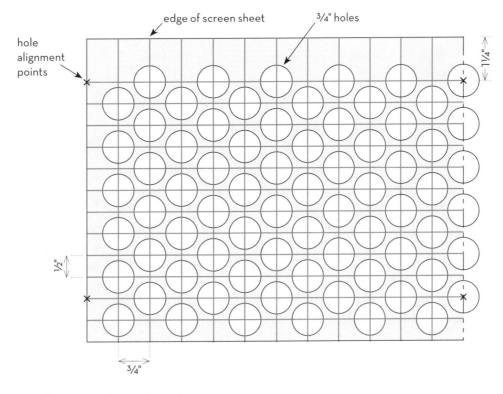

FIGURE 2.6 *Destemmer Screen Layout*

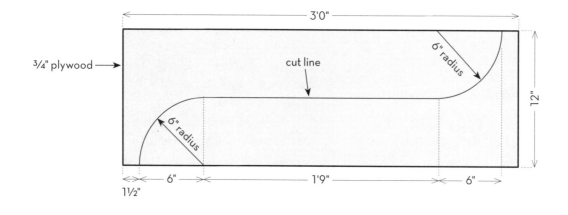

FIGURE 2.7 *Destemmer Screen Support Layout*

Laminate, page 29). Next, cut three 1×2 screen braces to length at 10½". Fasten the braces between the supports at the locations shown in figure 2.8.

Fasten the screen to the supports with screws. It helps to roll the ends of the plastic before trying to form them into curves. Be aggressive; you won't break it. Drill holes and countersinks at 3" on center along the screen, then fasten the screen to the supports with #8 × ¾" stainless steel wood screws, beginning at the outfeed end of the chute.

Cut the destemmer sides from ⅜" plywood, as shown in figure 2.8, and screw them to the outsides of the screen supports. Again, if you want to laminate your destemmer, install the laminate on the inside of the side pieces before attaching them to the supports.

. Cut a 2×10 at 12" long for a support for the crusher's hopper. Bevel one edge to match the hopper's long angled side (at roughly 30°). Install the hopper support by driving a pair of 1½" screws through the plywood sides and into each support end. Cut two lengths of 1×2 at 10⅝". Trim the tops of the 1×2s to match the steep angle of the short angled side (at roughly 45°). Install the 1×2s vertically on the inside of the plywood side pieces, opposite the 2×10 hopper support piece. Test-fit the crusher in this opening; it should fit snugly but be easy to remove. Also ensure that the crusher's drive rod assemblies don't hit the sides of the destemmer. The crusher just sits in the destemmer without any attachments necessary.

3. Install the legs.

To determine the length of the legs, you'll need to have decided upon a receiving bin for the crushed grapes and the dolly you'll use to move it. Set the bin of your choosing on your dolly (see page 73). Measure the height from the floor to the top of the bin, and add 4 inches; this is the length of the legs. Cut the four legs to length from the 1×4. Trim the bottom of each leg at a 10° angle. Trim the top of each leg into a half circle, and drill a ¼" hole in the centerpoint to accept a ¼" bolt.

Using the bottom of a leg as a template, mark a 10° angle on each end of the bottom of the destemmer box to locate

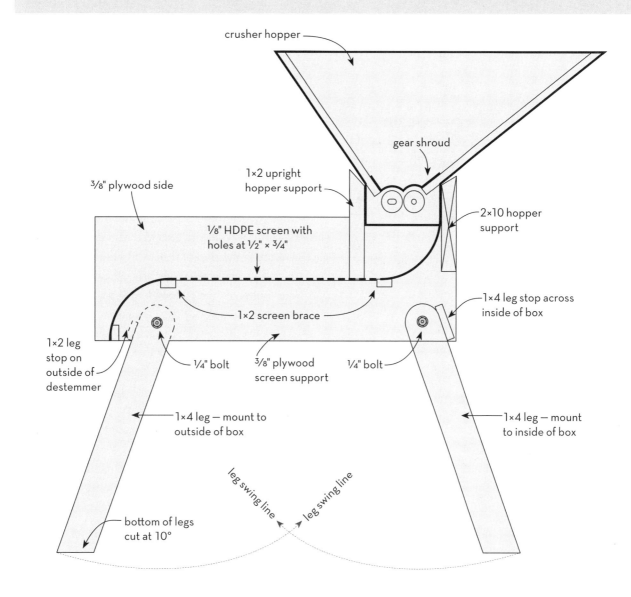

crusher hopper

gear shroud

3/8" plywood side

1×2 upright hopper support

1/8" HDPE screen with holes at 1/2" × 3/4"

2×10 hopper support

1×2 screen brace

1×4 leg stop across inside of box

1×2 leg stop on outside of destemmer

1/4" bolt

3/8" plywood screen support

1/4" bolt

1×4 leg — mount to outside of box

1×4 leg — mount to inside of box

leg swing line

leg swing line

bottom of legs cut at 10°

FIGURE 2.8 *Destemmer Cross Section*

the stops that will hold the legs in place when open. Cut a 10½"-long piece of 1×4 to provide a leg stop for the infeed-end legs. Screw this leg stop into place, aligning it along the 10° angle mark. Install the two back legs tight against the stop, on the inside of the box, using bolts with nuts and washers. On the outfeed end, bolt the remaining two legs into place, mounting them on the outside of the box. Cut two

lengths of 1×2 with a 10° angle on one end. Install these on the outsides of the destemmer box to serve as stops for the front legs once you stand the destemmer up on a flat surface and the legs fit the floor.

Once bolted in place, the legs should be able to fold up flush with the bottom of the destemmer box, one pair on the inside, and the other pair on the outside.

4. Build the motor mount.

The motor mount for the electric drill is made from a piece of 2×8 that is screwed (or clamped) to a 2×2 support fastened to the drive side of the destemmer box. If the drill has an auxiliary handle (the secondary detachable handle found on most ½" drills), it should be attached and pointed in line with the trigger handle.

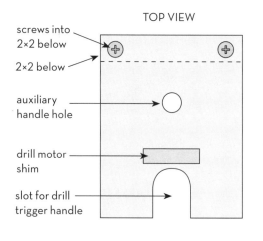

TOP VIEW

screws into 2×2 below

2×2 below

auxiliary handle hole

drill motor shim

slot for drill trigger handle

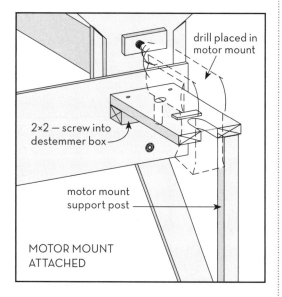

drill placed in motor mount

2×2 — screw into destemmer box

motor mount support post

MOTOR MOUNT ATTACHED

FIGURE 2.9 *Crusher Motor Mount*

With the drill secured to the drive shaft of the crusher and the crusher sitting in the destemmer box, carefully measure the distance from the outside of the destemmer box to the center of the auxiliary handle, as well as the handle's diameter. Transfer these measurements to the 2×8, and drill a hole that will snugly accept the handle. Then measure the distance from the outside of the destemmer box to the back end of the drill, and cut the 2×8 to this length. Cut a notch in the end of the 2×8 to receive the trigger handle snugly on both sides and loosely at the trigger. Install a shim to support the drill body as necessary to keep the chuck in line with the drive shaft of the crusher. Install the motor mount on the drill.

Last, cut a 2×2 motor mount support block, and cut a post that will support the motor mount down to the floor, taking care to keep the drill in alignment with the drive shaft. Screw the support block to the motor mount and through the destemmer box into the 2×2, and screw the post to the outside corner of the motor mount; when you disassemble the destemmer at the end of crush, just pull out the two screws that hold the motor mount 2×8 to the 2×2 support block and loosen the drill chuck from the drive shaft.

USE IT!

Set up the destemmer box with the receiving bin and dolly under it and the crusher set in the hopper supports. Set the drill in the motor mount, and then fasten it to the crusher drive shaft and screw the motor mount to the 2×2 support. I like to plug the drill into a switched cord, which allows me to turn it off and on with a flick of my

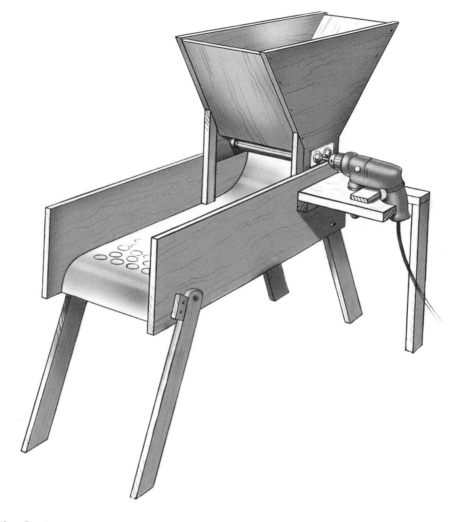

Grape Crusher-Destemmer

thumb. Adjust the speed of the drill with the hose clamp around the trigger and check the rollers for smooth operation.

Begin sorting and feeding the grapes into the crusher and watch with glee as they descend through the rollers and spill down onto the destemmer. Once the grapes are on the destemmer, use a squeegee or stiff broom on a handle to rake the crushed clusters across the screen. Push back and forth until the berries fall into the bin. Take a final pull toward the outfeed

end of the chute to pull the stems into their own basket or garden cart for disposal.

If you're crushing red grapes, once the bin is full, you will roll it over to your fermentation vessel and shovel the fruit in in preparation for starting the yeast on their happy adventure of sugar consumption. For white grapes, the dolly gets rolled over to the press to remove the rest of the juice from the skins before you inoculate the must with yeast. This is the time to give the must its first dose of potassium metabisulfite.

FOLDABLE, ROLLABLE WINE PRESS

THE QUINTESSENTIAL PIECE OF WINEMAKING EQUIPMENT is the press, used for squeezing the last bit of goodness from the grapes. Presses come in all shapes and sizes, but for the purposes of this plan, I've developed a press that will easily handle a ton or more of grapes per year with a minimum amount of work.

I identified three criteria for this design: (1) it needs to be easy and inexpensive to build with commonly available materials; (2) it needs to be as effective as comparably sized, commercially available presses; and (3) due to the lack of space we *garagistes* have for our passion and the fact that the press will be used only one month each year, it needs to be storable in a small space and be multifunctional (see Wine Hoist on page 70 and Four-Spout Bottle Filler on page 139). The press I designed folds up to a svelte 29" wide, 5'7" tall, and 5" deep. With a pair of casters on the legs, you can wheel it around the winery like a hand truck.

The press basket has an outside diameter of 16" and is 18" tall. It has a capacity of just under 13 gallons and is able to hold the skins of 250 pounds of crushed grapes (must). A steady press-and-rest method will result in a pomace cake about 2" to 2½" thick (depending on the variety of grape being pressed). For its mechanics the press relies on a 6-ton hydraulic jack. I recommend using a bottle jack with a screw-out extension that has a total jacking capacity of at least 15".

To simplify the building instructions, I have divided the project into three parts:

» Basket

» Press frame

» Drive assembly

MATERIALS

Basket

- Twenty-five 18" lengths 1×2 hardwood (oak preferred)
- Two Simpson Strong-Tie MSTC52 framing straps (or other steel framing straps of similar weight cut to 52¼" in length)
- Two ¼" × ⅝" pan-head machine bolts with lock nuts
- One hundred ⅝" #10 round-head stainless steel wood screws

NOTE: *For the basket, purchase 1×2 hardwood in increments of 3 feet. This will allow for negligible waste.*

Press Frame

- Two 21⅞" lengths 4×6 lumber (#1 Douglas fir preferred)
- Two 61½" lengths 4×4 lumber (#1 or #2 Douglas fir preferred)
- Four Simpson HUCQ412 joist hangers
- Eighty galvanized joist hanger nails or Simpson SD8 1¼" #8 screws
- One 4×4-foot piece ¾" ACX plywood
- Four pairs 3" butt hinges with ¾" screws
- Twelve 1¼" wood screws
- One 18"-diameter press pan (see note, page 44)
- One 3"×3" piece 24-gauge sheet metal (not galvanized)
- Four ⅝" sheet metal screws
- Two 1"×1½" J hooks
- Four barrel bolts
- Two 2"-diameter fixed rotation casters

NOTE: *Try using #1 Douglas fir for the four members of the press frame; I like its high strength and low cost. Very soft woods like some pines and cedar would not be effective at handling the pressures that you'll be exerting. Most hardwoods, although more expensive, would also be acceptable as well as attractive. Do not use pressure-treated materials for anything that may come near your wine.*

Drive Assembly

- One 4-foot length clear (no knots) tongue-and-groove 2×6 car decking
- One 2-foot length 2×6 lumber
- Twelve 2½" zinc-coated wood screws
- Two 1" black steel plumbing pipe floor flanges (not galvanized)
- One 1" × 3" steel pipe nipple
- One 1" × 7" steel pipe nipple
- One 1" × 12" steel pipe nipple
- Three 1" steel pipe couplings
- One ¾" steel pipe floor flange
- Four ¼" × 2" lag screws
- One ¾" steel close nipple (approx. 1" long)
- One 1¼" × ¾" steel bell reducer
- Four 3/16" × 1½" wood screws
- One ¼" × 1" thumbscrew
- One 6-ton hydraulic bottle jack
- One 17" length 2"-diameter PVC pipe
- One 3½" wood screw
- One 1" wood screw

Basket

BUILD IT!

1. Cut the staves.

Cut the twenty-five 1×2s to each measure 17⅞"; these will become the basket staves. Sand the staves to a nice smooth finish. Measure and mark 1½" from each end of the staves. This marks the location of the steel hoops you'll soon be installing.

2. Prepare the hoop straps.

The Simpson MSTC52 framing straps need to be rolled or bent into a hoop to create the supports for the basket, but it's a good idea to first drill the screw holes and mark the locations of the staves. Lay the straps side by side on a bench. On one strap, make a mark 1⅛" from one end. Starting from that mark, make a mark every 2" along the length of the strap. Use a square to draw lines across both straps at these marks.

Now measure in ¾" from the first mark, and make a mark at this point on the strap's centerline. Starting from that mark, make a mark every 2" along the centerline of the strap; these marks locate the holes for the screws that hold the straps to the staves. Finish by making a mark halfway between the end of the strap and the first mark. Clamp the two straps together and drill holes through both straps with a drill bit just large enough to allow the screws to slip though.

There are a number of ways to shape these flat straps into circles and bolt their ends together, including having a metal fabricator roll them into a hoop, but my plans involve making slight bends at each of the lines marking the edges of the staves. To do this, secure the straps in a vise and bend them 166° at each of the lines. (The marks you've made should be on the inside of the hoops.) You can make an angle gauge by cutting a piece of scrap 1×4 with a chop saw: Cut the end of the piece at 7°, then flip

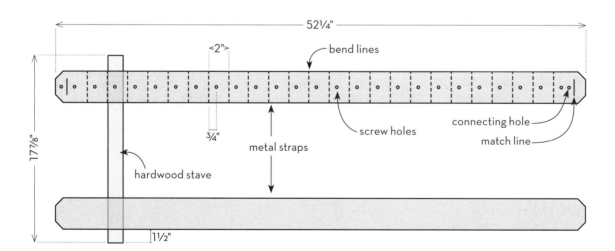

FIGURE 2.10 *Hoop Bending Strap Layout*

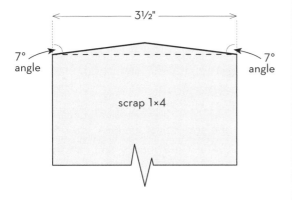

FIGURE 2.11 *Hoop Bending Gauge*

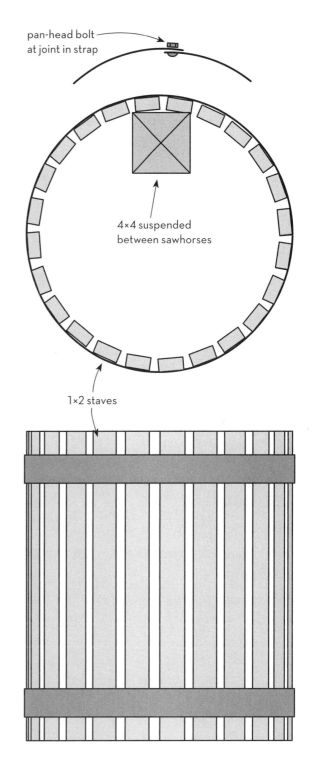

FIGURE 2.12 *Basket Assembly (and Finished Basket)*

it over and cut it again at 7° to create a point forming the angle gauge. The bends in the hoops don't have to be perfect but should be within a degree or two of 14°. You can fine-tune the hoop shape after the strap ends are bolted together.

Once you've made all the bends and each strap begins to look like a hoop, connect the two ends at the match lines with a ⅝" long machine bolt and lock nut. The first bends at each end of the straps should overlap. Align the bends at each end, clamp them together, and drill through the end hole to receive the bolt.

3. Assemble the basket.

To assemble the basket, lay one of the 4×4s of the press frame across a pair of sawhorses. Hang the two hoops on it, with the sections containing their end bolts aligned at the bottom. Slip a 1×2 stave under the straps and on top of the 4×4, with the marks on the stave facing up. Align the stave between a pair of lines marked on the hoops, with the marks on the stave aligned with the outer edges of the hoops. Drill a pilot hole into the stave, taking care not to drill all the way through it; a piece of tape on the drill bit to mark the appropriate depth is helpful. Then drive a 5/8" #10 wood screw though the hole in the strap and into the stave. Leave these screws slightly loose at this point. We'll square up the basket and tighten the screws when all the staves are installed.

Turn the hoops as needed to install staves at the 4 o'clock and 8 o'clock points on the basket, and then install all the remaining staves. The stave installed where the machine bolts hold the straps together will need a little carving to clear the bolt heads.

Remove the new basket from the 4×4 and set it on a flat surface, pressing down to even up the tops and bottoms of the staves and squaring the hoops to the staves. Now tighten all the wood screws, and voilà! The press basket is complete.

Press Frame

BUILD IT!

1. Construct the timber frame.

Now we'll put the press frame together. The basic frame is made of two 4×6 beams at 21⅞" and two 4×4 legs at 61½" (see figure 2.18, page 45). Position a Simpson HUCQ412 joist hanger (beam hanger) upside down at the top of each 4×4 leg, so the 4×6 top beam will sit flush with the tops of the legs. Drive joist hanger nails or Simpson SD8 screws into each hole in the joist hangers, including the triangular holes. (This gives the hanger full strength.) Rout, file, or rasp down the corners of the 4×6 top beam

ends to fit the curve of the hangers, so the beam will sit snugly into the hanger. Once it fits well, slip the beam into the hangers and fasten it to the hangers with the joist hanger nails or SD8 screws.

For the bottom beam, make a mark 16½" up from the bottoms of the legs. Position the two remaining joist hangers right side up on the legs, so the bottom of the lower beam will line up with the marks on the legs, and nail or screw the joist hangers into the legs. Fit this beam to the hangers, as you did for the top beam. Drop the lower beam into the hangers and fasten it with nails or screws in every available hanger hole.

Note that the hangers, being designed for 4×12s, will extend past the 4×6 beams. If the corners are sharp, it's a good idea to file them down to prevent injury.

2. Install the swing-out feet.

Following the template drawing in figure 2.13, cut the four feet from ¾" plywood, and notch the bottoms of the feet as

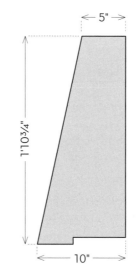

FIGURE 2.13 *Press Feet*

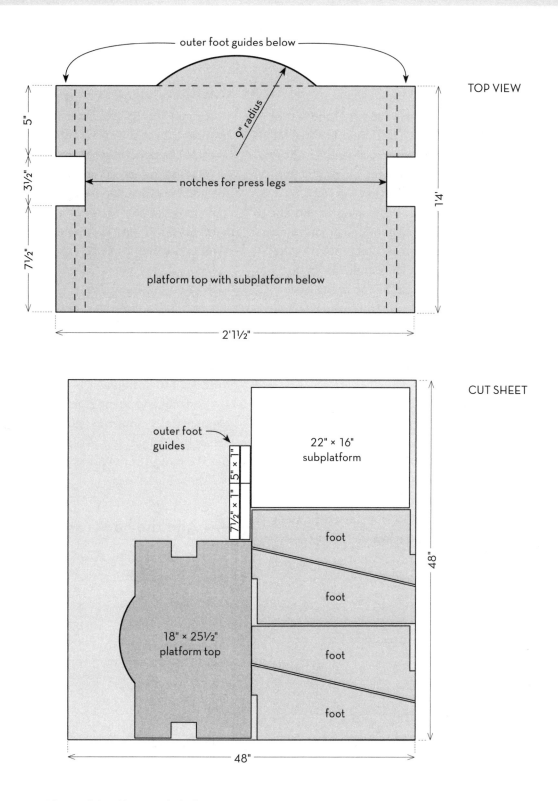

TOP VIEW

outer foot guides below

9" radius

notches for press legs

platform top with subplatform below

5"

3½"

7½"

1'4'

2'1½"

CUT SHEET

outer foot guides

22" × 16" subplatform

5" × 1"

7½" × 1"

foot

foot

18" × 25½" platform top

foot

foot

48"

48"

FIGURE 2.14 *Plywood Cut Sheet and Platform Layout*

shown. These will keep the press from rocking on an uneven crush pad. Sand the feet to the desired finish. Screw two butt hinges to each foot (see figure 2.18). Position the bottom hinge about 1" above the notch, and position the upper one just far enough below the top to clear the bottom of the beam hanger. Keeping in mind that there are two left feet and two right feet, attach the hinges on opposing sides of the feet appropriately. Stand the press frame on a flat, level floor and set one of the feet up against the leg, perpendicular to the beam. Confirm that the top of the foot extends ¾" above the top of the beam. Open the hinges and screw them to the inside face of the press leg. Repeat for the remaining three feet.

3. Build the press platform.

From the ¾" plywood, cut the platform top to size at 25½" × 18", and cut the subplatform to size at 22" × 16". In the platform top, cut out notches to fit around each leg, as shown in figure 2.14. Then fasten the subplatform to the platform top, using construction adhesive and 1¼" wood screws evenly spaced across the platform. Place the platform between the press legs and trace along the sides of the beam hangers. Using a jigsaw, cut slots in the platform to allow it to slide down easily over the hangers.

Center the 18" press pan on the platform, and trace the curve of the pan along the front edge of the platform top. Mark an intersecting line across the length of the platform top, 2" in from the front edge. Cut along this line, around the curve where it intersects the line, to create the curved front of the platform (see figure 2.14).

From the ¾" plywood, cut two outer foot guides to size at 7½" × 1" and two to size at 5" × 1". Glue and screw these outer foot guides to the outside edges of the platform bottom. They'll create slots for the swing-out feet when the platform is lowered into position.

Last, cut and shape a piece of 24-gauge sheet metal as shown in figure 2.15. Then screw this "spout" to the platform top, under the mouth of the press pan, with four ⅝" sheet metal screws.

4. Add the hooks and casters.

So that you can stow the platform when the press is in storage, install a 1" × 1½" J hook

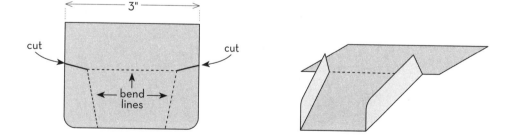

FIGURE 2.15 *Platform Spout*

into the front face of each leg, about 36" up from the bottom of the leg. The platform can be hung from the hooks at its leg notches, so line the hooks up to meet these slots. The J hooks are great during pressing for hanging rags, hand rakes for breaking up pomace, or other tools.

With the feet folded in, fasten a strip of ¾" plywood to each side of the bottom beam, between the tops of the feet. Install a barrel bolt on each strip to hold the feet closed for storage. Then install a caster at the bottom of the back face of each leg, so when you tip the frame back you can easily roll the press in and out of your storage place.

Drive Assembly

BUILD IT!

1. Build the press plate.

For the drive shaft, we'll start the mechanism at the bottom and work our way up.

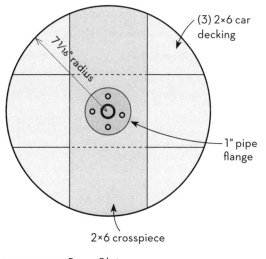

FIGURE 2.16 *Press Plate*

Start by cutting the 2×6 tongue-and-groove car decking into three 16" pieces. Fit the three pieces together to form a rectangle that measures 16" by about 15". Mark a light line between each pair of opposite corners; their intersection marks the centerpoint of the rectangle. Use the centerpoint to draw a 7¹⁄₁₆"-radius circle, and cut out the disk. This is the press plate as shown in figure 2.16. Place a 2×6 on top of the press plate, perpendicular to the car decking and centered across it; mark the curve of the press plate on each end of the 2×6, and cut the 2×6 along these lines. Secure this crosspiece in place with twelve 2½" wood screws, driving them through pilot holes.

NOTE: *If car decking is not available, ordinary 2x6s splined together with ¼" plywood rips would also work.*

2. Assemble the jack holder.

Clean all the steel pipe and fittings thoroughly to remove any residual oils that might remain from cutting and threading (see note on page 44).

Center a 1" steel floor flange on the top of the 2×6 crosspiece and screw it into place with four 2½" wood screws. The shaft becomes variable in length by using one or more of the lengths of pipe and couplings. Thread the pipe together and cap with the other 1" pipe flange. This flange will fit under the bottom of the hydraulic jack when pressing.

At the centerpoint on the bottom of the top beam of the press frame, fasten the ¾" floor flange to the beam using four ¼" × 2" lag screws. Then, finish the jack holder assembly with a ¾" "close" nipple and the

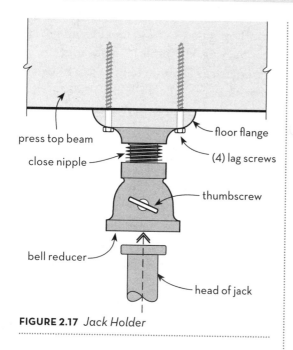

press top beam

close nipple

floor flange

(4) lag screws

thumbscrew

bell reducer

head of jack

FIGURE 2.17 *Jack Holder*

¾" × 1¼" bell reducer, as shown in figure 2.17. Check to verify that the top of the jack shaft will fit up into the bell reducer. If not, you may need to grind out the threads of the reducer, but they will usually fit without any work.

To hold the jack in the bell reducer, drill a hole through the front of the reducer and tap the hole for ¼" threads. Then screw a ¼" × 1" thumbscrew into the hole. Unscrew the shaft of the jack about ½", slip it into the reducer, and tighten the thumbscrew. The thumbscrew should fit under the lip of the top of the jack shaft, holding the jack in place.

NOTE: *I like to spray-paint the parts of the steel shaft assembly with several light coats of an industrial water-based paint after cleaning them well. Before painting, thread the parts together — hand-tightening only — to protect the threads and ensure that the pieces will turn easily unimpeded by the paint.*

3. Form the press pan spout.

To cut a notch for a spout in the press pan, make two vertical cuts about 2" apart in the side of the pan from the top lip down to the bottom of the pan, using a hacksaw. Fold this 2" piece down to an angle about 15° down from the bottom of the pan. You can reuse your gauge you used for the basket hoops to get it close. Then bend the sides of this spout up slightly.

NOTE: *There are several options for a press pan. A hot water tank overflow pan would work well, as would a stainless steel cake pan. You could also forgo a press pan, simply lining the perimeter of the press platform with some strips to contain the wine as it flows to the spout. I was lucky to have a winemaker give me one of his neutral 30-gallon barrels, so I cut the top few inches off the barrel (just past the second hoop) and now use that as a pan.*

4. Add a drive shaft holder.

A piece of PVC pipe screwed to the side of the frame serves as storage for the drive shaft when the press is folded up and rolled away. Drive a 3½" wood screw all the way through the pipe at the bottom, and drive a 1" wood screw through just the inner side of the pipe at the top.

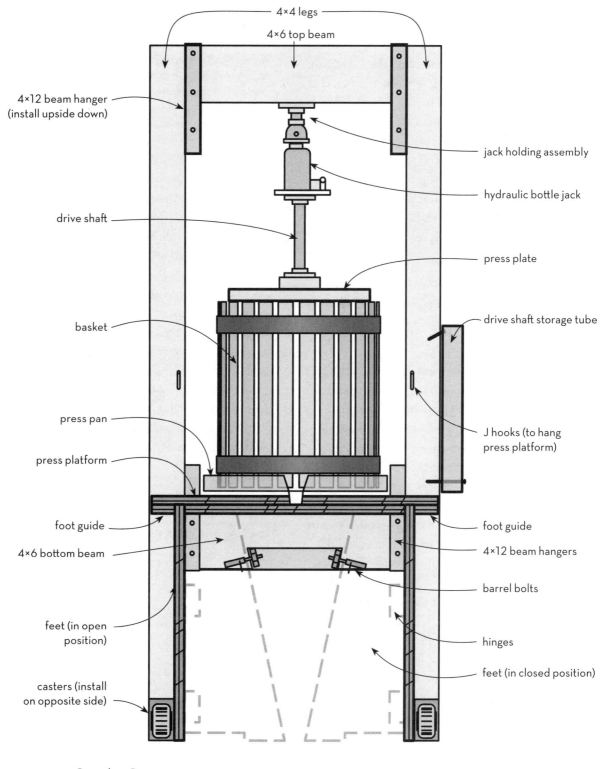

4×4 legs

4×6 top beam

4×12 beam hanger (install upside down)

jack holding assembly

hydraulic bottle jack

drive shaft

press plate

basket

drive shaft storage tube

press pan

J hooks (to hang press platform)

press platform

foot guide

foot guide

4×6 bottom beam

4×12 beam hangers

feet (in open position)

barrel bolts

hinges

feet (in closed position)

casters (install on opposite side)

FIGURE 2.18 *Complete Press*

USE IT!

Using the press is a lot of fun. First roll it out into position and unfold the feet. Drop the press platform down into position and adjust the feet to fit in the slots on the underside. Set the press pan in place and the basket into the press pan. Fit the jack in the bell reducer and tighten the thumb-screw. Give all of it a good wipe-down with some potassium metabisulfite and citric acid solution (see Sanitation in chapter 1, page 12). Place a bucket under the spout of the press pan.

✽ *To reduce the amount of larger solids and seeds falling into your pressed wine, try setting a stainless steel sieve on top of the bucket for the press juice to flow through.*

Attempting to leave as many seeds as possible in the bottom of the fermenter, pour the must into the basket. Install the 12" drive shaft on the press plate, and set it on top of the must. Fit the top flange of the drive shaft directly under the jack and pump the jack until it is snug. Pump the jack down to its full depth, pressing the wine out of the skins, then release the pressure and push the jack back up to its closed position. Rotate to lower the jack along the threaded jack shaft, then start jacking again. Once you've achieved maximum extension on the jack, unscrew the top flange from the drive shaft and add a 3" or 7" nipple and coupling (length of pipe threaded on each end), reinstall the flange, and recoil the jack to start the press again.

NOTE: *Some hydraulic jacks have a plug on the side that allows for filling the jack cylinder with hydraulic oil. If your jack has such a plug, I highly recommend wrapping the plug with a piece of heavy-duty plastic tape and covering the tape and plug with a hose clamp to ensure that it does not unexpectedly pop out in the middle of pressing that precious Syrah.*

You've undoubtedly seen photos of winemakers who end up with a very tall pomace cake in their basket. While this may look impressive, I don't recommend filling the basket that full. My ideal thickness for the pomace cake when I finish pressing is no more than 3 inches. More than that and you'll leave a lot of wine in the center of the cake and have a lot of work to do removing this beast from the pan. With the ability to remove the drive shaft and simply lift the basket off the pomace, it is easy to keep the cake thin. Then just lift the pan off the platform and dump the pomace into whatever receiving bin/wheelbarrow you care to use for transporting it to the compost pile.

✽ *When cleaning the jack, take care not to clean the hydraulic shaft. Cleaning off the hydraulic oil will cause the jack to stick, making retraction very difficult.*

CHOOSING FERMENTATION BINS

For red wine, a number of options exist for primary fermenters. The first priority should be that the material is "food grade." For small batches you can use white plastic food-grade buckets, which you can obtain from paint stores or, even less expensively, restaurants, bakeries, or other food-related establishments. As you make batches larger than the buckets will hold, I've found that the Rubbermaid Brute line of containers is an excellent option. At the time of this writing only the gray, white, and yellow models are rated NSF (safe for food contact). They come in a variety of sizes from 10 gallons to 44 gallons, and they are available with loose-fitting lids that allow CO_2 to escape during fermentation. You can nest them together to reduce the space needed to store them when they're not in use, and as an added bonus, you can bring them to the vineyard to transport fresh grapes or crushed fruit back to your winery.

Other options are available, such as stainless steel tanks and rope-handled plastic containers, but for cost and durability, the Rubbermaid Brutes are a great choice for the home winemaker.

Before "pumping" your crushed grapes into any fermentation containers, sanitize the containers well with a solution of potassium metabisulfite and citric acid and dump out the excess, as described in chapter 1 (see page 12). There's no need to dry them.

✳ *Don't fill the Brute fermenters any higher than the bottom of the handles. If you're using a different container, reserve at least 10 percent of the container's height for a rising cap of grape skins. Otherwise, the cap will float up and overflow the container.*

PUNCH-DOWN TOOL

A PUNCH-DOWN TOOL IS USED TO SUBMERGE THE FLOATING SKINS of the grapes several times a day during active fermentation. You can buy a stainless steel one like commercial wineries use, but since you're already making much of the equipment you need, you can build this one for a fraction of the cost and it will last for many years.

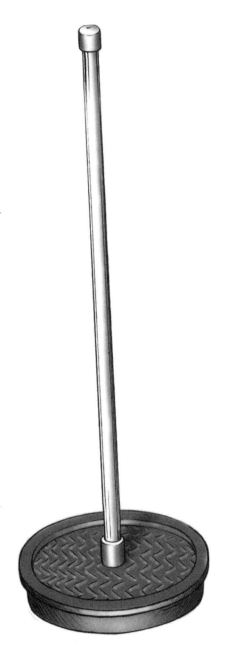

MATERIALS

- One 1" PVC cap
- One 3-foot length 1"-diameter PVC pipe
- One 1" PVC female slip by 1" male thread adapter
- One 12"-diameter fiberglass irrigation box lid (the green one that locks onto a round black plastic box)
- One 1" PVC threaded cap

BUILD IT!

Install the PVC slip cap on one end of the PVC pipe, and the male x female adapter on the other. (I just drive the fittings onto the pipe with a mallet rather than using any adhesives that may not be safe for food contact.)

Drill a hole in the center of the irrigation box lid that will snugly accept the threaded end of the adapter, and slip the lid over the adapter. Finally, screw the threaded cap over the male threads and tighten down securely.

NOTE: *If the adapter has too much play in the hole, you can make a short bushing from a piece of coupling so the threaded cap will clamp down on the lid more tightly.*

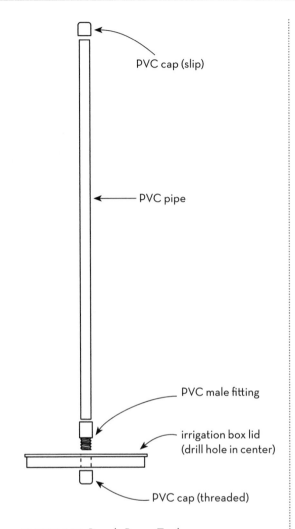

PVC cap (slip)

PVC pipe

PVC male fitting

irrigation box lid
(drill hole in center)

PVC cap (threaded)

FIGURE 2.19 *Punch-Down Tool*

USE IT!

The punch-down tool is very handy not only for punching down the cap but also for mixing in yeast, sugar, sulfites, or other agents you want to stir through the wine. To punch down, simply press the tool down into the must, being careful not to splash excessively. As you punch down, the surrounding cap will rise up, so this is when you'll be thankful you left plenty of headspace at the top of your fermenter. This tool is also helpful in pressing oxygen into the must, which helps keep the yeast actively reproducing and on their way to a strong finish.

✳ *For larger batches where the cap of skins can be fairly thick, you may find it handy to add a tee on the handle about 8" down from the top; then add an 8" piece of capped pipe into the tee to make an additional horizontal handle.*

Temperature Control

Different wines are better made with different rates of fermentation. For example, one technique for making red wines will involve performing a cold soak, then rapidly warming the must in order to inoculate it with the yeast, then encouraging the strong propagation of the yeast by keeping the must at a temperature between 80 and 90°F.

Then again, many white wines are better when fermentation is conducted much more slowly, by keeping the fermenting must at a cooler temperature, in the 60°F range.

The purpose of this book is not to guide your winemaking stylistic choices or methods but to provide you with means to your methods, so here's a simple technique to keep your whites cool, followed by a way to maintain a constant warm temperature for your red wines.

FERMENTATION COOLER

THIS IS SUCH A SIMPLE PROJECT that it doesn't require a materials list. Once you have your white grapes crushed and pressed, put the fermentation vessel into a container about twice the size of the vessel. Fill the larger vessel about three-quarters full with cool water and add some "ice bombs" — 2-liter plastic bottles filled with water and frozen. Keep a couple of extra bottles in the freezer so that you can regularly rotate ice bombs into the water bath and back to the freezer. Monitor the temperature of the must and add or remove the ice bombs as necessary to maintain your fermentation at a nice steady pace. If you wanted to reduce the rotations of ice, you could easily build a foam board box similar to the fermentation chamber (page 51) that sits over the top of the water bath.

Controlling the temperature of fermentation can be achieved using a water bath and ice bombs rotated from the freezer.

FERMENTATION CHAMBER

THIS CHAMBER WAS INSPIRED BY MY LITTLE SISTER'S EASY-BAKE OVEN and my brother's duck egg incubator. It's amazing how much heat a single 100-watt lightbulb will create, and you can harness that heat to keep your wine at just the right temperature for warm fermentation.

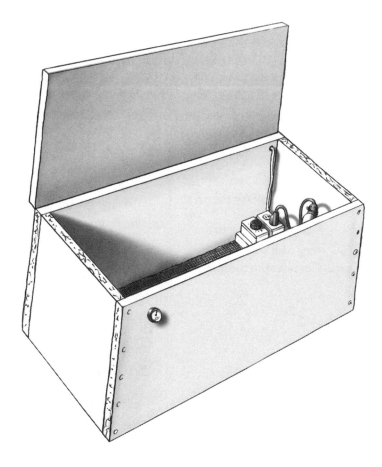

MATERIALS

- Two 2 × 8-foot sheets 1"-thick rigid foam insulation (foundation insulation board)

- Twenty 3" coarse-thread wood screws

- One 12" length 2×6 lumber

- One triple-gang electrical box with screws

- One 110V (line voltage) thermostat

- One duplex electrical outlet (with ground)

- One approx. 2-foot length 14/2 electrical cable (with ground)

- Wire nuts

- One duplex electrical outlet cover plate with screw

- Three-prong 120V plug

- One 8" length 1×2 lumber

- One clamp-on-style shop light with metal shroud

- One 100W incandescent lightbulb

- One approx. 24" × 48" piece carpet or other floor pad

BUILD IT!

1. Build the chamber box.

Cut the insulation boards into three 4-foot-long pieces. Cut the remaining piece into two 24" × 22" pieces. Carefully drive coarse-thread screws through two of the 4-foot pieces into the 22" pieces, forming a rectangular box (see figure 2.20). Be very careful not to strip the screw holes. Set the third 4-foot piece of insulation board aside for now; it will serve as the top of the box.

2. Make the wiring connections.

Attach the triple-gang electrical box to the 2×6 by screwing through the back of the box and into the board. Connect the thermostat to a duplex outlet as shown in figure 2.21, using short lengths (about 8") of the individual strands of wires pulled from the sheathing of the three-wire 14/2 electrical cable. Secure the wires together with wire nuts. From the thermostat, connect a 12" length of 14/2 cable to the thermostat and install a three-prong 120V plug on the other end.

NOTE: *This wiring is appropriate only in areas where 120V power supply is typical. For areas where 220V is standard, contact a licensed electrician for more information.*

✱ *A word of caution about working with electricity in your winery: Whenever you're using any electrical device in a garage, basement, or other location where moisture may be present, be sure all outlets and other sources of power are connected to a ground-fault circuit interrupter (GFCI)* **and** *a suitable breaker or fuse panel. If you are unsure about making any connections or permit requirements, contact a licensed electrician.*

3. Add the light fixture.

Cut the 1×2 to fit from the side of the electrical box to the end of the 2×6, and attach the 1×2 to the centerline of the 2×6, as shown in figure 2.21. Clamp the light fixture to the 1×2, install the lightbulb, plug the fixture cord into the thermostat-controlled outlet, and voilà, you have a wine incubator!

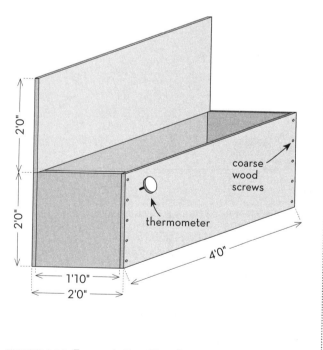

FIGURE 2.20 *Fermentation Chamber*

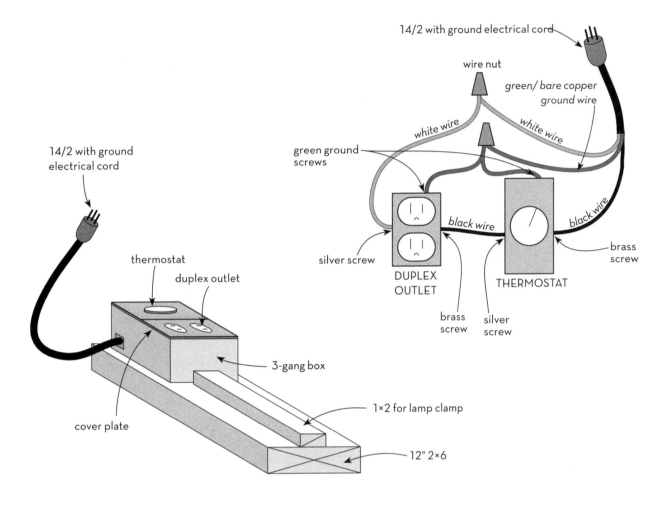

14/2 with ground electrical cord

wire nut

green/ bare copper ground wire

white wire

white wire

green ground screws

black wire

black wire

brass screw

silver screw

DUPLEX OUTLET

THERMOSTAT

brass screw

silver screw

14/2 with ground electrical cord

thermostat

duplex outlet

3-gang box

1×2 for lamp clamp

cover plate

12" 2×6

FIGURE 2.21 *Fermentation Chamber Thermostat*

USE IT!

Place the bottomless chamber on the carpet scrap/pad. Lower your carboys or fermenters into the chamber, adjust the thermostat to the desired temperature, plug in the thermostat, and close the lid. To really trick this out, you can insert an analog thermometer on a 45° angle down through the upper front corner, opposite the light, so that you can monitor the chamber temperature without removing the cover.

When it comes time to move the carboys or fermenters, it is much easier and safer for your back to lift the chamber off the wine rather than lifting the wine out of the chamber (the main reason for not having a bottom on it). To store the chamber, just remove the screws and stack the pieces flat or on end.

CHAPTER THREE

MOVING WINE

FROM THE MOMENT THE GRAPES ARE PICKED, the winemaker is continually challenged by having to move the grapes, must, wine, barrels, carboys, bottles, and other vessels around the winery. In the vineyard, a few bucketfuls of grapes quickly become too heavy to lift when combined in a bin. In the winery, once crushed and destemmed, the grapes go to the primary fermenter or, in the case of white wines, directly to the press. From the press, the must goes to a secondary fermentation container to begin the oxygen isolation ritual.

Up to this point, the movement of the wine is called "transferring." From here on, though, it's "racking." After the pressing, the must settles out for a short period of time and then the winemaker will "rack" the wine off its lees. Racking essentially draws the wine off the sediment and places it into a clean vessel to age and clear further. Typically winemakers rack the wine several times during the aging process in an effort to produce a very clear, sediment-free beverage. Winemakers should strive to develop excellent technique to rack off the most amount of wine as possible, leaving the sediment at the bottom of the aging vessel. Equally important to good technique is minimizing the exposure of the wine to oxygen during the racking process.

In this chapter we'll discuss a number of different ways to move grapes, must, and wine. The more techniques you master, the more easily and successfully you'll move the product, while improving quality and saving your back.

At the Vineyard

When picking grapes in the vineyard, it's common to drop the fruit into a 5-gallon bucket. Once full, this bucket will weigh 20 to 25 pounds. As my crew and I pick our grapes, we combine them in a bulk container that will hold no more than 125 pounds, which is about all two people can carry from the head of the row back to our vehicle. The 25-gallon Rubbermaid Roughneck bins I described in chapter 2 work perfectly for this. You can

If you're fortunate enough to have a vineyard nearby where you can get your grapes, treat your grower well. What you lack in volume can be made up many times over through appreciation.

expect 10 to 12 gallons of red-grape must from this full bin, and a gallon or so less of white-grape must. I also use the 32-gallon Rubbermaid Brute cans (that double as my fermenters) to transport my grapes.

Back at the Winery

Once back at the winery, my crew and I carefully lower the bins onto a hand truck that converts to a four-wheeled cart. A small hand truck like this is indispensable for loads greater than 100 pounds. I make it my goal to lift as little as possible.

I roll the bins over to the crusher-destemmer, weigh them, and set them up on an inverted garbage can or sawhorses to start the processing.

As described in chapter 2 (page 35), after being crushed, the grapes fall through the destemmer into a receiving bin (another 25-gallon Roughneck in my setup), which sits on a dolly below the destemmer. The dolly is very easy to build.

From Fermenter to Press

Once the fermentation is slowing and your sugar levels are approaching 1° Brix, you'll move the fermenter over to the press. Rubbermaid makes nice little dollies for its Brute containers, but by following the general plans for the dolly on page 56, you can make several fermenter dollies with some casters and pieces of plywood for a fraction of the price of the store-bought versions. These can also double as dollies for carboys when the fermenters are put away for the season. Whenever I see an old office chair or other salvage item that has casters on the bottom, I always scrounge them for some additional dollies. I've even used an old skateboard!

WINERY DOLLY

MOVING HEAVY STUFF AROUND, especially fragile glass carboys and fully loaded fermenters, is much easier and safer if you have a dolly to set them on. A very funny video on YouTube has a frequently quoted line that goes something like, "Making wine is 49 percent cleaning stuff, 49 percent moving heavy stuff around, and 2 percent drinking beer." With this simple little platform on wheels, your heavy stuff will glide across the floor of your winery, allowing you more time for the beer. I shoot to increase the beer ratio to about 4 percent.

MATERIALS

- Four 2"-diameter pivoting casters (two with locking wheels)
- Sixteen ¾" screws to attach casters to platform
- One 16" × 24" piece ¾" plywood
- Primer and paint (optional)

NOTE: *You could use smaller casters, but they are less likely to navigate over bumps in the floor and things like mats or extension cords, so I don't recommend them.*

BUILD IT!

Fasten a caster to each corner of the plywood, with the two locking casters on the same end and the edges of the caster mounting plate about ¾" in from each side.

If desired, paint the dolly with some primer and gloss paint to help with cleanup and keep it looking good.

USE IT!

You'll find that this little workhorse will help you move all kinds of bins, equipment, and other stuff around your winery.

RACKING CANES & HOSES

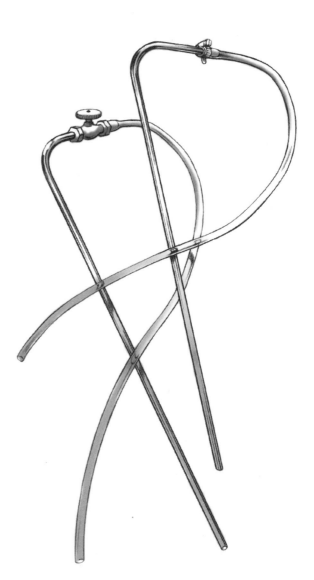

AS YOUR WINEMAKING PROGRESSES to the point that you want to move a significant amount of wine gently from one container to the next, you need a couple of racking canes and tubing. Most homebrew stores carry plastic racking canes in 5/16" and 3/8" outside diameters. Some of the better shops have them in stainless steel. Plastic canes are fine for the beginner, but as you begin to master the technique of racking, you'll find that they are too small, take too long, and break much too easily.

You can make durable ½"-diameter racking canes from thin-wall stainless steel tubing that is available from many metal suppliers. You'll also need one or two pieces of 5-foot-long, flexible plastic tubing to use with most carboys and barrels. With two pieces, you'll also need a barbed coupling. Bending the top 6" of the racking canes to a right angle is a bit tricky, but if you follow these simple steps, you should be successful in making some very nice canes that will last a long, long time.

MATERIALS

- One 3" × 9" piece ¾" plywood
- Two 3-foot lengths ½"-O.D. (outside diameter) stainless steel tubing
- 1 pound superfine sand
- One ½" chrome quarter-turn stop valve (female threaded on one side, compression fitting on the other)
- One ½" stainless steel or brass male-thread by barb fitting
- One (or two) 5-foot length ½"-I.D. (inside diameter) plastic tubing

BUILD IT!

1. Cut and position the plywood bending form.

Cut the plywood to form a quarter circle with a 3" radius on one end, leaving a straight leg 6" long. Place the plywood in a vise with the curved end up and toward the center of the vise. Leave enough space between the metal shaft of the vise to allow you to slip the stainless steel tubing down between it and the plywood.

2. Fill the tubing with sand.

Tape one end of the stainless steel tubing closed. Using a small funnel, fill the tubing with superfine sand, tamping the tube to compact the sand every couple inches. Once the tube is full, tape off the other end to hold the sand in place. The sand will help keep the tubing from kinking or buckling as you bend it.

NOTE: *You should be able to find superfine sand in the garden department of a local hardware store. Be sure that it is very dry. If it is not, spread it out on a cookie sheet and bake in an oven for a few minutes.*

3. Bend the tubing.

You will want about 3" to 6" at the end of the racking cane to be at a right angle to the main shaft of the cane. This helps keep your hoses from kinking as they are connected to the canes. Slip the sand-filled tube down into the vise between the plywood and the center bar of the vice; if you can see the weld-line of the tubing, make sure it faces

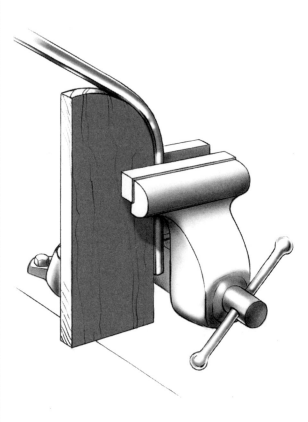

Slowly bend the sand-filled tube around the plywood form.

the plywood, as you'll want it on the inside of the curve. Gently and slowly bend the tube over the curve of the plywood. Watch the tubing as you bend it, and release pressure if you see a kink or deformation begin to form. If the tubing appears to be flattening out on the bend, try to reshape it back into round by squeezing the sides with the vise. Again, go slowly, and you'll end up with a very nice racking cane.

Build a second racking cane like the first one, and you'll have a pair of very durable, efficient pieces of wine-moving equipment.

4. Install a valve and fitting.

A valve on one of the racking canes will give you great control of your racking, especially if the valve closes quickly. The quarter-turn valve works well for this. To install it onto the racking cane, remove the nut and compression ring from the valve, place them over the racking cane's short end, and connect the valve's compression side to the compression nut. Tighten down the nut securely, using two wrenches. On the other side of the valve, install the barbed fitting on the threaded inlet of the valve, again, using two wrenches. Also use a single wrap of Teflon tape wrapped around the male threads to seal the connection. Only one valve is necessary for a racking setup of two canes and flexible hoses.

By installing a quarter-turn valve on one racking cane, you will gain excellent control of the racking process and avoid back-siphoning when racking from a container that is lower than the receiving one.

5. Connect the hose.

You'll also need a length of hose to connect one cane to the other. You should have a minimum of 5 feet of hose to do a basic racking using a siphon.

NOTE: *Clear poly tubing works well for connecting racking canes. However, if you decide to advance to using a vacuum pump (which I highly recommend; see page 64), you may want to upgrade now to fiber-reinforced poly tubing, which is less resistant to collapse under suction. You may also want to consider getting two 5-foot lengths of tubing to extend your wine-moving range to 10 feet. I recommend using a barbed coupling to connect them; by using two lengths and a coupling, rather than a continuous 10-foot length, you have more flexibility in your system, and you can hang them up vertically to dry after you clean them.*

Let Gravity Be Your Friend

Some commercial wineries are set up to move their must and wine by siphoning, which uses gravity alone and never subjects the wine to pumping. The principal of siphoning is pretty simple: liquid moves from an upper container to a lower one when gravity causes the pressure of the liquid in the upper end of the tube to be greater than the pressure in the lower container.

You can start a siphon in a number of ways:

1. With racking canes attached to tubing, put one end into the upper container, lower the other end below the upper container, and suck on the lower end until the liquid is drawn to the level of the wine in the upper container. Before the wine gets to your mouth (or a moment later, if you like), place the end of the tubing in the lower container. This process isn't recommended due to the risk of contaminating your wine with mouth-borne bacteria.

2. Put the racking cane into the sealed upper container through a two-hole bung or cap, and put the other end of the tubing into the lower receiving vessel. Blow or pump some air into the full container through the free hole until the siphon begins. Allow the "blow" hole in the bung to remain clear to allow air to be drawn in to keep the siphon flowing, or, conversely, seal the hole to stop the flow.

3. Fill your racking canes and tubing with water or wine. With your thumb sealing the end that will be inserted into the lower receiving vessel, place the upper end into the upper container. Place the other end into the lower container and remove your thumb. A nice steady flow will begin.

4. Use a siphon pump (see page at right).

LOADING THE FERMENTER

Commercial wineries use what is called a must pump to move wine from their crusher-destemmers to their fermenters. Must pumps usually require a minimum of 2" hoses and fittings and very expensive in-line pumps. On a home winemaking scale, you can move must faster than some low-end must pumps simply by using a 2- or 3-quart kitchen pot with a comfortable handle. If you want a pot to use exclusively for your winery, pick one up at a thrift store. Otherwise, there's likely a "must pump" pot in your kitchen. I brag that my must pump moves 10 gallons of wine in a minute, and I get a good workout at the same time.

SIPHON PUMP

YOU CAN LIKELY FIND A PREFAB SIPHONING DEVICE (one such product is called the Auto-Siphon) at your local homebrew shop. But similar pumps are easy to build with some off-the-shelf products from a hardware store. The siphon pump design shown here uses tubing that allows for nearly 50 percent more capacity and transfer speed than the commercially available pumps, for a bit less money to boot.

MATERIALS

- Two rubber ½" cone washers with ¾" O.D. (outside diameter)
- One length ½"-O.D. racking cane or rigid tubing
- Wine cork (used is fine)
- One 24" length ¾"-I.D. (inside diameter) clear plastic tubing

BUILD IT!

Slip the cone washers over the bottom end of the racking cane (the cane must be dry). Insert the wine cork approximately ⅜" into one end of the ¾" tubing, so that it is well seated. Just above the cork, drill a ⅜" hole all the way through the tubing. Trim the cork flush with the end of the tube (see figure 3.1 on page 62).

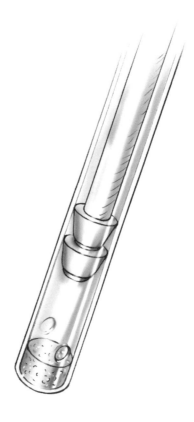

USE IT!

Apply a small bit of cooking oil to your finger and use it to lubricate the outer edges of the cone washers that are seated on the racking cane. Push the racking cane down into the ¾" tubing. Move the racking cane up and down to slightly lubricate the interior of the tubing. Push the racking cane to the bottom of the pump. With the racking cane connected by a hose to a second racking cane in the receiving vessel, insert the pump assembly into your full vessel. The pump will displace some of the wine, so be careful not to cause an overflow. Slowly raise the cane part of the pump, filling the larger tube, and then push the cane back down until wine flows over the top of the cane and the siphon is started. Be vigilant about keeping the holes of the pump below the surface of the wine so as to not lose the siphon, and above the lees in the bottom to keep from transferring sediment to the receiving vessel. To stop the flow, simply lift the pump out of the wine.

You can speed up the siphon by pumping the racking cane up and down, but be careful not to pump so vigorously that you pull a cone washer off the racking cane or pop the cork out of the larger tube. A few cut-off pins pushed through the outer tube into the cork will help prevent this from happening.

I've found that this device is also very useful for filling containers such as hydrometer jars for testing sugar levels or other times when you need a fair amount of a sample that would take a number of dips with your wine thief. It slips easily through the grape cap in a primary fermenter to get into the liquid without getting clogged up with skins as could happen with the use of a wine thief.

✱ *If you want to siphon clear wine that has no sediment, pull out the racking cane and cork plug, flip the clear tube over, and insert the cane into the opposite end. You should be able to pull out nearly all of the wine with no residue left over.*

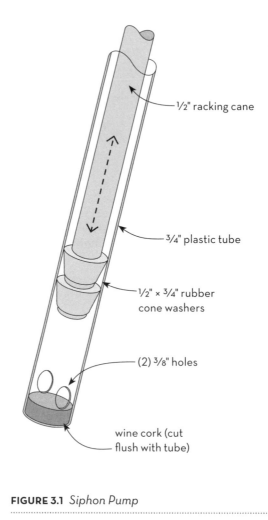

½" racking cane

¾" plastic tube

½" × ¾" rubber cone washers

(2) ⅜" holes

wine cork (cut flush with tube)

FIGURE 3.1 *Siphon Pump*

Pumping with Power

There are a number of pumps you might be inclined to use for transferring and racking your must and wine. Many are designed specifically for use with wine. The important thing to keep in mind when exploring a pump system is what the pump will do to your wine. The more a pump jostles, stirs, and "beats" the wine, the more damage can result. This is why the Gravity Guys who tout their wineries for relying on the pull of the earth for moving wine claim that their wines are somehow "better." But it is a theory that has been shown to have merit, so consider pumping with minimal disturbance to the wine and minimal exposure to oxygen.

Some of the pumping options include:

Impeller pump. An impeller pump is relatively inexpensive but probably the most abusive to your wine. It operates with a fanlike driver that pushes wine like a fan blows air. The pump needs to be primed, that is, you must feed wine to the impeller in order for it to be able to push the wine to the empty container. As such, it is installed between the two containers.

Diaphragm pump. The setup of a diaphragm pump is basically the same as that of an impeller pump. Some diaphragm pumps are self-priming, meaning that they will pull the wine from the donating vessel without having to be fed wine. Others need to be primed. Inside the pump is a rubber bladder that works like a heart, quickly pulsing the wine through the lines. Diaphragm pumps can be found with electric or compressed-air drives and are the most common type of pumps found in smaller commercial wineries. While they are very effective at moving wine gently and quickly, they are relatively expensive and singularly purposed.

Vacuum pump. A vacuum pump is basically a reverse compressor. It can create very high vacuum pressure and, unlike a vacuum cleaner, can run for a long time with the vacuum hose shut off without overheating. Wine never touches the pump itself; it is installed downstream of the receiving container, so it is a very gentle way to move wine. A common myth holds that a vacuum pump creates a perfect vacuum in the receiving container, such that no air exists, which could cause a carboy to implode. In fact, all a vacuum pump does is reduce the pressure in the receiving container, causing wine to be drawn from the donating container in much the same way

that a siphon works, except it can work horizontally or uphill.

There are a number of designs for vacuum pumps, one of which uses a piston with alternating valves. The piston dropping down draws air into the cylinder and the exhaust valve closes, and then the piston rises up and pushes the air out the exhaust valve, in much the same way that the engine of a car works. Others use fans or other means of pulling air through the pump and exhausting it through an outlet of some sort.

Vacuum pumps have become this *garagiste*'s preferred pump of choice. They can be found for reasonable prices at discount tool houses, online, and from heating contractors. They are versatile, and if you get a piston-drive pump, not only can you vacuum, you can also use it in reverse to move wine as described in the #2 option of "Let Gravity Be Your Friend" on page 60, in the event that the receiving container is an open container. Bear in mind, though, that for a piston-drive vacuum pump to work, either the receiving container or the donating container must be closable to maintain the pressure differential. With all other vacuum pumps, the receiving container must be a rigid, closable container — unlike glass carboys or wood barrels, thin plastic carboys and containers can't handle the vacuum pressure and may collapse — so plan your racking and equipment accordingly.

VACUUM PUMPING SETUP

A VACUUM PUMPING SYSTEM IS PRETTY EASY TO ASSEMBLE, but using it takes some practice in order to shut it off at just the right time to keep from drawing a large amount of air through the wine at the end of the process. So this project gets one wine bottle for the Build It! section and another one for the Use It! section.

MATERIALS

- One vacuum pump

- Pressure gauge for the pump (optional)

- Regulator (optional; a needle/ball valve can be used)

- One ⅜" barbed x male-threaded brass pipe fitting (sized to fit the inlet of the pump)

- Two 5-foot lengths ⅜" I.D. (inside diameter) plastic tubing

- One ⅜" × ⅜" barbed coupling

- One 3" length ¾" PVC pipe

- One ¾" slip × ½" threaded PVC tee

- One ¾" × ½" PVC reducing bushing

- One ⅜" hose barb × ½" male threaded connector

- One hollow universal bung sized to fit your rigid, closed container (size 6.5 for carboys)

- 100% food-grade silicone sealant

- Two ½" I.D. cone washers with ⅞" O.D. (outside diameter)

- Two ½" racking canes

- One overflow container (large jar, 1-gallon jug, small carboy, et cetera)

- Two 1-hole bungs (for overflow container)

- Two ⅜" × ¼" barb × barb elbows

- Four ⅜" hose clamps

- One short piece ¼" rigid tubing

- ½" flexible tubing (to connect racking canes)

- Remote switch extension cord (optional)

✳ *Vacuum pumps are commonly used by HVAC contractors, by auto mechanics, and in the medical profession (where they are called "aspirators"). Most are very sensitive to moisture, so be sure to install an overflow container between the pump and the receiving vessel. A pump rated for 2.0 to 2.5 cfm will serve a winemaker well for many years.*

BUILD IT!

1. Set up the pump and tubing.

If you're going to use a regulator and pressure gauge, install them on the pump inlet. Then connect the 3/8" barbed x male threaded fitting to the inlet. Install a short piece of 3/8" tubing over the fitting; you'll connect the pump to the overflow container via this tubing when you're ready to use the pump. As you become more and more proficient at vacuum racking, you'll find that positioning your overflow container in various places in your winery will be beneficial. For most operations, however, the overflow container will be placed right next to the pump or even connected to a rack that holds them both together.

2. Assemble the transfer gun.

Glue the 3" piece of PVC pipe into the 3/4" PVC tee fitting. Glue the 3/4" × 1/2" reducing bushing into the opposite end of the tee. Screw a 3/8" barb x male threaded connector into the threaded 1/2" fitting of the tee, and connect one 5-foot length of flexible 3/8" tubing to it.

Using an X-Acto-type knife, carefully cut out (*not* cut off) the bottom of the universal bung so the PVC pipe fits snugly in it. Slip

the bung over the PVC pipe and fill the bung with silicone sealant or construction adhesive and allow to dry.

NOTE: *At this point you may want to consider using up the rest of the silicone caulk by making some extra custom silicone bungs as described in chapter 4 (see page 78).*

Slip the two cone washers, with their sides tapering downward, over the racking cane with the valve installed, and slip the cane and washers through the reducer bushing in the top of the racking gun.

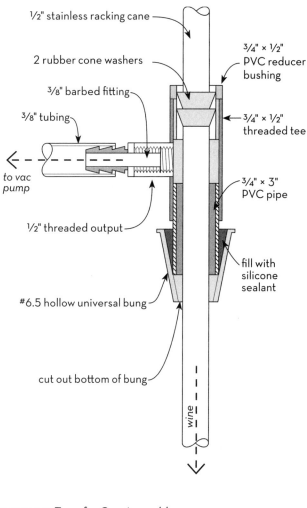

FIGURE 3.2 *Transfer Gun Assembly*

3. Set up the overflow container.

Make an overflow container from a 1- or 2-quart glass or rigid plastic jar by drilling a pair of holes in the lid sized to match the diameter of a one-hole bung with a ¼" hole. Insert a piece of ¼" O. D. plastic tubing into one of the bungs so it extends to near the bottom of the jar when the top is installed. Install the ⅜" × ¼" barb x barb elbows into the top holes of both bungs and insert the bungs into the holes in the lid. Install the lid on the jar.

Connect the 5-foot length of ⅜" tubing extending from the transfer gun to the fitting in the bung that has the plastic tubing dropping down into the container. Connect the ⅜" tubing installed on the pump inlet to the fitting of the other bung.

Install hose clamps on all tubing connectors to ensure a tight seal.

USE IT!

✳ *It takes a bit of practice to learn to pump wine with this vacuum racking setup without pulling the lees from the donating container and large amounts of air at the end of racking, so it's a good idea to practice the pumping a few times with water before undertaking the job with your wine.*

✳ *After getting to know your pump and developing your technique, you'll be able to reliably predict when to turn off the pump so that you can rack off the last bit of wine without any air bubbles or lees.*

Connect the two racking canes with the ½" tubing. Insert the racking cane with the valve attached to the transfer gun into the receiving container, making sure it is tightly seated. Insert the other racking cane into the donating (full) container, taking care not to cause an overflow.

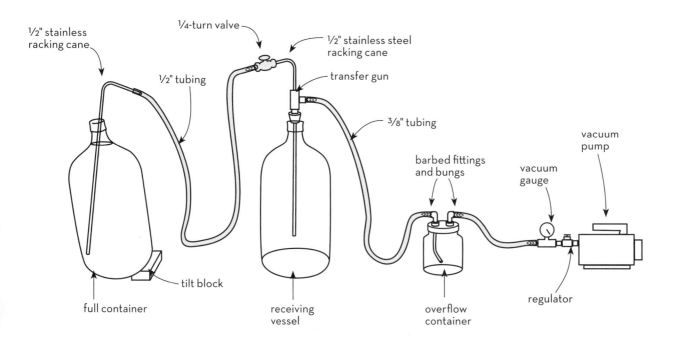

FIGURE 3.3 *Vacuum Racking Setup*

Open the valve on the racking cane and turn on the vacuum pump, and the flow of wine will begin. If you are racking off the lees, keep the bottom of the racking cane in the donating container above the lees.

When the transfer is nearing completion, keep in mind that shutting off the pump does not immediately stop the vacuum; the wine will continue to flow for several seconds while the vacuum diminishes. If the donating container runs out of wine and there is still a vacuum on the line, air will be sucked through. To avoid this, simply pull the transfer gun off the receiving vessel as the last bit of wine is drawn from the donating vessel to break the vacuum and immediately stop the flow. Or better yet, just shut the valve you installed on the top of the racking cane when you see the final bit of wine coming near.

The quarter-turn valve on the racking cane also prevents back-siphoning of wine in the event that your receiving vessel is higher than the donating one. When your transfer is completed, just give the valve a quick turn and the wine in the hoses remains where it is until you relocate the racking canes to a position that will reduce the siphoning potential.

A side benefit to vacuum racking is that the vacuum is great at pulling CO_2 out of solution during the racking process. The first couple of times you rack a wine, you'll see a fair amount of foaming caused by the wine releasing carbon dioxide. If the foaming rises to the bottom of the transfer gun, some foam may enter the vacuum line. Turning off the pump as the foam approaches the transfer gun will almost immediately stop the foam from increasing. This is where running the pump on a switched extension cord is really handy; it lets you stay near the vessels for maximum racking control rather than near the vacuum pump, which may be several feet away.

A second technique that this system can perform during and at the end of racking is an operation called vacuum degassing. Simply by turning off the valve on your racking cane and allowing your vacuum pump to continue to run, you will be pulling a strong suction on the wine and removing the residual dissolved CO_2. After about 20 seconds the tiny foam-sized bubbles become larger, indicating most of the CO_2 has been released. Then, just open the valve to draw in more wine, and repeat the process as necessary to fully degas the wine.

One last note on setting up the vacuum pumping system for racking: be sure to set the vacuum pump on a surface other than the surface your wines are on to avoid vibrations that could disturb the lees and reducing the effectiveness of a clean racking.

A piston-driven, oilless vacuum pump equipped with a needle valve regulator

Pushing Wine

There may be times when vacuum transfers aren't suitable — when the receiving vessel is going to be an open container, or when it cannot withstand the negative pressures of a vacuum, as would be the case with a plastic carboy or thin-walled stainless steel tank. The transfer gun of the vacuum pump system (page 65) works well for this situation as well, except it is installed on the full container rather than the empty one. If your vacuum pump has outfeed capability, you can simply put the fittings on the outfeed and essentially "blow" the wine using positive pressure instead of negative pressure. If the vacuum pump does not have outfeed, you can use a small air compressor instead. Start with the regulator or ball valve closed, and slowly open it just enough to start the wine flowing. Too much pressure and the transfer gun will pop off the container and stop the flow. You might want to keep a hand on the transfer gun to keep it seated or to release pressure in the tank by pulling it off as necessary. With practice, you can learn to control the flow by adjusting the regulator valve and releasing pressure as needed through the gun.

As we all know, minimizing exposure to air and oxygen is generally good winemaking practice. If you would prefer not to expose your wine to the air required for this method of pushing wine, a tank of compressed nitrogen or argon can be safely substituted for the compressor. You can find such tanks at welding supply shops or other gas suppliers. Typically you purchase a tank and regulator; when you use up the gas, you remove the regula-

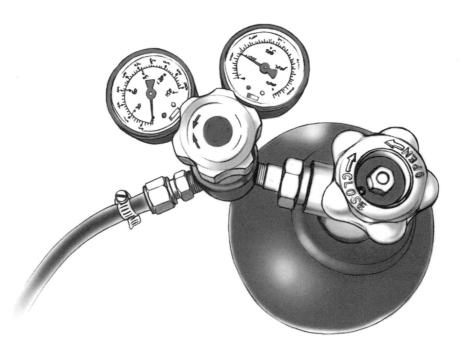

FIGURE 3.4 *Nitrogen regulator and setup*

tor and exchange the empty tank for a full one. If you're looking at getting a used tank or regulator from a third party, be sure to have it checked out by a compressed gas supplier. When full, compressed gas tanks are under enormous pressure, and a faulty tank can easily turn into a bomb. For home winemaking purposes, a 46- or 80-cubic-foot tank is quite adequate.

There are two gauges on the regulator; one shows the internal pressure of the tank, the other the pressure in the line feeding the gas. To set up your tank for wine transfers, install a ⅜" barbed fitting on the regulator and attach a ⅜" flexible tube to it with a hose clamp. Attach the other end of the tube to your transfer gun's vacuum pump fitting. Following the same protocol as when using a compressor, open the main valve of the tank, and then slowly open the regulator until wine just begins to move.

Once you have an inert gas setup like this, you'll find many uses for it, from sparging the headspace of tanks and barrels to replacing air in your bottles just before filling them. Using inert gas will dramatically improve your winemaking prowess and practice, and though the initial expense is costly, the reward is great.

A final word about gas tank safety: be sure to strap the tank to a stable support to keep it from inadvertently tipping over, breaking off the regulator or valve, and becoming an uncontrolled missile. When it's not in use, be sure to shut the tank's valve as well as the regulator.

> Using inert gas will dramatically improve your winemaking prowess and practice, and though the initial expense is costly, the reward is great.

Lifting Wine

There are lots of times when it is necessary to lift a full carboy, barrel, or tank, and it can be scary to try to do that by hand. Not only do you run the risk of spilling that precious nectar, but there's also a potential for damaging a barrel, shattering a carboy, or even injuring yourself. Therefore, a lift, or wine hoist, is a very handy device to have. There are engine hoists on the market for hundreds of dollars, but if you've built the foldable, rollable wine press described in chapter 2 (page 36), you already have the frame of a great hoist. With a simple attachment, you'll be lifting heavy stuff with ease.

WINE HOIST

THIS PROJECT DOUBLES UP THE FUNCTIONS OF THE PRESS you built in chapter 2. The sturdy frame of the press can easily be converted into a crane to lift your vessels or other heavy stuff off the ground (or your winery dolly) to allow you to siphon or rack to another container below.

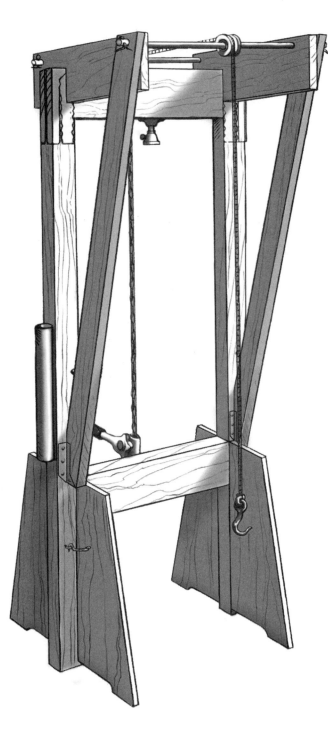

MATERIALS

- Press frame (page 36)
- Four hook-and-eye latches
- Two 6" × 18" pieces ¾" plywood
- Two 4-foot lengths 2×4 lumber
- Two Simpson U24 (2×4) joist hangers
- Twenty Simpson #8 × 1¼" screws
- Six 2" wood screws
- Two 28" lengths ⅝" solid steel rod
- Two 2" or 3" pulleys with ⅝" shaft holes
- Four cotter pins
- One ¼" × 2"-diameter screw eye with lag screw threads
- One come-along hoist or winch
- Four ⅝" flat washers

BUILD IT!

1. Cut and fit the plywood support arms.

Begin by setting up the press frame, without the platform. Secure each foot to the adjacent frame leg with a hook-and-eye latch to lock the feet in place.

In each piece of ¾" plywood, cut out a 3½" × 3½" notch 3½" from one 6" end. This notch in the plywood "arm" will slip over the top beam of the press frame (see figure 3.5). You want a snug fit here, but not so tight that the plywood arms are hard to remove. In each upper corner of the arms, mark a spot 1¾" in from each adjacent edge, and drill a ⅝" hole in each location. Slip the arms over the inside edge of the legs, next to the top beam, with the arms extending away from the side of the press that has the casters.

2. Make the diagonal supports.

Use a miter saw to cut the bottom ends of the two 2×4s at 13°. Square up from this cut approximately 2" in from the front edge of the 2×4 and make a vertical cut to fit the post of the press frame. Install a U24 hanger on these supports and screw it into place with the #8 screws. Tack the bottoms of these hangers along the centerline of the press legs and even with the top of the bottom 4×6 beams. Then with the ⅝" holes in the support arms aligned with the centerline of the 2×4 supports, mark the top, front edge, and hole of each arm. Then cut and drill in these locations.

3. Install the rods and pulleys.

Place each ⅝" steel rod in a vise and drill a ⅛" hole through the rod 1" in from each end. (It's helpful to first "nick" the rod with a center punch or other hard, pointed tool to help keep the drill bit from slipping off the rod.) File a flat spot for the pulley set screw to engage in the center of the steel rod. Slip each steel rod through one side of a diagonal 2×4 and a plywood arm, add a pulley, then slip the rod through the other arm and the other diagonal support. Slide a washer

over each outside end of the rod, and insert the cotter pins through the ⅛" holes to secure the rod. Tighten down the screws of the two pulleys at the flat spot you filed so they are centered on the rods.

Swing the diagonal supports over to the press leg and secure the attached U24 joist hangers to the legs with the #8 screws.

Install the screw eye into the bottom beam on the side with the casters, and your hoist is done.

USE IT!

Unwind the cable from the come-along, and hook the stationary end of the winch into the screw eye. Run the cable over the pulleys and down to the waiting container. Any number of ways to connect the container to the hook can be devised, from using ropes to nylon strapping to choker cables.

For lifting a carboy, I find it works well to set the carboy in a milk crate with straps around the handles of the crate. There are also nylon strapping carboy-carrying slings that can hook onto the come-along cable. For lifting a barrel, run a strap or rope through each corner of the barrel dolly (see page 73) and onto the hook.

When you're ready to lift, set the ratchet lock of the come-along in the correct position and pull down on the handle. Follow the manufacturer's instructions for lowering the container properly. Usually you release the lock and press a key while raising the handle. (As with any procedure, it helps to practice; try raising and lowering an unbreakable weighted load before trying to lift your wine.) Once your vessel is raised up, you can roll a cart under it and then move it over to its final destination.

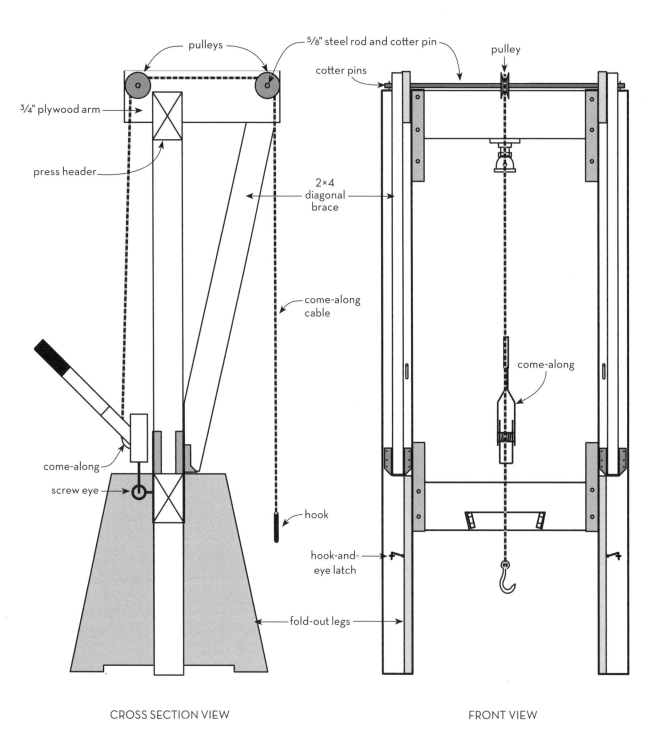

pulleys

⅝" steel rod and cotter pin

pulley

cotter pins

¾" plywood arm

press header

2×4
diagonal
brace

come-along
cable

come-along

come-along

screw eye

hook

hook-and-
eye latch

fold-out legs

CROSS SECTION VIEW

FRONT VIEW

FIGURE 3.5 *Wine Hoist*

BARREL DOLLY

USING BARRELS IN YOUR WINEMAKING ADVENTURES is a great step up in the production of high-quality wines. But moving a barrel full of wine around your winery can be a difficult task. You can lift them with a hoist, as described in the preceding project, but getting them to the hoist isn't easy without the right equipment. Small wineries use pallet jacks and larger ones have forklifts. By making a barrel dolly for each of your barrels, you can move your barrels around with ease.

While barrels are inherently strong due to their shape, I find that they are best supported when cradled along their metal hoops, distributing the weight over a greater length, as opposed to letting them sit with all their weight on just a few spots of the wood staves while being held in place by wedges or blocks. This dolly design accomplishes that goal as well.

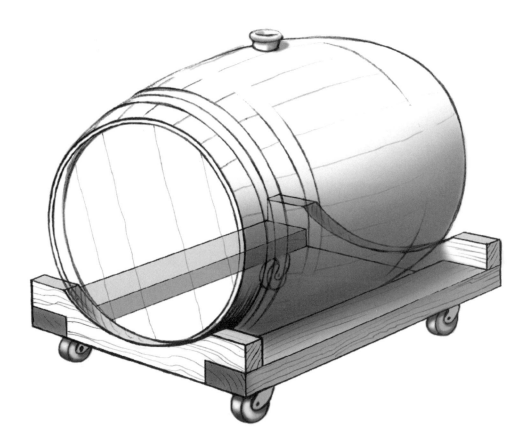

MATERIALS

- One 8-foot length 2×4 lumber
- Four 2" swiveling casters
- Eight 2½" wood screws
- Sixteen 1" round-head wood screws

BUILD IT!

1. Cut the straight side pieces.

Barrels from different manufacturers come in different shapes and sizes, so each dolly should be built to fit a specific barrel. Start by setting the barrel on a flat surface, like a workbench or counter, and roughly measure its length. Cut a couple of 2×4 pieces slightly longer than the barrel and place them flat on the bench, one on each side of the barrel, just touching the side at the bilge (the widest part; see figure 10.1 on page 183). Using another piece of 2×4 to align the 2×4s with the end of the barrel, push the two side pieces so they are flush with the barrel at one end. At the other end, lay another 2×4 across the side pieces, flush with the end of the barrel, and use it as a straightedge to mark the top of the two side pieces, so they'll be flush with the end of the barrel. Cut the side pieces to the marked length and put them back in place, against the barrel's bilge, on the bench.

2. Cut the cross supports.

Measure across the two ends of the side 2×4s, and adjust them until the measurement at each end is equal, meaning they are parallel. Using this measurement, cut two more lengths of 2×4 to be the barrel cross supports.

Now you need to find the diameter of the barrel at the hoop. Rather than just estimate, tape a piece of string to the head hoop, and wrap the string around the barrel until it meets itself. Mark that point on the string with a felt marker and then lay out the string on your work surface and measure this length. To determine the radius of this circumference, divide this length by 6.28 (2 × pi).

Set each cross support flat on the bench with a short piece of scrap 2×4 perpendicular to it, centered on the centerpoint. Use a square to mark this scrap at a point that is the length of the radius plus 1½". Drive a short nail into the scrap piece at this point. Hook a tape measure on this nail, pull the tape out the length of the radius you calculated, and lock the tape at that measurement. Holding the body of the tape, with a pencil on the radius measurement, swing an arc across the support 2×4 and mark the curve. Cut out the curve, and then notch the bottom corners of the cross support to fit the dolly side pieces, at 3½" × 1½". Trace this shape onto the other cross support and cut it to match.

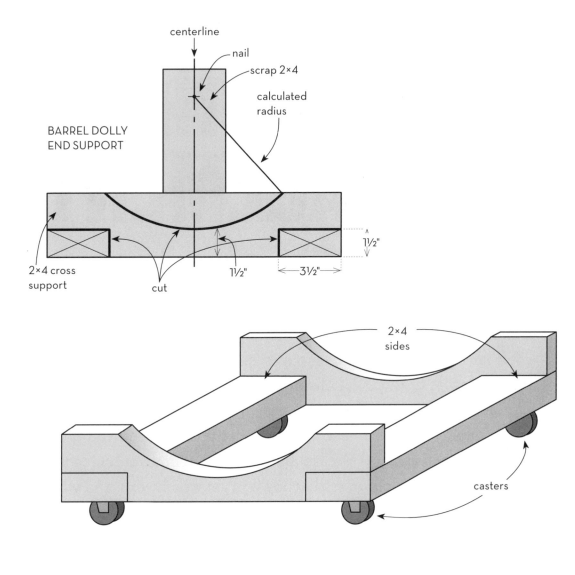

centerline

nail

scrap 2×4

calculated radius

BARREL DOLLY END SUPPORT

2×4 cross support

cut

1½"

1½"

3½"

2×4 sides

casters

FIGURE 3.6 *Barrel Dolly Assembly*

3. Assemble the dolly.

Set the two cross supports on edge with the curves facing down. Fasten the side 2×4s into the notches, using two wood screws per joint. Now attach one swivel caster on each corner, and your barrel dolly is ready to cradle your barrel and roll around the winery with ease. You may be tempted to offer barrel rides to your kids, but wait until the barrel is empty.

CHAPTER FOUR

CONTAINER MANAGEMENT

GOOD CONTAINER MANAGEMENT IS CRUCIAL TO MAKING WINE. When it's time to rack wine, you must have the right-size container to move the wine into. If you're making fairly small batches, and only a few at a time, container management isn't as difficult as when you are making 50 or more gallons of many types of wine at a time. Careful planning is necessary to ensure you have enough of the right size and type of containers when you need them. From the time when you order your grapes to when you cork the last bottle, you will find yourself scratching your head to figure out which carboy will get which wine and what to do if there is too little or too much wine to fill it. Here are some tricks that have helped me solve the perennial puzzle of container management.

I advocate having several different sizes of containers available. And one tactic I use is to make my wines in same-size batches each time. I have found that 250-pound and 100-pound orders of grapes work well. A basic rule of thumb is that 10 pounds of grapes will crush down to 1 gallon of must. So, when crushed, the 250-pound batches fit into my 32-gallon fermenter, with adequate space for the cap to rise. And 100 pounds crushes to 10 gallons, easily fitting into a 20-gallon fermenter with lots of punch-down room.

Once pressed, a 100-pound batch of white grapes will yield 6 to 8 gallons of must. I'll ferment this must in two 5-gallon carboys under an airlock with plenty of headspace for yeast foaming. Upon completion of fermentation, I'll rack the wine into a 6- or 6½-gallon carboy, and any remaining will go into 1-gallon jugs or 1.5-liter or 750 ml wine bottles with rubber stoppers.

A 250-pound batch of red grapes will press out to between 15 and 18 gallons of wine, so three 6-gallon carboys work well. Three-gallon carboys and 15-gallon demijohns are also invaluable to have in the mix, although they're hard to come by now.

Add into this menagerie of containers some barrels, and you'll have lots of options. A 50-liter barrel works well for a 250-pound batch of grapes, leaving a gallon or two for topping up and rotating through. (With a barrel, it's a good idea to make slightly more wine than the barrel will hold to be sure you can continue to feed the angels their share and keep them topped up.) For 100-pound batches, 23-liter barrels are a good fit. A doubled 250-pound batch will work well with a 100-liter barrel.

The head-scratching fun really begins when you have 10 or 20 containers you need to rack and only two or three empty ones. If you're really good, you can maneuver the wine from container to container without ever doing a double racking. This involves careful consideration of which vessel is going to be needed after you finish racking the current batch. So ask yourself, "If I rack that Syrah from the 6½-gallon carboy into the 6-gallon carboy, what am I going to fill the 6½-gallon carboy with?"

Topping Up

At some point you may find yourself having to rack to a container that is too big, or to multiple small containers, and then, after cleaning the vessel, doing a double rack back into the original container. In this case, you may find yourself with too much headspace and in need of topping up (winemakers keep the level of wine to

within an inch or so of the top of the vessel to minimize air exposure). You can use some of last year's similar wine to top up your container, but sometimes that will take several bottles and you may not want to sacrifice today's joy of a finished wine for delayed satisfaction.

There are a number of alternatives to using wine to top up your containers, called *ullage preventers*. The commercially available ones are essentially rubber bags that are inflated with air and set in a barrel or other vessel to take up the empty space. They are very expensive.

So how do home winemakers top up their wines? One popular method is to purchase glass marbles, sanitize them well, and carefully drop them into the container, displacing the ullage.

Another alternative is to get cork overruns from your favorite local winery. Wineries generally order more than they can use, and they shouldn't keep them for more than the current year, so usually they have some corks to discard. Corks are nice in that they float, so you can insert your racking cane down through them when racking time comes. And when you're done, you just throw them out or into the same kind of wine they were in before. When they're not in use, store the corks in a tightly sealed container with a bit of sulfite solution to keep them germ-free. Change out the solution every two to three months to ensure its effectiveness. And soak them well in potassium metabisulfite before dropping them into your wine. A nifty trick to make it easy to get corks out of a carboy or barrel is to string them on a line: just drill a small hole through the length of each cork, feed a fishing line through them, and, after putting the cork string into the carboy, tie the end of the line around the neck of the carboy.

Another alternative is to make your own "corks" for topping up from 100 percent food-grade silicone caulk, which is available at most hardware and paint stores. Trim the tip of the caulking tube to a large opening, and squeeze out ¾"-diameter balls onto a sheet of waxed paper. Let them cure for several weeks to be sure all the acetic acid has off-gassed before using them. Then connect them with a piece of heavy fishing line. They clean up well and can be used over and over.

For larger containers such as barrels, another option is to use an empty bag from a box wine. Put the bag into the barrel that needs topping and blow into the bag (or use nitrogen or argon) with the valve open, and voilà, instant ullage preventer. (This doesn't work for carboys, however, as the valve is larger than the mouth of the carboy.)

Air Locks

An air lock is a simple device that inserts into a bung. It has a hole in its center, and its purpose is to allow a wine's CO_2 and other gases to escape while not allowing air to enter the container. There are a number of different types of air locks, and they are all very inexpensive, so stock up — you'll want more than the number of vessels you have. You can also find "breathable" bungs that perform the same function without an air lock, with a one-way valve built into the bung, but they are much more expensive than a regular bung and air lock. Also, I have heard a report of an instance where a winemaker using breathable bungs in glass carboys experienced a sudden tempera-

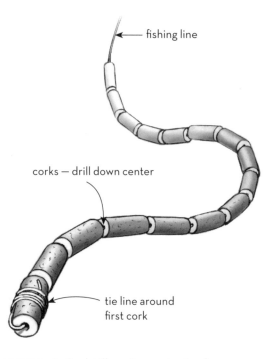

fishing line

corks — drill down center

tie line around first cork

FIGURE 4.1 *Cork Ullage Preventer (corks on a string)*

ture drop in his winery. As the volume of the wine reduced, the bung sealed so tight that the carboys broke. With an air lock, the water in the air lock would have been drawn into the wine, and when it was gone, air would have been drawn in, but the wine would likely not have been ruined.

In a pinch, if you find you don't have an air lock for a container, you can fashion one by inserting a tube or barbed connector into a one-holed bung and then connecting a flexible tube to it. Run this tube down into a container with water in it, with the water container set lower than the wine vessel to reduce the potential of the water being siphoned into the wine with atmospheric changes. Gas will be able to escape the wine, but air is precluded from entering the wine container.

Oaking Wines

For home winemakers with batches too small to fill a barrel, or if the budget doesn't allow for small-format barrels, it's common practice to replicate the aromas and flavors that commercial winemakers get from barrel-aging their wines by adding oak to the wine instead of adding wine to the oak. Several manufacturers make oak augments, including dust, chips, cubes, spirals, balls, slats, and staves, that can be added to your wine. The degree to which the oak is toasted affects the flavor profile, so it's a good idea to get an understanding of which level of toast will work best for your winemaking style.

When I bought my first little bag of oak cubes, I was flabbergasted at how much a tiny bit of wood scraps cost. I had recently picked up a full-size neutral barrel from a winemaker to make a half-barrel planter with, and I decided to break down the other half to try to make and toast my own oak. We'll discuss how you can cut and toast your own oak for enhancing your wines in chapter 10 (page 193). A half barrel will provide you with many, many years of oak at virtually no cost.

The Home Winemaker's "Barrel Room"

When talking about container management, one of the home winemaker's biggest challenges is where to put all those containers full (and empty) of their fermenting and aging wines. The commercial winery typically has a specially designated air- and humidity-controlled space for their aging wines, typically called their barrel room. As a home winemaker you can easily build your own barrel room that is much simpler and smaller than commercial versions but is no less useful.

The home winemaker's barrel room

BARREL ROOM

THIS HOME BARREL ROOM IS MADE TO STORE scores of gallons of wine in a very efficient space. It is cooled with a small window air conditioner, and it allows you to access all the containers in it without having to move any full ones. Armed with a vacuum pump, you should never have to lift a full carboy, barrel, keg, or other heavy vessel again.

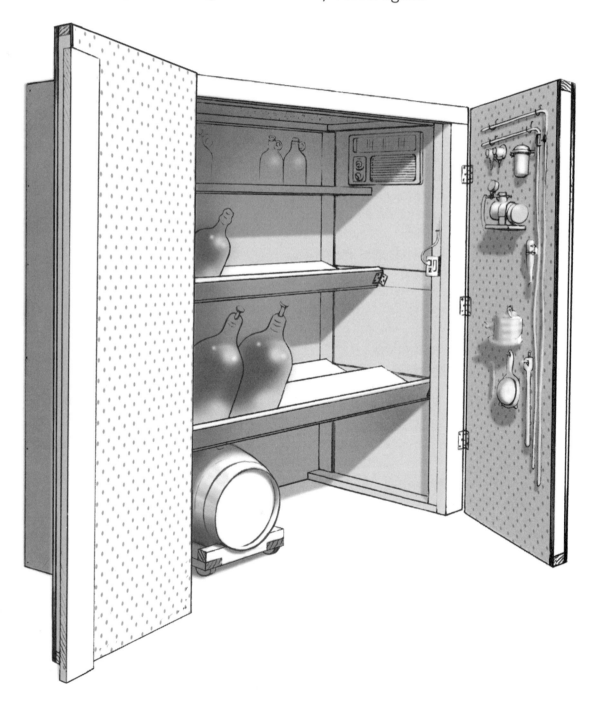

MATERIALS

- Eighteen 8-foot lengths 2×4 lumber
- Five 4 × 8-foot sheets ½" plywood or oriented strand board (*not* particleboard)
- One 8-foot length 2×12 lumber
- Two 4 × 8-foot sheets ¼" pegboard
- 16d framing nails
- 3½" wood screws
- 1½" wood screws
- Six Simpson A23 angle clips
- Three 2 × 8-foot sheets 1½"-thick rigid foam insulation
- Two 4 × 8-foot sheets 1" thick rigid foam insulation
- Six 3½" butt (door) hinges
- 32 lineal feet self-adhesive weatherstripping
- Two 36"-long rubber door sweeps
- One cane bolt (mounts to door and holds bottom in place)
- One small window air conditioner (5,000 BTU)

BUILD IT!

NOTE: *These plans assume that the barrel room will be built with its back against a wall that has already been insulated. If not, then frame a wall that will constitute the back wall and insulate it with a minimum of R-13 (3½"-thick) fiberglass insulation. Also, this barrel room is designed to be built at 8 feet tall. If your ceiling is lower than that, adjust the height measurements accordingly. Additionally, you will need to have a supply of 110V power available for the window AC unit.*

1. Frame the side walls and ceiling.

Start by laying out the dimensions of the barrel room on the floor. It should be 2'6" deep and 6'4" wide. Of course, you could also make this larger or smaller based on your own wine production.

Cut four of the 2×4s at 7'7½" (or the height of your ceiling minus 5"). Then cut four 2×4s at 2'6". Lay two of the longer 2×4s flat on the floor and two of the shorter ones on edge across the ends to form one side wall for the barrel room. Nail these together, and stand the assembly up in the location where a side wall will be. Nail or screw the wall framing to the floor, square with the back wall, shimming the bottom as necessary to make the front of the wall plumb in both directions. If backing, such as studs, top or bottom plates, or other framing material, exists in the back walls, nail the side wall to it as well. If not, you should screw it to the shelf supports later. Repeat with the remaining cut 2×4s to make the other side wall.

NOTE: *If the bottom 2×4s will sit on a bare concrete floor, use pressure-treated lumber for those pieces, to prevent rot.*

Cut two of the 2×4s at 6'4" long. Nail them on top of the two side walls, at their ends, spanning the distance between them, to frame the ceiling. On the top 2×4s of the side walls, fill in the spaces between the ceiling 2×4s with lengths of 2×4, effectively doubling the top pieces. If your ceiling is higher than the barrel room, install a piece of plywood to form the "roof" on top of the framed ceiling.

Cut two pieces of plywood at 2'6" × 8' and fasten them to the side walls, and the barrel room starts to take shape.

2. Build the shelves.

The shelves are going to be built on a slight angle, which will allow the carboys to be stacked closer together while still allowing you access to insert a wine thief or racking canes into them without moving them. To build the shelf supports, cut five 2×4s to match the inside width along the back wall between the two side walls (which should be about 6'1"). Rip the top edge of two of these 2×4s at a 15° angle. Locate the studs in the back wall, and using one 16d nail or 3½" wood screw at each stud, nail the two angled shelf supports to the back wall, one at 2'4" and one at 4'6" above the floor, with the angled edges sloping down to the front.

Cut two lengths of 2×4 to match the inside width of each side wall. Install these 2×4s between the front and rear side-wall studs, again at 2'4" and 4'6".

Cut the remaining plywood into three pieces that are each 1'2" wide and 6'1" long. Pair each plywood piece with one of the 2×4s you cut to match the inside width of the back wall of the barrel room. For each pair, set the 2×4 on edge, and set the

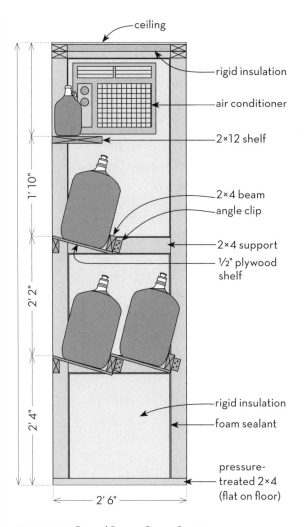

FIGURE 4.2 *Barrel Room Cross Section*

plywood piece on top of it, with one edge flush with the face of the 2×4. Fasten them together with 1½" wood screws set every 6 inches. Next, flip these assemblies over so the 2×4 is on top of the plywood. Mark a line ¾ inch in from the long edge of the plywood, on the side opposite the 2×4, and parallel to the long edge. Start a 1⅝" screw every 6 inches along the line. On the outer faces of the 2×4s, nail on an A23 clip.

To install the shelves, set the back lower shelf in place and drive the screws that you

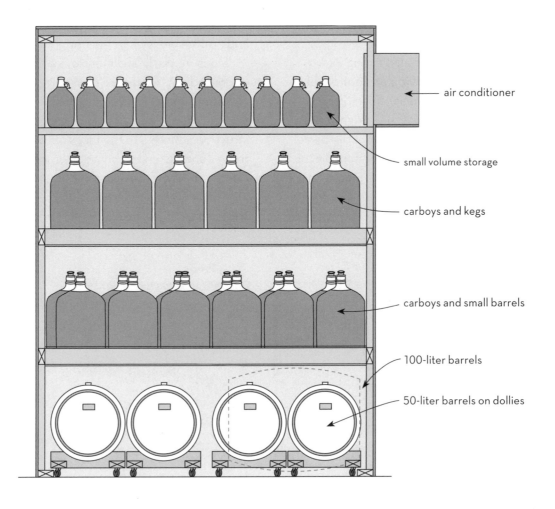

air conditioner

small volume storage

carboys and kegs

carboys and small barrels

100-liter barrels

50-liter barrels on dollies

FIGURE 4.3 *Barrel Room Front View*

started in the plywood into the angled 2×4 support on the back wall. Then fasten the front of the shelf to the side-wall supports through the A23 clip on each end. Install the front lower shelf in the same manner. Then install the middle shelf. You should be able to stand on the lower shelves to install the middle one. When you're finished, you should have three slanted shelves with a 2×4 front edge that will hold carboys in place at approximately 15°.

The top shelf, built with the 2×12, is installed level to store jugs, bottles, and other smaller containers. Cut the 2×12 to length, and notch the back corners to fit around the 2×4 studs. To secure the shelf, screw through the side walls and into the ends of the 2×12 shelf with 3½" wood screws. Along the back of the 2×12, "toenail" some screws on a diagonal into the back wall studs.

Fill the wall and ceiling cavities with pieces cut from the 2 × 8-foot sheets of rigid insulation, using construction adhesive.

3. Construct the doors.

Build the two door frames using 2×4 uprights and, for the top and bottom of the frame, a 2×4 that has been ripped in half lengthwise. Cut the upright 2×4s 2¾" shorter than the height of the barrel room, and cut the top and bottom pieces at 37¾". Lay the door frame pieces on the floor, square them up with a framing square, and fasten them together using two 16d nails or 3½" screws through the top and bottom pieces into the uprights.

Measure the final dimensions of the doors and cut two pieces of ½" plywood to match. These are for the outsides of the doors. Liberally apply wood glue or construction adhesive to the faces of the door frames and fasten the plywood to them using screws or nails. Flip the doors over and install some scrap pieces of 2×4 at strategic locations inside the doors to allow

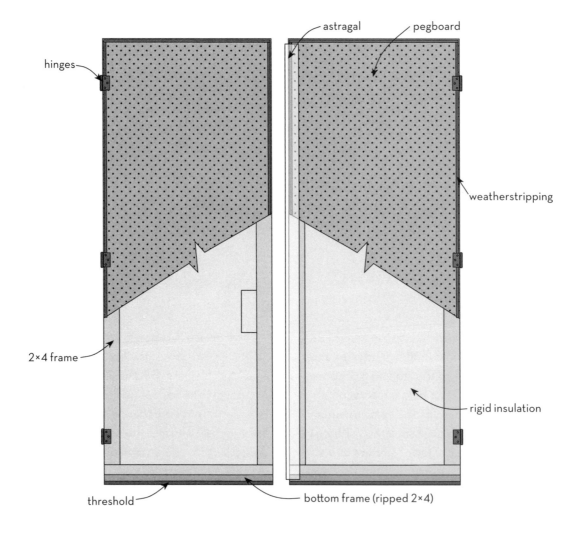

FIGURE 4.4 *Barrel Room Doors*

you to screw various devices to the doors in the future.

Cut and install the 1" rigid insulation in the interior cavity of the doors, and then screw the cut-to-fit ¼" pegboard over the insulation. Rip a 4"-wide piece of ½" plywood, just shorter in length than the door frame, and screw it to the inside (pegboard side) of the door that will close first (this is called the *astragal*). Be sure to set the astragal low enough at the top so that when the door closes, it ends up below the ceiling framing of the barrel room.

4. Hang the doors and install the AC.

Install three butt hinges on the inside face of each door, with the tops of the hinge pins pointing up.

Place some ½" plywood scraps on the floor at the opening to the barrel room and stand the first door in place, plumbing up the hinge side with some shims as necessary. Once it's plumb, mark the top and bottom of each hinge on the framing and lay the door back down. Remove the hinge pins, and install the jamb sides of the hinges on the framing (note: there's no need to mortise for the hinges), leaving the screws just slightly loose. Stand the door back up, set the hinges together, and reinstall the hinge pins; then tighten up the screws into the jambs. Repeat this process with the second door, while maintaining about ¼" between the leading edges of the two doors.

Install the cane bolt on the door without the astragal, and install the weatherstripping as shown in figure 4.4. On one side wall, near the top, install a small window-style air conditioner by cutting through the plywood and installing the unit per the manufacturer's instructions. Now you're about done.

NOTE: *If you like, you can paint the barrel room. I recommend using a primer and some enamel on the shelves in particular to make cleanup easier.*

USE IT!

Your new barrel room will hold a lot of wine. The lower floor level will allow for barrels or carboys on their respective dollies to roll out easily for access. Barrels of up to 30 gallons can be stored in this space. The second level with the double shelves can accommodate twelve 6½-gallon carboys, or you can make a modified barrel dolly without wheels that just sits on the shelf to support a small-format barrel. All told, nearly 200 gallons of wine in various phases of development can be stored in a safe, cool 60°F environment.

Racking is made particularly easy with a vacuum pump and transfer gun (see page 64) or, if you plan well, simply by using gravity to take wine from one level to the next. Once empty, the carboys lift out easily for cleaning. Never again will you need to lift or even move a full carboy!

With a few pegboard hooks, the doors become an excellent place to hang racking canes, tubing, wine thieves, large spoons, and any other equipment you may need for working with the wine, keeping it organized and out of sight. On the outside, a towel bar, coat hooks, and thermometer with remote sensor to the inside can be installed, along with all the gold medals you'll win from your fantastic wines.

ORGANIZING YOUR EQUIPMENT

A well-organized winery will make your tasks move more smoothly and ensure that your equipment is not lost when vitally needed. By lining your barrel room doors with pegboard (see page 84), you will create a large, easy-to-access hanging surface for a lot of your equipment. In this photo, the racking canes are set in a pair of hooks, and then the attached hoses hang straight to dry thoroughly and prevent curling, making running the lines much easier. A funnel hangs below the transfer guns, and a canister filter is stored next to a spray bottle filled with sanitizing solution. The vacuum pump sits on a small wood shelf and is strapped to the pegboard with plastic zip ties. Below the pump is its overflow container held to the pegboard with a nylon strap with plastic snap buckles that come apart for easy transfer to the sink for cleaning. Also hanging from the door are vacuum tubing, a screen filter, a stirring rod, and a flashlight for inspecting the insides of the barrels.

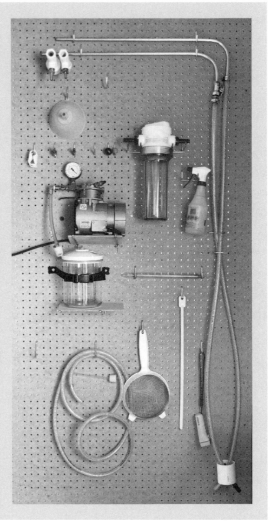

Stockpiling Bottles

Most of us *garagistes* prefer to reuse bottles rather than buy new bottles. They are easy to acquire from a number of sources (see Sourcing Bottles, page 122). As all these bottles come pouring in, you need to be able to store them for bottling day. One option is to keep them in wine boxes stacked against a wall. The downside of wine boxes is that they don't allow you to easily identify which kinds of bottles are in which box. Sorting bottles at bottling time can be a very tedious task, so I like to do a basic sort as they come into the winery either from my kitchen or from restaurants.

A rough diamond-style bottle rack solves most of these issues and looks good in the winery as well. Bottles can be stacked on top of each other, sorted by shape, color, and even punt size and neck shape.

DIAMOND WINE BOTTLE RACK

THIS RACK WILL HOLD FOUR CASES OF BOTTLES in each full diamond and between 15 and 21 bottles in each smaller triangle, for a total capacity of about 364 bottles.

MATERIALS

- Two 12-foot lengths 2×10 lumber
- Four 8-foot lengths 2×10 lumber
- 16d nails or 3½" wood screws
- Two Simpson A35 angle brackets
- Six 4" wood screws
- Six 1⅜" wood screws
- Polyethylene sheeting (optional)

BUILD IT!

1. Construct the rack.

The following numbers correspond to the numbered pieces in figure 4.5:

❶ Cut one of the 12-foot 2×10s into two pieces at 67½" each. These will become the top and bottom of the rack.

❷ Cut the other 12-foot 2×10 into two pieces at 64½" each. These are the sides. Lay the top, bottom, and sides on the floor and fasten them with 16d nails or 3½" wood screws, driving the fasteners through the tops and bottoms into the upright pieces. Square up this frame by measuring diagonally between opposite corners, adjusting the frame until the two measurements are equal.

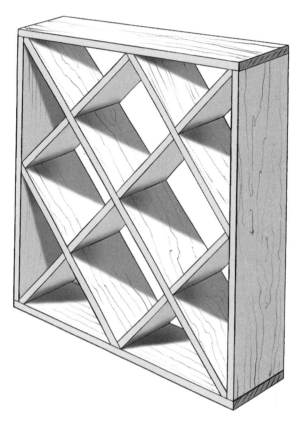

❸ Cut one of the 8-foot 2×10s to length at 91". Measure back ¾" from each end and cut on this line at a 45° bevel out toward the ends. Flip the piece over and cut the same angle on the other side, effectively forming a V point on each end. Slip this piece into the frame, extending from one corner to the opposite one, and nail or screw it in place. Mark the centerpoint of this piece along its front edge.

❹ Cut another 8-foot 2×10 into two pieces at 47" each, by cutting one end

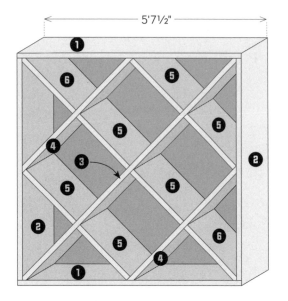

5'7½"

FIGURE 4.5 *Diamond Wine Bottle Rack*

2. Install the rack.

Stand the new diamond rack up against the wall where you plan to install it. Locate a couple of studs to fasten the rack to. Nail or screw a metal angle bracket to the shelf at these two locations, and fasten the brackets securely into the studs with some 2" screws.

USE IT!

After you've cleaned the bottles, store them in the diamond rack, at the ready for bottling. To keep critters out in the interim, you could hang a piece of polyethylene sheeting over the face of the rack.

When stacking bottles in the rack, it's a good idea to insert Bordeaux-style bottles (the ones with squarer shoulders) with their necks out and the Burgundy-style (like Chardonnay), Hock-style (like Riesling), and champagne-style bottles with their necks pointing toward the wall, as these latter types can tip forward and cascade out onto the floor.

square and the other on a similar 45° point with the 47" measurement being to the long point of the piece. Install these pieces parallel to the long diagonal piece, and fasten them in place with the nails or screws.

⑤ From the remaining 8-foot lengths of 2×10, cut six pieces at 21¼" each. The ends of these should be left square. Install these six pieces perpendicular to the diagonal pieces, at each end of the #4 pieces and aligned on the centerpoint of the #3 piece, completing four diamonds in the center of the larger frame, and fasten them in place.

⑥ From the remaining 2×10, cut two pieces with the double 45° cut similar to the #3 piece on one end. Measure from the cut 21¼" and cut this end square. These are the remaining pieces that get installed at the opposite corners from the #3 piece.

SILICONE BUNGS

SILICONE BUNGS HAVE BECOME THE CADILLAC of barrel and carboy closures, and as such they are fairly expensive in comparison to the rubber bungs on the market. Of course, you can make them and save yourself some money!

Most hardware and paint stores stock 100 percent silicone caulk. Be sure to check the product label to confirm that the caulk is rated safe for food contact.

I use silicone sealants for lots of things around the house and rarely does my project require a full tube. That moment becomes a Bung Opportunity. Here's how to do it.

MATERIALS

- 100% food-grade silicone sealant
- One or more 5-ounce waxed paper cups

BUILD IT!

Put the tube in your caulking gun and trim the tip to a medium-sized opening. Put the tip down all the way down into the bottom of the cup and fill the bottom completely, and then leave the tip at the bottom of the cup, moving it in a slow circular motion, as the caulk fills the cup from the bottom up. If you try to fill from the top, you'll end up with lots of voids on the sides and inside the bung.

When the sealant reaches about the halfway point, slowly begin to withdraw the tip while continuing to push caulk out. After the sealant has filled the cup about two-thirds full, you can stop the flow and just make a little swirl, like the top of a soft-serve ice cream cone.

Allow the sealant to cure for a minimum of two months, then carefully tear away the paper cup. With a pair of scissors, trim up the top corners of the bung, and you've got yourself a nice, smooth little bung. Let the bung air-dry until no hint of acetic acid can be smelled before using it.

USE IT!

Just push the silicone bung down into the bunghole of your barrel and you've got a nice tight seal.

VARIATIONS

Carboy Bung

In order to make a bung that fits your carboys or other containers with smaller holes, you may need to make a mold. To do this, mix up some plaster of paris into a relatively creamy consistency. Lightly coat a bung that fits your container with some cooking oil, and press the bung down into the plaster. Allow the plaster to set up for a couple days, and then carefully remove the bung, leaving its impression in the plaster, like a cup in a cupcake pan. Lightly sand the inside of the mold with some very fine sandpaper. Coat the mold with a little cooking spray, and then fill it with silicone sealant as described above. You could reuse the mold over and over to use up those half-empty tubes of silicone sealant left over from other projects.

Transfer Gun Bung

Once you have filled the cup or mold with the sealant, immediately push a 2"-long piece of ¾" PVC pipe down through the sealant to the bottom of the cup. Once the sealant is cured, remove the excess sealant from the inside of the PVC pipe with a pen knife, then assemble the rest of the transfer gun as described on page 65.

One-Hole Bung

Once you have filled the cup or mold with the sealant, insert a short piece of ⅜" flexible tubing down through it. Once the sealant is cured, cut the tubing flush with the top of the bung, and push out the sealant inside the tube with a rod, like a small Phillips screwdriver or a drill bit. This arrangement will work to hold an air lock securely in the bung.

CHAPTER FIVE

THE HOME WINE LABORATORY

MAKING GOOD WINE AT HOME doesn't require an extensive education in chemistry or other microbiological sciences, but gaining a basic understanding of what is going on and how, why, and when to test and adjust your wine is vital. Once again, there are some great books on the market that will present the basics and the details of wine analysis. Here, we are going to set up your lab, make some of the testing equipment for a fraction of the cost of store-bought versions, and get you organized to analyze your wine efficiently.

Measuring Sugar

There are a couple of pieces of equipment that the winemaker uses to determine the amount of sugar in grapes, juice, must, and wine. One is a hydrometer, the other a refractometer. A hydrometer is a long glass sealed tube with a weighted bottom and graduated markings along its upper portion. Most winemakers commonly use the triple-scale hydrometer, which indicates specific gravity, degrees Brix, and potential alcohol. I recommend that every winemaker have a good-quality hydrometer. That said, hydrometers tend to break at the worst possible times, and depending on where you live, it can take a long time to get a replacement. Therefore, you may need to make one in a pinch.

Only a few analyses are needed for making good wine. These include tests to determine levels of:

» Sugar
» pH
» Malic acid
» Free sulfite
» Titratable acidity

HYDROMETER

WHILE FAIRLY RUDIMENTARY, this simple DIY hydrometer will get you through until you have a replacement manufactured hydrometer in hand.

MATERIALS

- One approx. 12"-long drinking straw or other rigid plastic tube (a broken plastic racking cane works too)
- Modeling clay, Play-Doh, glazing compound, or other moldable material
- Distilled water
- Sugar
- Jar
- Graph paper
- 12" ruler

NOTE: *If you're stuck and don't have any modeling clay, you can make a bit with ¼ cup of flour, ¼ cup of warm water, ⅛ cup salt, and ¾ teaspoon vegetable oil.*

BUILD IT!

Stick a blob of the clay on the bottom of the tube. You might also want to put a very small amount in the top of the tube to keep liquids out.

Lower the tube into a full jar of distilled water. The water line should be near the top of the tube. If not, add more clay to the bottom of the tube to weight it down. The correct amount to add is just enough to sink the tube to within ½" of the top of the water. Mark the water line on the tube with a permanent felt-tip marker; this is the 0° Brix mark. Remove the tube and dump out the water.

Mix up a solution of 24 grams of sugar in 100 ml of distilled water. Fill the jar to the top with this solution and lower the

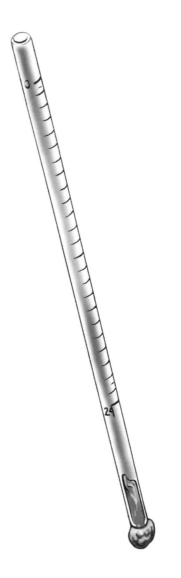

hydrometer into it. Allow it to come to rest and mark the water line with the marker. You now have it marked for 0° Brix and 24° Brix.

The Brix scale is a straight-line scale, so you want to mark the straw from 0 through 24. Rather than doing the math, set the hydrometer on a piece of graph paper and note the 0 and 24 marks. Place a ruler on the graph paper at an angle so the 0" mark of the ruler aligns with the graph grid line of the 0°B mark on the hydrometer and the 12" mark aligns with the 24°B grid line. Transfer every half-inch mark of the ruler down to the hydrometer and mark it on the tube. Then just number every fourth calibration mark from 0 through 24 and it's calibrated.

USE IT!

Whether you are using a DIY hydrometer or a glass hydrometer, float the device in relatively clear liquid in a hydrometer jar (a clear tube just a bit larger in diameter and taller than the hydrometer).

NOTE: *Hydrometer jars are very cheap, so I recommend just buying one with your hydrometer. If you're stuck without one, however, put a wine cork in a 14"-long piece of clear plastic tubing and cut the cork off flush with the bottom of the tubing. For a base, drill a ¾" hole though a 2" square or circle of ½" plywood, and glue the tube into the hole.*

✳ *Drawing a sample of fermenting red wine for checking sugar levels is fairly difficult due to all the skins and MOG (matter other than grapes) in the must that clog up your wine thief. Plus your sample should have as few solids in it as possible to get an accurate reading. A trick I've found that allows for obtaining a clean sample is to punch down the cap just prior to drawing the sample, place a stainless steel kitchen strainer on top of the must, and pull the sample with a turkey baster.*

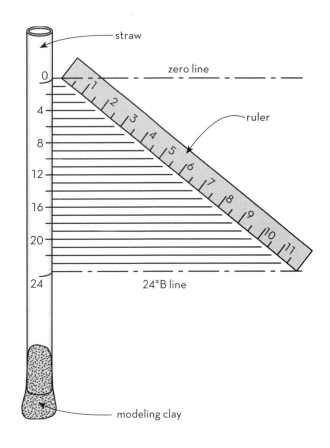

FIGURE 5.1 *DIY Hydrometer*

Refractometer

The refractometer is the other device that winemakers use for measuring sugar. This instrument is a calibrated prism that refracts light and indicates the amount of sugar present in the juice. You put a couple drops of the juice on the prism, close the cover, look through the scope, and read the scale. As your must is fermenting, alcohol will skew the reading, so you need to refer to a compensation chart to obtain the actual reading.

As is the case for any piece of equipment, calibrating your refractometer is critical to obtaining good results.

A refractometer is very handy for field testing in the vineyard. You take a very random sampling of grapes that are going to be picked together, put them in a small ziplock bag, and mush them up and mix well. Then snip a corner from the bottom of the bag, let a few drops of juice fall on the prism, and read it.

As is the case for any piece of equipment, calibrating your refractometer is critical to obtaining good results, so at the beginning of each season, make up a standardizing solution of a known amount of sugar in grams mixed with 100 ml of distilled water and take a reading with your hydrometer. Use this solution on your refractometer and adjust the calibration to match the hydrometer. Some winemak-ers I know have several hydrometers and measure the same solution with all of them, then average to arrive at their refractometer calibrations. You should also calibrate at zero with distilled water placed on the clean prism.

Note that some refractometers compensate for temperature while others do not, so follow the manufacturer's instructions for adjusting your readings if needed.

Measuring pH

The pH of a solution gives the winemaker an indication of its relative acidity. A wine with too low a pH will be tart, bitter, or "green" tasting, and one with too high a pH will be flabby and not capable of long-term storage. Getting grapes with the proper range of pH for the varietal is great but not always possible, particularly for a home winemaker.

You can measure pH using paper litmus strips, but they can be difficult to read with a colored wine, and they don't provide the real accuracy you will need for pH determination and the other tests you will be using this measurement for. Therefore I recommend that all home winemakers consider a good-quality pH meter as essential a piece of equipment as their hydrometer.

A pH meter is an electronic device that has a small glass probe at the bottom of a shaft. Typically it has a couple of calibration screws and a digital readout.

There are a few types of pH meters to be aware of when you're looking for the one that is right for your needs. One is a pen-like all-in-one meter that is very handy for checking pH in the vineyard or whenever it is important to have a pocket-size meter. Due to its low price, it's a good meter to get when you're first starting out with wine-making, and it makes a great backup meter as you get more advanced.

Another type is a handheld model with a cable that extends from the electronics module to the probe. A third type is a benchtop model that is larger and typically much more expensive than the other two. The pen-type and handheld models are typically powered by batteries, and the benchtop model more commonly uses 12V DC power.

Your pH meter should have the appropriate range, accuracy, and resolution for winemaking. The range should be from 0.00 through 14.00, the accuracy should be +/- 0.01 pH, and the resolution 0.01 pH. Temperature compensation is desirable but not absolutely required.

The glass probes of the pH meter are very sensitive and can be damaged if they dry out or are exposed to oils on your fingertips. Some manufacturers will void the warranty if their probe is allowed to dry out, so take care to keep it submerged in the appropriate solution, such as a pH probe storage solution, tap water, or a pH 4.0 buffer solution. Do *not* store a pH meter in distilled water, as it will damage the probe. Follow the manufacturer's directions for maximum longevity of your probe.

When you first get your meter, you'll want to follow the manufacturer's instructions for calibrating it. Know that it will take an hour or more simply for the meter to stabilize and come to rest at a steady reading. Then you can calibrate it. This is done by inserting the probe into standardizing buffer solutions of pH 7.01 and pH 4.01. These solutions need to be fresh and so generally are not used more than once,

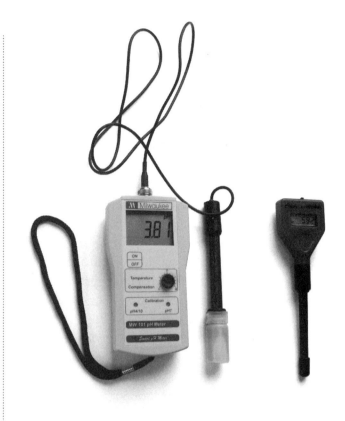

Handheld and pen-type pH meters

unless the calibration is being done only a few days after a previous calibration. One manufacturer recommends keeping the standardizing buffers from the previous calibration to use as a prerinse for the meter, before you insert it into fresh buffer solution. I keep used buffer solutions in small, dark-colored bottles for this purpose. A calibration should be good for a week or two, but if it has been longer than that since you used your meter, it's good practice to recalibrate it.

The standardizing buffer solutions are available in bulk or in individual sachets designed for single-use applications. If stored properly, the bulk solutions should last a reasonable length of time for a frequent tester.

Total Titratable Acidity

Titratable acidity (TA) is a measurement of the acidity in your juice, must, or wine, based on the concentration of the acid in solution. It's read in grams per liter or percent. For example, the TA of a must might be 7.2 grams per liter (also parts per million) or 0.72%.

The primary chemical for testing TA is 0.10 normal sodium hydroxide (NaOH). ("Normality" is a way to express the concentration of a substance in solution.) You can purchase this solution premixed, or you can make it by dissolving 4 grams of solid-form NaOH in 100 ml of distilled water. **Caution: Use lab gloves and goggles when using solid NaOH and read all MSDS sheets**. This solution is fairly stable and should last about a year. Before using this solution, it is good practice to standardize the actual concentration of the NaOH; see Standardizing Sodium Hydroxide Solution on page 107.

Ask a dozen winemakers how they test for TA, and you'll get a dozen different protocols. This is how I do it:

1. Place 100 ml of distilled water into a 250 ml beaker, Erlenmeyer flask, or comparably sized glass jar.

2. Add 5 ml of wine sample to the distilled water, and mix thoroughly by stirring or swirling.

3. Place the pH meter probe in the water and wine solution.

4. Fill a 10 ml pipette or syringe with the NaOH solution, noting the exact amount in the pipette or syringe. Slowly add drops of the NaOH solution to the water and wine solution, swirling after each drop to mix it in, until the pH meter reaches 8.20.

5. Check the pipette or syringe to find out how many milliliters of NaOH you added to the wine and water solution. Multiply this number by 0.15, giving you the percent of titratable acidity.

If your standardization of the NaOH proves your actual concentration is not 0.10N (normal), then use this formula to calculate the TA instead:

$$V_{NaOH} \times N \times 7.5 / V_s$$

where:

V_{NaOH} = volume of NaOH used in ml

N = normality of NaOH

V_s = volume of wine sample used

WHEN MAKING TITRATIONS AND OTHER TESTS, a lab support stand is handy to have around. This version consists of a steel rod and heavy base to which you can clamp different pieces of equipment.

MATERIALS

- One 8" x 12" piece 1/2" plywood or HDPE plastic
- One 16" length 3/8" solid steel rod
- 3/8" thread-cutting die with handle
- Two 3/8" nuts
- Four rubber cabinet door bumpers

BUILD IT!

Drill a 1/8" hole in the plywood or HDPE, centered on the 8" dimension and 3/4" in from the edge. If you're not using a drill press, work carefully to drill a straight, perpendicular hole. Now, using the 1/8" hole as the centerpoint, and using a 5/8" spade bit, drill a hole 3/16" deep into the bottom of the plywood or HDPE. Do not drill this hole too deep. It's meant to allow you to recess the bottom nut of the steel rod into the stand base. Complete the hole by enlarging the 1/8" hole, drilling all the way through with a 3/8" straight bit.

* *If you use plywood for the base of your lab stand, you can paint it after drilling the hole for the stand. I prefer white paint, as it makes it easy to discern color changes in solutions.*

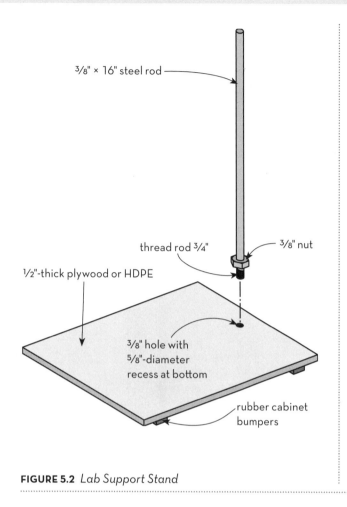

3/8" × 16" steel rod

thread rod 3/4"

3/8" nut

1/2"-thick plywood or HDPE

3/8" hole with 5/8"-diameter recess at bottom

rubber cabinet bumpers

FIGURE 5.2 *Lab Support Stand*

On one end of the steel rod, use the die tool to cut threads up to 3/4" up the rod. Install one of the nuts at the top of the threads. Insert the threaded end of the rod down through the 3/8" hole, install the other nut on the rod, and tighten it up into the recessed base hole.

Install a cabinet door bumper at each corner on the underside of the base, and your stand is ready for use.

USE IT!

You can purchase (or make) a number of different types of clamps that work well to hold various types of test tubes, pipettes, burettes, pH meter probes, and so on. You should have at least two of these clamps, and a third could be useful.

Malic Acid

Malic acid is one of a number of acids commonly found in grapes. It produces a crisp "green apple" flavor, and depending on your style of wine, this may not be desirable. Winemakers frequently inoculate their wines with malolactic bacteria to ferment this malic acid, which converts it to a smoother, almost buttery-tasting lactic acid. When the fermentation appears to be complete, it's time to test for malic acid to confirm the process is complete before adding potassium metabisulfite to protect the wine.

MALIC ACID TEST

THIS TEST IS FOR ANY WINES you wish to put through malolactic fermentation (MLF). It's easy to perform and gives you a colorful, almost artistic result. You can buy a malic acid test kit, which should include everything you will need, or you can assemble the pieces and reagents from various sources. Chromatography solvent emits strong fumes, so perform this test in a well-ventilated area.

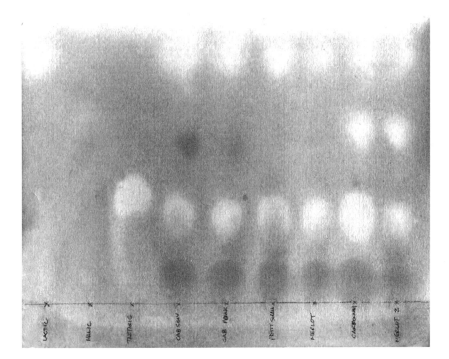

MATERIALS

- Chromatography paper
- Capillary tubes
- Malic, tartaric, and lactic acid chromatography standard solutions
- Chromatography solvent
- One 1-gallon widemouthed plastic or glass container with lid (approx. 8" tall)
- Stapler

USE IT!

Mark a light pencil (not pen) line along the chromatography paper's long dimension, about ¾" in from the edge. On this line, mark a series of small *X*s, beginning about ½" in from the left edge and spacing them 1" apart. You'll place the standard solutions of tartaric, malic, and lactic acids at the first three *X*s, so mark a *T*, *M*, or *L* under them. Under the remaining *X*s, identify each of the wines you will be testing.

Collect very small samples of each wine you will be testing. Small paper cups labeled with a felt-tip pen are handy for this.

Fill a capillary tube about half full with your first wine sample; just place the end of the tube in the wine, and it will fill by itself. Put your finger over the upper end to hold the wine in the tube, set the tip of the tube on the appropriate *X* on the paper, and allow the wine to soak into the paper to form a dot no bigger than ¼". Repeat this process for each wine sample and each acid solution standard; use a fresh tube for each wine sample. Allow these dots to dry, and repeat this application at least two more times with each sample, taking care to keep the dots no bigger than ¼". This multiple application concentrates the sample and gives a stronger result.

While the samples are drying, pour about ¼" of the solvent into the gallon container, taking care not to breathe the strong fumes.

Once the samples are dry, roll the paper into a circle, with the two edges butted together, and staple them to form a tube. With the pencil line horizontal and on the bottom edge, lower the paper tube into the gallon container so the edge is completely immersed into the solvent. Close the container, and wait for the paper to absorb the solvent all the way up to its top. This usually takes 8 to 12 hours, but it can take more or less time. Do not let the paper sit in the solution longer than is needed for the solvent to reach the top of the paper,

or the samples may be diluted or encroach on each other.

Remove the paper and hang with a clip (perhaps on the lab support stand; see page 97). Allow it to dry, which can take as long as 24 hours. Once the paper is dry, examine it. Above the tartaric, malic, and lactic acid standards, you'll find a yellow blotch at a particular height. Look for similar yellow blotches above your wine samples. A blotch at the level of the malic acid standard blotch indicates that malic acid is still present in your wine, and malolactic fermentation has not finished. A blotch at the level of the lactic acid standard blotch, with no blotch at the level of the malic acid standard, indicates that malolactic fermentation is complete.

The chromatography solvent is very stable and will last indefinitely, so once the test is completed, pour the unused portion back into the solvent bottle.

✴ *Instead of using disposable capillary tubes, you can obtain a small hypodermic needle from your doctor and rinse it with distilled water between uses.*

✴ *For individual samples, cut a 1" wide piece of the chromatography paper, and place the sample at the bottom as described above. Stand the paper in a 100 ml graduated cylinder with ¼" of the solvent. Cover with a cork or other top to contain the fumes.*

CHROMATOGRAPHY CHAMBER

MOST CHROMATOGRAPHY TEST KITS supply you with a plastic jar for soaking the paper in solvent, but the jar is usually opaque, which makes checking on the absorption of the solvent difficult. Using a clear glass jar instead can help, but even so, the jar takes up a fair amount of room for a test that you'll do only once or twice a year. So, as an alternative to the jar, I have developed this thin-profile chromatography chamber.

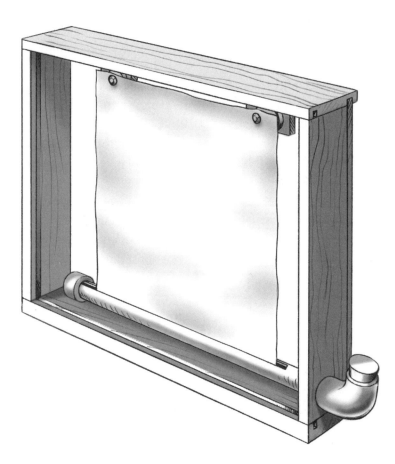

MATERIALS

- Various scraps ¼", ½", and ¾" plywood
- One 12" × 12" piece ⅛" clear Plexiglas
- Wood glue
- ⅞" brads

- One 18" length ½" PVC pipe
- One ½" PVC cap
- PVC adhesive
- One ½" PVC elbow

- One piece chromatography paper
- Wine bottle cork
- One ¾" rubber stopper
- Two thumbtacks

BUILD IT!

1. Cut the chamber box parts.

Cut the base of the chamber from ¾" plywood at 1½" × 11". Cut the two sides from ½" plywood at 1½" × 10". Cut the top from ½" plywood at 2" × 11".

Set your table saw blade ¼" above the table, and use it to mill a ⅛"-wide, ¼"-deep groove along the long dimension, ¼" in from one edge, on each of these four pieces. On the top piece, cut a similar groove on the other long side, and widen it with another pass or two of the saw to make it slightly more than ¼" wide. This groove will slip down over the back of the chamber.

Cut the back from ¼" plywood at 11" × 11". Cut the Plexiglas down to 10½" × 10½".

2. Assemble the chamber box.

Glue and nail the side pieces to the base, then glue and nail the back to the sides and base. The back should extend ¼" above the sides. Slide the Plexiglas down into the ⅛" grooves of the sides and base. Apply some compatible adhesive into the ⅛" groove in the top piece, and slip it over the Plexiglas and back panel and onto the sides. Let the adhesive dry.

3. Create the solvent reservoir.

Make a mark on the PVC pipe 11½" from one end. Measure the outside diameter of the pipe, and set the fence of the table saw so that it is half this distance from the center of the blade. Set the blade so that it is just high enough to cut through only one wall of the pipe. Cut a slot in the pipe up to the 11½" mark; when the blade gets to that mark, carefully lift the pipe up off the blade, starting from the end in your hands and keeping the leading end firmly on the table until the pipe is clear of the blade. Use caution that the pipe does not kick back at you while performing this maneuver. Install the PVC cap on the cut end of this pipe, using PVC adhesive.

Measure the diameter of the PVC cap and drill a hole at the bottom of the right-hand chamber side piece, just above the base, to receive the pipe. Cut the pipe off at 10¼" (including the cap), and use PVC adhesive to install the PVC elbow on the uncapped side, with the slot in the pipe and the free end of the elbow both pointing up. Slide this solvent reservoir assembly into the chamber.

4. Add paper supports.

Remove the Plexiglas front and chamber top. Set a sample piece of chromatography paper in the slot of the reservoir and mark the top edge of the paper on the back panel. Cut two 1" × 1" pieces of ¼" plywood, and glue them to the back panel at the marked line. Then cut a ¼"-thick piece from each end of the cork, and glue them to the plywood pieces.

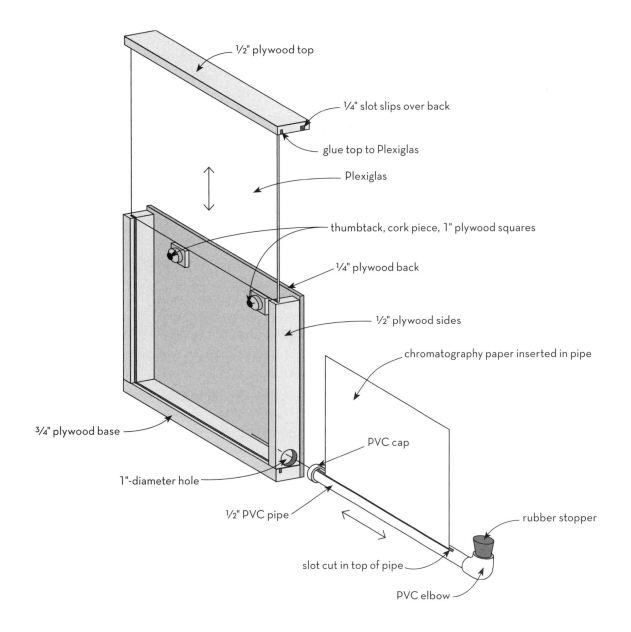

½" plywood top

¼" slot slips over back

glue top to Plexiglas

Plexiglas

thumbtack, cork piece, 1" plywood squares

¼" plywood back

½" plywood sides

chromatography paper inserted in pipe

¾" plywood base

PVC cap

1"-diameter hole

½" PVC pipe

rubber stopper

slot cut in top of pipe

PVC elbow

FIGURE 5.3 *Chromatography Chamber Assembly*

USE IT!

Prepare your chromatography paper as outlined in the malic acid test project (page 99). Pull the PVC reservoir partway out from the chamber, and pour the chromatography solvent into the elbow to fill the reservoir half full. Plug the top of the elbow with the ¾" rubber stopper, and slide the reservoir back into the chamber. Slip your test paper into the slot in the reservoir, so it touches the bottom. Secure the top of the paper in the chamber with thumbtacks pushed into the corks. Install the Plexiglas front and let the test run its course.

Once the solvent reaches the top of the paper, remove the front and, without removing the thumbtacks, gently slip the paper out of the reservoir. Pull the reservoir out of the chamber, and return the unused portion of the solvent to its bottle. Replace the Plexiglas front to allow the paper to dry overnight.

Testing for Free Sulfites

Sulfites (SO_2) have been shown to be an excellent addition to wines to preserve them, stop bacterial and unwanted yeast growth, and remove oxygen and other undesirable elements. Sulfites can be added in the form of potassium metabisulfite tablets (commonly known as Campden tablets) or potassium metabisulfite powder. There is much information about the use of sulfites in winemaking on the Internet and in winemaking books and magazines, so here we'll just explore when and how to perform the testing for free SO_2.

Some assumptions I make about sulfites are:

» At crush there is virtually no free SO_2 in the must.

» Depending on the type of grape (white or red), the pH of the must, and/or the condition of the grapes, an addition of potassium metabisulfite or Campden tablets should be made at crush to preclude a case of the wine-tainting nasties. This addition would normally range between 35 and 50 parts per million.

» Upon completion of fermentation, nearly all the SO_2 will have either become bound or blown off in gaseous form. If malolactic fermentation (MLF) is to be conducted at this time, no additional SO_2 is added until MLF has completed. The pH is then checked and SO_2 is added (in amounts appropriate to the wine type and pH), assuming there is no residual SO_2 in the wine.

» At each subsequent racking, restore the sulfite level to the level determined to be appropriate. At this time it is good practice to perform a test to determine the residual amount and the addition that should be made to restore the desired level.

FREE SO$_2$ TESTING SETUP

PERFORMING THE TEST FOR FREE SO$_2$ IS FAIRLY SIMPLE as long as you have the appropriate equipment. A commercially available setup to determine sulfite levels by aeration/oxidation can cost as much as $500, although some manufacturers (having realized that it is easy to make such setups from basic materials) now offer setups for closer to $100. Still too rich for my blood, so here's how to make one for even less (much less). In addition to the materials listed below, you should also have a 10 ml syringe and 10 ml pipette and pipette bulb handy.

MATERIALS

- Two 4–6 oz. glass jars
- Two 2-hole rubber bungs/stoppers to fit the jars (with ¼" holes)
- One 12" length ¼"-O.D. (outside diameter) glass tubing
- One aquarium air pump
- One 24" length ¼"-I.D. (inside diameter) flexible plastic tubing
- One egg timer (or other 10-minute timer)

NOTE: *You can make your own two-hole bungs from silicone; see page 89. Use ¼" plastic tubing for the holes. And if you prefer, you can substitute for the jars with 200 ml #32 test tubes and rubber stoppers supported by your lab support stand (see page 97).*

MATERIALS, continued

Chemicals

- 3% hydrogen peroxide solution (available at any drugstore)

- Methyl red–methylene blue indicator solution (from wine or chemical supply stores)

- 25% phosphoric acid solution (available from hardware stores in the tile department, or from chemical supply stores)

- 0.01N NaOH (dilute 0.10N solution, one part 0.10N NaOH to nine parts distilled water)

BUILD IT!

1. Prepare the glass tubes.

Set up the two jars with rubber bungs seated snugly in them. For the purposes of this design, we'll call the jars Jar #1 and Jar #2, with Jar #1 assigned to receive the wine sample. Be sure the holes in the rubber stoppers will snugly accommodate the glass tubing.

For each jar, cut a length of glass tubing so that it extends from just above the bottom of the jar, through the hole in the stopper, to just about ½" above the stopper. To cut the tubing, score it with a file or sharp knife, then hold it in both hands with your thumbs on each side of the score mark and quickly snap it. Cut a third, short piece of glass tubing that is about ¾" longer than the height of the stopper.

Use a propane torch (or other gas flame) to melt one tip of each of the two longer glass tubes to make the hole very small, but not closed up. Hold the tubing with leather gloves or pliers so you don't burn your fingers. These lengths of glass tubing will serve as *impingers*.

2. Assemble the setup.

Insert the impingers through one of the holes in each stopper. Insert the shorter glass tube through the other hole in Jar #1's stopper. You may want to use some lubricant like petroleum jelly or mineral oil to help with this.

Connect the aquarium pump tubing from the short glass tube in Jar #1 to the impinger of Jar #2. Connect the pump to the impinger in Jar #1, and you're ready to start the test.

USE IT!

Start by taking the pH of your wine sample; you'll adjust the SO_2 based on the pH.

Place 10 ml of the 3% hydrogen peroxide into Jar #2. Add three or four drops of the methyl red–methylene blue indicator solution. Swirl well to make sure it is mixed thoroughly. This solution should be a light pink color. Now add a drop or two of the 0.01N NaOH, until the solution turns a light bluish gray color. Put stopper (with impinger) on Jar #2.

Place 20 ml of wine into Jar #1. Measure out 10 ml of the phosphoric acid, and turn on the aquarium pump. Add the phosphoric acid to the wine and immediately put the stopper in the top of the jar, and the test has begun. Start the timer and let the air from the pump bubble the solutions in both jars for 10 minutes. As you do this, Jar #2 will trap the free SO_2 in the solution and will turn it back to the pink color. (Note: if the solution does not change color, it most likely has no residual free SO_2.)

Fill a 10 ml pipette (with pipette bulb on top) with the 0.01N NaOH solution, taking note of exactly how much NaOH it contains. Once the time has elapsed, turn off the pump and titrate the pink hydrogen peroxide solution, swirling the solution after each drop of NaOH. When the solution returns to its bluish gray color, stop titrating, and note the volume of NaOH you used in milliliters.

To determine the amount of free SO_2 in the wine in parts per million, multiply the volume of NaOH (in ml) used in the titration by 16. Subtract this amount from the desired level for your wine, and add potassium metabisulfite accordingly.

✳ *If your NaOH solution proves to be different from 0.01N after standardizing, use this formula to determine free SO_2:*

$$\text{Free } SO_2 \text{ (ppm)} = N \times V_{NaOH} \times 1600$$

where:

N = *normality of NaOH*

V_{NaOH} = *volume of NaOH used in ml*

STANDARDIZING SODIUM HYDROXIDE SOLUTION

Winemaking labwork uses various strengths of sodium hydroxide (NaOH) for a number of tests, and this reagent is somewhat unstable, especially in dilute form. Therefore it is important to know with confidence what the strength of your solution actually is. A simple titration will give you that information quickly. To do this, you'll need some potassium hydrogen phthalate (KaPh), also known as potassium acid phthalate. For our purposes, a 0.1N solution of KaPh works well, but the formula compensates for other strengths if you aren't able to get 0.1N. In addition, you'll need some phenolphthalein indicator.

To perform the standardization, carefully measure 10 ml of KaPh solution into a 50 ml beaker or small glass jar. Add five drops of phenolphthalein and swirl to mix thoroughly.

Fill a 25 ml pipette or burette with your NaOH solution, and note the starting volume in the pipette. Titrate by dripping the NaOH slowly into the KaPh, swirling the jar after each drop to mix it in, until the solution changes to a pink color. Once the solution is permanently pink, stop titrating, note the remaining amount of NaOH in the pipette, and calculate the total amount used.

Perform this calculation to determine the actual normality of the NaOH:

$$N_{NaOH} = V_{KaPh} \times N_{KaPh} / V_{NaOH}$$

where:

N_{NaOH} = normality of NaOH

V_{KaPh} = volume of KaPh

N_{KaPh} = normality of KaPh

V_{NaOH} = volume of NaOH used

GRAM SCALE

EVERY LAB SHOULD BE EQUIPPED for weighing reagents, additives, and other items. A digital scale is helpful, and there are some interesting spoon scales on the market now. You can also make this nice scale that's accurate to 0.5 gram using scraps lying around your shop. This may not be adequate for very small SO_2 additions, but for most other measurements it is perfectly functional.

MATERIALS

- Scrap ½" plywood
- Wood screws
- Scrap ⅛" plywood
- One small, squat plastic cup (with a volume of about 6 fluid ounces)
- Heavy string
- One paper clip
- One clothespin
- One 1¼" 3d finish nail

BUILD IT!

1. Build the scale structure.

Cut two pieces of ½" plywood at 1" × 6", one piece at 12" × 3", and one piece at 1" × 1". Glue the 1" × 1" piece to one end of one of the 1" × 6" pieces to serve as a shim block. Screw the 1" × 6" pieces into the long side edge of the 12" × 3" piece, near each end, to form the uprights of the scale.

Cut the ⅛" plywood on a long diagonal to create the balance arm. The actual dimensions aren't terribly important, but it should be about 12" to 15" long. Drill a hole near the wide end of the balance arm where you want the cup to hang.

2. Add the cup and clothespin.

Measure around the top of the cup and mark it in thirds. Just below the rim of the cup, at each mark, drill or punch a small hole large enough for a double piece of the string.

Cut three lengths of string about 12" long. On both ends of the strings, tie an overhand loop knot, ensuring each string is the same length and short enough to allow the cup and strings to hang freely from the balance arm. For each string, push the loop through one of the holes in the cup, then run the other end of the string through the loop. Bring the three strings together at the top and tie them together.

Bend one of the paper clips to form an S hook, and use it to suspend the cup (via the knotted strings) from the hole in the balance arm. Attach a clothespin to the bottom of the balance arm, about 2" from the S hook. Pick up the balance arm between your thumb and forefinger (or use a pair of calipers if you have them), holding it near the top edge and between the S hook and the clothespin. Move your thumb and finger to find the balance point, where the arm feels relatively level. If necessary, you can move the clothespin a bit or trim a bit off the arm. Once you get a good approximate balance point, mark it, and drill a ⅛" hole through the arm at that point. The location doesn't have to be precise, as we'll set the clothespin at the balance point next.

Drive the 3d finish nail into the center of the 1" × 1" shim block, but not all the way through both pieces, ensuring the nail is perpendicular to the block's face. Then slip the balance arm over the nail. Mark the top of the balance arm on the upright from which it is suspended. Remove the balance arm and measure the distance to the mark you just made. With the whole assembly sitting on a level counter, mark the other upright the same distance up and make a "balance" mark.

3. Calibrate the scale.

Replace the balance arm on the upright, making sure it's not touching the uprights. Find the sweet spot for the clothespin to perfectly balance with the cup. Once you have it balanced, mark the cup side of the clothespin on the bottom of the balance arm as your zero grams spot. Then calibrate additional points along the balance arm by using a U.S. nickel for a 5-gram weight, a penny for a 2.5-gram weight, and a standard-size #1 paper clip (uncoated) or U.S. dollar bill for a 1-gram weight. A standard business card (not a thick one) also weighs 1 gram, so for a 0.5-gram weight, cut a card in half.

You can use water for additional units of measure, knowing that 1 milliliter weighs 1 gram and pipetting various volumes into the cup.

Once you have the arm marked in 0.5-gram increments, you have a handy little scale for use in your wine lab.

USE IT!

To weigh an unknown amount of material, place it in the cup and move the clothespin to balance the balance arm at the balance line on the left upright. To measure out material to a preset weight, place the clothespin at the desired weight and fill the cup until the arm is balanced. Pouring from a larger container into the small cup can be difficult, so try placing your dry material on a folded piece of paper before pouring it into the cup. For wet material, a pipette, syringe, or small turkey baster will do the trick.

CHAPTER SIX

SPARKLING WINE
(Méthode Champenoise)

S PARKLING WINE HAS BEEN A TRADITIONAL CELEBRATORY libation for hundreds of years, and the toast of choice for most festivities. Making sparkling wine is similar to making white wines in the initial steps, but once the wine has fermented and cleared, some additional steps and equipment are necessary to produce a successful mouthwatering sparkler.

Champagne, made in the Champagne region of France, traditionally is made from Chardonnay, Pinot Noir, or Pinot Meunier grapes picked early, at a sugar level of about 19 to 20° Brix. The grapes are crushed and pressed, and the must is fermented dry and allowed to bulk-age in neutral barrels or inert tanks. Once the wine is clear, it is bottled in champagne-style bottles, along with a *liqueur de tirage* of sugar and yeast, and then capped with crown caps or corked with plastic corks and wire hoods.

The wine is aged for six months to a year (or more), with the bottles on their sides. While the yeast ferments, the additional sugar in the bottle develops the carbon dioxide bubbles. As fermentation completes, the yeast will settle on the sides of the bottles, imparting an improved mouthfeel and rounding out the wine.

Riddling

Riddling is the process of gradually tipping the bottles of sparkling wine from horizontal to vertical, neck down, over a period of a few weeks. Winemakers insert the bottles into an adjustable riddling rack, which holds the bottles at an ever-increasing pitch. Through the course of the riddling they regularly give the bottles a quick turn to work the sediment free from the sides, so it can begin its descent down to the necks of the inverted bottles. The sediment acts a bit like sandpaper against itself; if the bottles were simply inverted completely in one step, some sediment might remain stuck to the bottle.

RIDDLING RACK

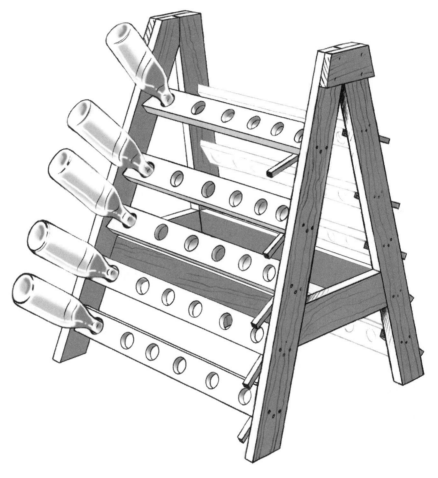

THE RIDDLING RACKS COMMONLY FOUND IN THE CAVES OF REIMS and in other parts of France are made from long boards with angled holes drilled through them. This riddling rack accomplishes the same job with little material and also functions as a bottle storage rack when not in use for riddling.

MATERIALS

- Four 42" lengths 1×6 lumber

- Ten 33" lengths 2×4 lumber

- One 24" length 1×4 lumber

- 1³⁄₈" wood screws

- Twenty ¼" × 1½" lag screws with washers

- Three 36" lengths 1×6 lumber

- Wood glue

- Twenty 6" lengths 1×2 lumber

- Ten ¼" × 1½" eyebolts

BUILD IT!

1. Cut and drill the legs.

Cut the ends of the 42" 1×6 legs at a 15° angle. On the end that will be the top, square down the leg off the 15° cut and make a cut that will leave 4½" flat at the top of each leg (see figure 6.2).

Mark the centerline down the length of each leg. Make a mark on the centerline 6½" down from the top of the leg; this represents the centerpoint for the top 2×4 riddling bar. Mark centerpoints for the other four riddling bars, every 7½" down from the first mark. Drill ¼" holes through the legs at these marks.

2. Drill the riddling bars.

To make the holes for the bottle necks in each of the ten 2×4 riddling bars, mark the centerline down the length of each bar. Mark six holes on the centerline at 5" on center, starting 4" in from each end, as shown in figure 6.1a. Drill a 1½"-diameter hole through the bars at each mark.

Mark an *X* on the end of each bar by drawing lines between opposite corners.

The spot where the lines intersect is the centerpoint. Drill a ³⁄₁₆" pilot hole at each centerpoint.

3. Drill the riddling bar adjustment holes.

Cut a piece of 1×4 to length at 5½" (or cut a piece of cardboard to 3½" × 5½") to use as a drilling template for the angle adjustment holes in the legs. Mark and drill the holes in the template, as shown in figure 6.1b. At each riddling bar location, set the template flush with the outside edge of the leg, aligning the ¼" pivot hole with the hole you already drilled in the leg. Mark the other three holes and drill ¼" holes through the leg at the marks.

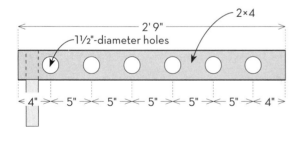

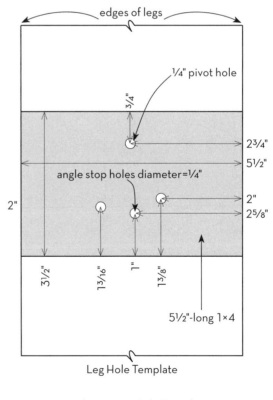

4. Assemble the rack.

Cut two 1×4 top ties to join the leg pairs, as shown in figure 6.2. These get 15° angle cuts on the ends and measure 9" along their short top edges. Fit the leg pairs together and fasten them to the top ties with three 1⅜" wood screws driven into each leg.

Install the riddling bars between the leg pairs, screwing the lag screws with washers through the outsides of the legs and into the pilot holes in the ends of the bars. Tighten the lag screws snug, so that the bars can rotate with just a little resistance. Cut the 1x6 stretchers at 33" and install them between the leg pairs as shown in figure 6.2, using glue and screws. Be sure to locate the stretchers so they won't impede the rotation of the bottles. Finally, cut the third 36" piece of 1×6 into two angled cross braces and install them to fit between the stretchers at each end of the rack, using glue and screws.

5. Add the adjusting levers and eyebolts.

Attach two 6"-long 1×2 adjusting levers to the undersides of each riddling bar, 1" from the ends. You use these to rotate the riddling bars to change the angle of the bottles. Set the riddling bars at the desired angle and insert the ¼" eyebolts into the adjustment holes in the legs for the bars to rest on.

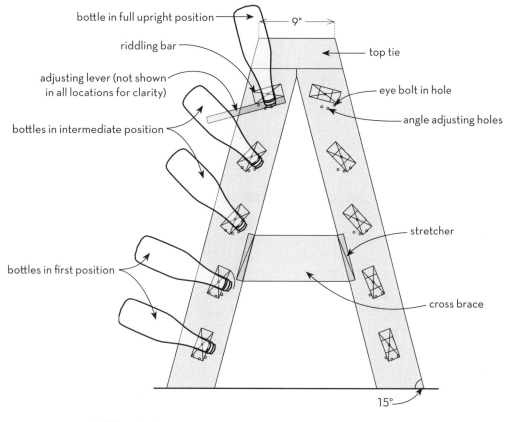

bottle in full upright position

riddling bar

adjusting lever (not shown in all locations for clarity)

bottles in intermediate position

bottles in first position

9"

top tie

eye bolt in hole

angle adjusting holes

stretcher

cross brace

15°

FIGURE 6.2 *Riddling Rack*

USE IT!

Once you're ready to start riddling the wine, insert the bottles neck-first into the holes in the 2×4 riddling bars, with the bars at the most vertical setting to hold the bottles horizontal, and just slightly pointed down. Begin riddling by giving each bottle a sharp quarter turn, turning them all in the same direction. The next day, repeat the operation, but turn the bottles sharply in the opposite direction. I like to associate the direction with odd or even days, so for example on the twenty-first of the month I would turn the bottle to the left and on the twenty-second to the right. Turning the bottles effectively uses the lees to scrub themselves loose so they'll slide down to the necks. This action should not cause the lees to become cloudy.

After about a week of riddling at this angle, rotate the racks upward, using the adjusting levers, and relocate the eye bolts in the holes to increase the angle of the bottles. Now, at this steeper angle, when you turn each bottle, include a short 1" drop of the bottle back into the rack as you complete the twist. This will jar the lees a bit and encourage their descent toward the neck.

After another week, increase the bottle angle to near vertical, and continue turning and dropping the bottles. After three weeks, the wine should be very clear and all the sediment should be in the necks of the bottles. If there is still some cloudiness, or the sediment hasn't made it all the way to the neck, continue the riddling until it has completed settling.

Congratulations! You are now ready for the thrill of disgorging.

Variation

Those of us who make smaller batches can build half of this rack and fasten it to a wall or vertical legs. You can always add on the other half as your passion increases your production!

Disgorging

Now that the riddling is done, the sediment is lodged in the cap and neck of the bottle. Getting it out is the next trick. This process, known as disgorging, involves freezing the sediment so that it forms a solid plug, which you can remove. After disgorging, you'll top up the bottle with your chosen *dosage* (wine or other solution; see page 117) and recap or recork it.

Prior to disgorging, it is important to cool the wine down as much as possible (without freezing it). This keeps the carbon dioxide bubbles in solution when you open the bottle. A warm wine will gush and spray during the disgorging process, so that you lose much of your bubbly, not to mention the sparkles. You can chill the wine bottle, inverted, in a refrigerator, in a snowbank, or just outside on a cold day or night.

The next step is to freeze the sediment in the neck of the bottle. To do this, you'll need a freezing pool with a brine solution that is about 1" deep. You could rig up a bucket or cooler for this, but the bottles tend to tip and slide around. A proper disgorging freezer will expedite the process and keep you focused on the more diligent task of disgorging and adding your dosage.

DISGORGING FREEZER

FREEZING THE SEDIMENT INTO AN ICE PLUG can be done efficiently if you have a freezer built specifically to accomplish this task. We'll supercharge the freezer by keeping the brine chilled with a slab of dry ice below it. (Be sure to wear heavy gloves when handling dry ice; bare hands may get you results similar to licking a frozen flagpole.)

MATERIALS

- One small plastic pan (such as a kitty litter pan)
- 3/8" plywood
- 3/4"-thick rigid foam insulation
- Water-resistant carpenter's glue
- Two small butt hinges, with fasteners

BUILD IT!

1. Construct the plywood box.

Measure the width and length of your pan just below the lip on the top. These will be the dimensions of the insulated interior of the freezer box. Then set the pan on a table and measure the height of the pan, from the table to the bottom of the lip. Add 1½" to the width (short side) measurement and 2" to the height measurement, and cut two pieces of 3/8" plywood to this size. Add 2¼" to the length (long side) measurement and 2" to the height measurement, and cut two more pieces to this size.

Glue and nail the long pieces over the ends of the short pieces to form a rectangle. Then make a bottom for the box by measuring, cutting, and fastening a piece of plywood to the rectangle.

2. Insulate the box.

Line the inside bottom of the freezer with a piece of ¾" rigid insulation. Cut another piece the same size as the first, then cut out and remove an 8½" × 5" rectangle from its center. Insert the larger piece on top of the bottom layer of insulation. Cut insulation strips to size to line the sides of the box, keeping them ½" below the top of the wood frame, and glue them in place. Insert the pan into the freezer so its lip rests on the insulation along the sides and its bottom sits on the insulation with the recessed cutout.

3. Create the lid.

Cut a piece of plywood to size for the lid, matching the outside dimensions of the box. Install the lid with two hinges along one long side of the box. Drill 1½" holes into the lid, spaced 4" apart. The necks of the bottles will extend down through these holes and into the plastic pan. If the depth of the pan is deeper than would allow the bottle caps to rest on the bottom of the pan, then make the holes a bit bigger. You may want to experiment with a scrap to determine the best hole size for this. You should be able to set 6 to 12 bottles in the lid, depending on how large the pan is.

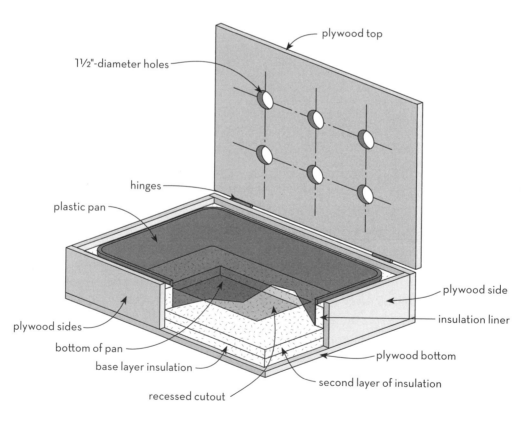

FIGURE 6.3 *Disgorging Freezer Assembly*

USE IT!

Open the lid and remove the plastic pan. Insert a slab of dry ice into the recess below. (Standard dry ice slabs are about 8" × 4½" and ¾" thick. Check with your supplier and if necessary you can modify the recessed opening in the insulation board.) Dry ice is extremely cold and will burn your skin, so, once again, be sure to use heavy gloves when handling it. You might also want to keep it in a ziplock freezer bag, to contain CO_2 fumes and reduce its sublimation.

Replace the pan and fill it with crushed ice, then sprinkle coarse salt over the crushed ice to make it even colder. The amount of salt you will need will depend on how much ice you need to fill the pan, but for a rule of thumb, use about 20 percent salt-to-ice ratio. Stir the salt into the ice to mix thoroughly. Close the lid and you should be ready to go. This brine solution may get as low as –20°F and the dry ice will keep it there.

You should have chilled your wine in a refrigerator or freezer, as mentioned earlier, to save the CO_2 and wine during disgorging. Carefully transfer the inverted chilled bottles to the disgorging freezer. Allow the bottles to sit for 5 to 10 minutes, checking the progress of the freezing in the neck. As the sediment freezes, you'll see an ice plug form. Keep in mind that it will freeze from the outside in; give it some time even after you see the beginnings of an ice plug.

Now that the sediment and wine in the neck of the bottle is frozen, you're ready to pop the cap and shoot out the plug. If you're not well prepared for this step, you'll have a big mess on your hands (not to mention your walls, ceilings, floors, and the rest of yourself). So prepare yourself by getting the following ready before you start disgorging:

» **Dosage.** This is the wine you'll use to replace the frozen plug. It could be the wine from the first bottle you disgorge, a still white wine, or any number of other solutions you can prepare to perfect that sparkling beverage. Blend your preferred amount of SO_2 into the dosage as well. You may also add sugar to the dosage to increase the residual sugar of the wine.

» **Ten ml syringe.** This works well to quickly top up the uncapped bottle with the dosage.

» **Corks or caps.** True champagne corks, not to be confused with wine corks, are much bigger and need to be inserted with a special corker. You can also use plastic stoppers, which you insert with a rubber mallet, or crown caps. If you're using corks or plastic stoppers, you'll need to secure them with wire hoods to ensure that they don't pop out. A baling wire twister works well for this purpose. Be careful not to overtighten, though, or the wire will break. Most important is to be sure that the type of cork, stopper, cap, or wire hood you want to use will fit your bottles before you begin disgorging.

» **Disgorging key.** It's important to pry off the caps starting from the side away from you. Using a typical bottle opener will cause the wine to spray back at you and make a huge mess. Disgorging keys are hard to find on the market, so I've included plans for making one on page 118.

» **Disgorging receptacle.** This is where the plug of frozen sediment will shoot (see page 120). Having one will keep your work space clean and tidy and make cleanup a snap.

DISGORGING KEY

A DISGORGING KEY IS A HANDY TOOL for disgorging your bubblies. A scrap of HDPE plastic is perfect for this design; a ½"-thick white plastic cutting board works great. I've provided a full-scale template of the key for your convenience.

MATERIALS

- One 3½" × 7" piece ½" HDPE plastic
- One ⅞" × ⅞" piece 12-gauge steel plate
- One ¾" pan-head wood screw
- One 12" length leather thong or fine rope

BUILD IT!

1. Form the handle.

Trace or copy the template (figure 6.4), transfer it to the HDPE, and cut it out. Shape the handle to fit your hand comfortably; a belt sander set on its back works well if you don't have a spindle or other table-type sander.

2. Shape the metal piece.

Cut or grind a slight curve into one side of the metal piece, checking the curve as you work to make sure that it fits the curve of the bottle neck just below the lip. File or grind a bevel into this curve at approximately 45°. Drill a ⅛" hole into the center of the metal piece, and countersink the hole to receive the screw head. (You can make the countersink by using a ¼" high-speed bit and drilling just slightly into the metal.)

3. Complete the tool.

As shown in figure 6.4, fasten the metal piece to the HDPE handle with the curved side toward the handle and the bevel out, driving the pan-head wood screw through the predrilled hole to set the metal piece slightly outset from the head of the key. Drill a hole through the handle, thread the leather thong through it, and tie the two ends together, forming a wrist strap.

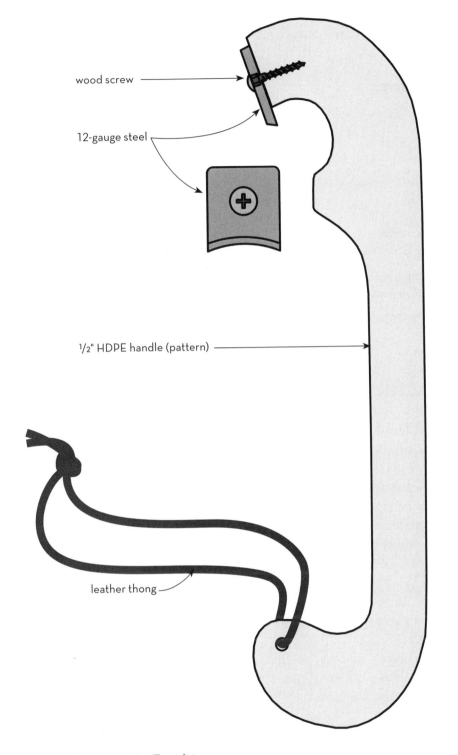

wood screw

12-gauge steel

¹/₂" HDPE handle (pattern)

leather thong

FIGURE 6.4 *Disgorging Key Template*

DISGORGING RECEPTACLE

THE FIRST TIME I ATTEMPTED TO DISGORGE WINES, I ended up with frozen gunk all over me, the floor, the ceiling, my wife's car, and places I'm still discovering years later. I solved that problem with this very simple disgorging receptacle.

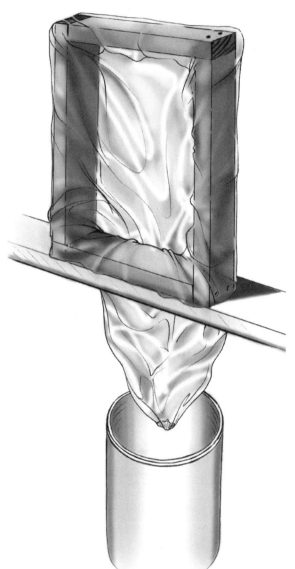

MATERIALS

- Wood screws
- Four 12" lengths 1×2 lumber
- Stapling gun and staples
- One 13-gallon plastic bag (of the kind used to line a kitchen trash can)
- One 36" length 2×6 lumber
- Bucket

BUILD IT!

Screw the 1×2s together pinwheel-fashion, (i.e., screw the side of the first piece into the end of the second piece. Rotate them 90° and screw the side of the second piece into the end of the third piece, then the side of the third piece into the end of the fourth piece, and finally the side of the fourth piece into the end of the first piece) to create a square that is 12¾" × 12¾".

Pull the opening of the plastic bag through the square frame, wrap it tightly around the frame, and staple it in place. Screw this frame to the center of the 2×6 and flush with its front edge.

Clamp the 2×6 to sawhorses, a narrow table, or other solid structure so the center of the square is at waist height (32" to 36" above the floor).

Cut a small hole in one corner of the bottom of the bag, and place a bucket under that corner. Arrange the bag so that the cut corner is the lowest part of the bag, which will allow the melting plugs to drip into the bucket.

USE IT!

Remove the bottle with the frozen sediment from the disgorging freezer, and dip the neck in a shallow pail of room-temperature water to rinse off the brine and slightly thaw the plug so that it releases from the glass. Keeping the bottle inverted at about 75°, place the bottom of the bottle against your thigh and hook the disgorging key over the bottle cap. The hand you are holding the bottle with should be under the neck, so that you can cover the top with your thumb as soon as the plug shoots out. The disgorging key in your other hand should be nearly horizontal.

With a quick motion, rotate the bottle up and, when it points into the disgorging receptacle, snap the disgorging key to pop off the cap. Immediately after the plug shoots out (and into the receptacle), cover the top of the bottle with your thumb to prevent excess wine from spraying out. Allow the pressure to subside a moment (slowly releasing your thumb for two seconds to release the pent-up pressure), and you are ready for your dosage.

There are a number of great online videos demonstrating this technique; search for "disgorging champagne" to see some veteran disgorgers in action.

ADDING THE DOSAGE

To keep the wine from foaming up excessively when adding the dosage, it's good practice to keep the bottle at an angle and let the liquid flow down the neck rather than just pouring the dosage in directly. Cork or cap the bottle as soon as possible after adding the dosage, so as to not lose any additional CO_2 from the wine.

CHAPTER SEVEN

FILTERING, BOTTLING & LABELING

So NOW YOUR WINE IS RESTING COMFORTABLY in the barrel room and the flavors have blended, the wine has cleared nicely, and you're thinking about a new crop of fruit coming in soon. It's time to clear out the barrel room and make way for the next batch. It's time to bottle!

Sourcing Bottles

Purchasing bottles can add significant cost to your winemaking, so home winemakers commonly recycle wine bottles and refill them. There are a lot of places to get free wine bottles. A bartender friend of mine stashes them in a box and lets me know when I can pick them up. The winery at the vineyard where I purchase my grapes has bottles from its tasting room available for me whenever I ask. Recycling centers will sometimes let you sort through their glass to pick out a case or two of bottles. Then there are the bottles that you purchase and friends save for you. Mother's Day and Easter brunches at local restaurants are great opportunities for stocking up your champagne bottles, and venues for wedding receptions will frequently be a good

source. It doesn't take long to accumulate wine bottles in the colors and shapes you need for bottling your wine.

I use the diamond racks (see plans in chapter 4) in my winery to sort and stockpile bottles. The dead-leaf-green Bordeaux bottles go in one compartment, brown Burgundy bottles with no punt go in another, and so on.

Bottle Types

I'm a bit of a traditionalist when bottling my wines. I like to put Bordeaux varietal wines and blends in Bordeaux bottles, Burgundies in Burgundy bottles, and German varietals in Hock or German bottles. Color is not as much of an issue for me; it tends to be decided by how many of each empty bottle type and color I have on hand on bottling day.

Bordeaux bottles are mostly cylindrical in shape and have more sharply rounded shoulders. They are slightly smaller in diameter than Burgundy bottles and stack well in a diamond rack.

Burgundy bottles are tapered from about their bottom third up to their neck. They are roughly the same height as Bordeaux bottles. Being tapered, Burgundy bottles are not terribly stable if set on top of each other on a shelf or in a diamond bin, so I highly recommend stacking them necks-to-the-wall to keep them from sliding out and hitting the floor.

Hock or German bottles have very long necks and usually are much taller than Bordeaux and Burgundy bottles.

Typical varietals for Bordeaux bottles are Cabernet Sauvignon, Merlot, Cabernet Franc, Malbec, and Petit Verdot. Burgundy varietals are Chardonnay, Pinot Noir, Syrah, and Petit Sirah, among others. Riesling is commonly put in Hock bottles. For non-grape wines, I feel it is the vintner's call (that is, whatever is on hand).

Removing Labels

Of course, part of the hassle of collecting used bottles is cleaning them and removing the labels. Making this task as fast and painless as possible is important, especially when you're staring at hundreds of bottles to delabel. I've experimented with a number of ways to remove labels and have come to the following process as being the most efficient (so far).

The first consideration when saving bottles is to collect ones with labels that are easy to remove. Some wineries pride themselves on using special plastic or foil-backed paper and glue that would take

From left to right: Bordeaux, German (Hock), and Burgundy

an atomic bomb to get off. You'll quickly identify these brands and send their bottles on their merry way to be recycled. I don't waste my time on them. Second, be sure that the adhesive and label materials you use for your own wine labels come off simply by soaking. Third, rinse the bottles well before moving them to your stockpiles to make final cleaning of them quick and painless.

I start by filling a plastic garden cart with bottles. I like using a cart because I can wheel it around from the diamond storage racks to the hose outside to the sink for cleaning. A large bin on a dolly would work almost as well, however. Once I've loaded the cart with about four cases worth of bottles, I fill the cart with hot water and let the bottles soak for at least 24 hours, and preferably 48 hours.

Notice that I always fill the cart with bottles *before* filling it with water. The weight of the upper bottles keeps the bottles below from floating up, allowing them to fill. For label removal, the hot water on the inside helps soften the adhesive and facilitates removal. The same principle applies for cleaning bottles in the sink: bottles first, then hot water.

When I'm ready to delabel, I wheel the cart over to near my winery sink. My sink has two compartments, and I reserve one compartment for scraping and rinsing the bottles and the other for stacking the delabeled bottles to be cleaned. I use a utility knife loaded with a large curved linoleum blade. I stick the tip of the blade under the foil neck capsule and give it a quick slice, and then I peel it off and drop it into a trash bucket next to the cart. Then I work the curved part of the blade under a corner of the label, and it becomes almost immediately apparent whether the label will peel off intact or I'll have to scrape it off. Once the label is removed, I scour off the residual adhesive with some steel wool and give the bottle a quick rinse under some warm water. I finish with a quick visual check of the inside of the bottle for debris and bugs, then I set the delabeled bottle on its side in the sink.

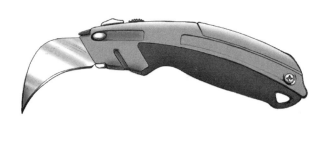

Delabeling knife

Once into a good rhythm I can remove labels from two or three bottles per minute until the sink is full of empty, relatively clean bottles.

Cleaning Bottles

With a sinkful of bottles, a bit of percarbonate oxygen cleaner and a fill with hot tap water starts the cleaning process. I keep the percarbonate cleaner at as low a level as possible — roughly a half tablespoon — to minimize foaming. Suds make rinsing more tedious.

The next step is to empty the bottles that are submerged in the sink, examining them once again for residue, bits of labels, spiders, or other gunk that may have eluded prior screening. If I see any residue, a bottle brush takes care of it. I add about a half cup of hot tap water for a first rinse, followed by another final rinse. Then I place the bottles on a bottle tree to drain. I'll wait to sanitize them until immediately prior to filling them with wine.

Note that there is a difference between cleaning, sanitizing, disinfecting, and sterilizing. Cleaning is the complete removal of soil, debris, food, and so on. Detergents used for cleaning bind water with oils in the debris and facilitate rinsing them away with clean water, but they do not necessarily sanitize. Sanitizing is reducing the number of microorganisms to a safe level given the use the equipment is destined for. Disinfecting is the removal of all debris or particles and the destruction of vegetative cells, but not spores. Sterilizing is the statistical destruction (99.99%) and removal of all living organisms. It has been said that no known human pathogens can survive in wine with typical alcohol and pH levels.

BOTTLE TREE

A COMPACT BOTTLE TREE WORKS WELL FOR DRYING BOTTLES after you've cleaned them, and it provides another layer of utility in the bottle sorting process. This bottle tree will hold up to six cases of wine bottles and allow you to move those bottles around the winery with ease, whether to further sorting and storage or on to the bottling line.

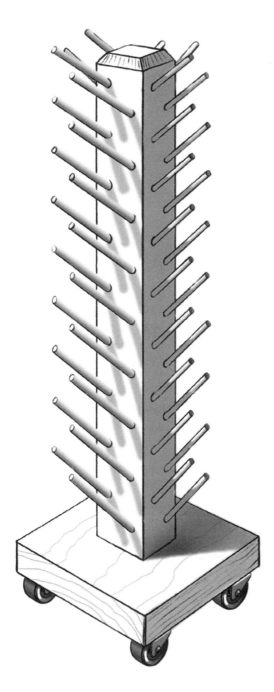

MATERIALS

- Scrap 2×4 and 1×2 lumber
- Four 1½" wood screws
- One 40" length 4×4 lumber
- One 12" length 2×12 lumber
- Four 3½" wood screws
- Twelve 36" lengths ⅜" hardwood dowels
- Wood glue
- Four small casters, with screws

BUILD IT!

1. Create a drilling jig.

There are 72 holes to drill on an angle; a jig makes this job a bit more precise and easy. Drill two ⅜" holes through the 2×4 scrap piece, ¾" up from the end and 1" in from the sides. Keep these holes as perpendicular to the 2×4 as possible. Use a miter saw to cut the end of the 2×4 off at a 45° angle, giving you a triangular piece of 2×4 with two holes.

Cut two pieces of scrap 1×2 at 4" in length, and screw them to the triangular piece of 2×4, as shown in figure 7.1, making sure the ends of the 1×2s are aligned with each other. Do not let the screws intersect the two holes. The right-angle point of the 2×4 triangle should be centered along the length of the 1×2s. This is your drilling jig.

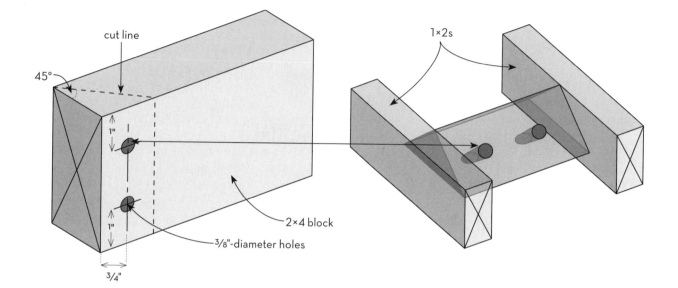

cut line

45°

1"

1"

3/4"

2×4 block

3/8"-diameter holes

1×2s

FIGURE 7.1 *Bottle Tree Drilling Jig*

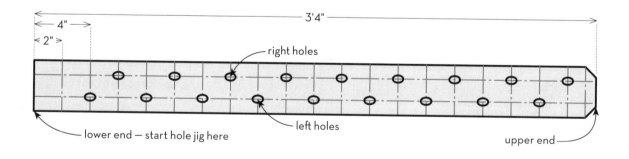

3'4"

4"

2"

right holes

lower end — start hole jig here

left holes

upper end

FIGURE 7.2 *Bottle Tree Hole Pattern*

2. Drill the 4×4 post.

Use a small square to mark a line around what will be the bottom of the 4×4, 2" up from the bottom. Then mark a line around the 4×4 every 2" up, until you reach the top. If you want, you can use a router to mill a chamfer or bull nose on the top edges of the 4×4 for a finished look.

Wrap a piece of tape around a ³⁄₈" drill bit 2¹⁄₈" up from the tip to mark the drilling depth for the holes. Place the jig on one face of the 4×4, with the ends of the 1×2s aligned on the first 2" mark and the holes angling down toward the 4" mark. Using the jig as a guide for the drill angle and location, drill one hole into the 4×4 using the "left" hole of the jig. Then slide the jig up the 4×4 to the next 2" mark and drill one hole using the "right" hole in the jig. Continue in this manner up to the top of the jig, alternating holes as you go. Repeat the drilling process for the other three faces of the 4×4.

3. Add the tree base.

Draw lines between opposite corners on the 2×12 to make an X. The intersection of the two lines marks the centerpoint. Use a scrap of 4×4 or your square to mark the location of the 4×4 post, centered over the centerpoint. Fasten the base to the post with four 3¹⁄₂" screws driven through pilot holes.

4. Install the dowels and casters.

Cut the ³⁄₈" dowels into 72 pieces at 5⁷⁄₈" each (there should be zero waste from the 36" dowels). Put a bit of wood glue on one end of each cut dowel and drive it into a

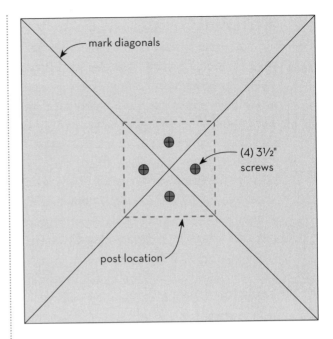

FIGURE 7.3 *Bottle Tree Base*

hole in the post. Install the four casters to the base of the tree, using the provided screws. Locate these as far out to the corners of the base as possible for maximum stability.

USE IT!

This bottle tree works well not only for drying, sorting, and moving bottles but also for hanging and drying rags, bottle brushes, test tubes, jars, hoses, and all sorts of other equipment. Paint it green and put some lights on it during the holidays. Have fun!

Filtering

As you prepare a wine for bottling, one of your protocols may include filtering. Filtering isn't necessary for many wines, as they will clear themselves quite nicely through bulk aging (and fining), but you will find that they really sparkle after a run or two through a filter.

It is important to note that filtering is not intended to clear a wine. Attempting to filter a wine whose solids have not settled out will result in clogged filters, wasted time, and much frustration. In fact, I recommend that you perform a clean racking just before filtering so that you can work with clear wines that will flow through the filters easily.

Commercial wine filters are typically "plate" filters in which a number of thick compressed paper filters are sandwiched between layers of rectangular plates.

There are a few designs made for home winemakers and they work well, although they may be a bit drippy and are fairly expensive.

To be effective, filtration should be done with the aid of a pump. Trying to filter by gravity alone will take a very long time. As I described in chapter 3, a vacuum pump is a great choice for home winemakers and will fulfill all of their pumping needs. With that a given, let's put together a filtering system that will make your wines get top ratings in the Appearance category in any wine competition.

WINE FILTER

A BASIC WHOLE-HOUSE WATER FILTER CAN WORK QUITE WELL for filtering wines and costs quite a bit less than the small home winery versions on the market. It also has fewer parts, and the filter cartridges will be available at your local hardware store. You'll use coarser filters (in the range of 5 microns) for initial filtering and finer filters (1 micron or less) for a final polish. The higher the micron designation, the coarser the filter. (Anything over 5 microns is a waste of effort.) You can run the wine through the coarse filter first and then switch out the cartridges, or you can put the two filters together in tandem to speed up the process. I don't recommend attempting to do a fine filtration without first running the wine through a coarse filter.

MATERIALS

- Two plastic ½" barbed fittings sized to fit your chosen water filter
- One cartridge-type household water filter, with filter cartridges from 5 microns to 0.5 micron
- Teflon tape
- Two ½" hose clamps

BUILD IT!

Insert the plastic barbed fittings into the inlet and outlet fittings of the water filter, wrapping the threads of the fittings with Teflon tape. Install the desired filter cartridge: coarser for initial filtering and finer for a final polish.

Set up your vacuum pump as you would for vacuum racking (see page 64), except install the filter in-line between the two

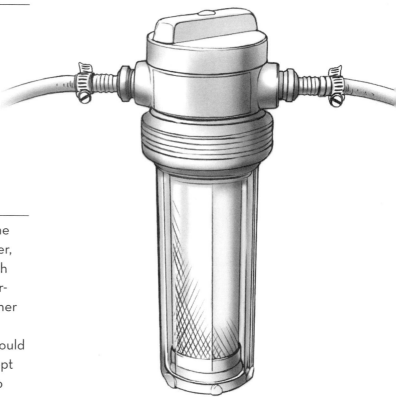

containers. (This is where it is nice to have two pieces of 5-foot-long hose instead of one 10-foot-long one.) Push the tubing over the barbed fittings and secure with the hose clamps, making sure that the racking cane's hose is connected to the filter inlet and the transfer gun's hose is connected to the outlet.

Hang the filter on the door of your barrel room on a pair of long pegboard hooks (or set it on a counter or other means of support), and you're ready to . . .

USE IT!

Start by racking the wine to be filtered off the lees into a clean, sanitized container.

Fill the water filter canister with water to wet the cartridge for a few minutes (or as directed by the manufacturer). Meanwhile, mix up a gallon or so of sanitizing solution (see page 13). Place the racking cane in the sanitizing solution upstream of the filter, and place the transfer gun into a rigid container like a glass carboy downstream of the filter. Turn on the vacuum pump and pull the sanitizing solution through the filter and into the carboy, until the solution has drained out of the filter canister. Turn off the vacuum pump.

Move the transfer gun to another empty, sanitized, rigid container and turn the pump back on to begin filtering the wine.

Cleaning the filter is relatively painless. Use the vacuum pump to pull out as much wine as possible into a third container, understanding that this last bit will suffer too much exposure to air to be worth bottling — but it will be great to taste and share with your helpers. Once the filter canister is mostly empty, insert the racking cane into the cleaning solution you cleaned the filter with originally, and reverse the hose connections on the filter so that the racking cane is connected to the outlet and the transfer gun is connected to the inlet. Now backflush the filter with the sanitizing solution (that is, run the solution backward through the filter to remove the sediment coating the outside of the cartridge), followed by a clean water rinse, and you're all cleaned up. Remove the cartridge and allow it to dry thoroughly before putting it away. (Another good use for the bottle tree!)

Bottling

A successful bottling day starts with careful planning. Bottling can be a lot of fun and a good experience to share with friends and family, but it can turn ugly if everything isn't carefully thought through beforehand. Here's a checklist of the things you'll want to check and double-check before that fateful, exciting day arrives.

☐ Take your final measurements of pH, TA, and SO_2, and calculate any SO_2 additions you want to make. Make any necessary last-minute adjustments of SO_2, potassium sorbate, sugar, and so on.

☐ Perform any blending or sweetening trials you want to make, and calculate blending ratios, if you plan to make your blends on bottling day. If you're blending in advance, have the blends in their respective containers, with each clearly identified.

☐ If you're going to sparge your bottles or transfer your wine to the bottling line with inert gas, check the tank to make sure you have enough gas.

☐ Calculate the number of gallons/liters of wine you will be bottling and double-check that figure against the number of bottles you have cleaned and ready for filling. Make a list of the wines and which bottles you will use for them. Remember, 1 gallon will fill five bottles, and 1 liter fills 1⅓ standard bottles.

☐ Be sure all of your corks/closures and capsules are on hand in sufficient quantities.

☐ Make sure your corker is clean and in good working order.

☐ Prepare for capsules and labeling. I like to install my capsules and labels in the bottling process, so I have my labels printed, capsules purchased and counted, and label adhesives mixed and ready, as well as having a stockpile of propane bottles to fuel my hot plate for shrink-wrap capsules.

☐ Make up enough sanitizing solution for sanitizing your bottling filler, hoses, bottles, and other equipment.

☐ Make sure you have an organized place in your cellar for the new wines.

☐ Have plenty of snacks and beverages prepped for the crew.

The flow of my winery on bottling day is shown in the illustration on page 132.

❶ Cleaned and sorted bottles are stockpiled and placed on the rinser-sparger, one case at a time.

❷ Wine is pumped/siphoned from the barrel room to the reservoir of the bottling machine.

❸ Bottles are rinsed with the sanitizing solution and sparged with nitrogen.

❹ Sanitized and sparged bottles are placed on the bottling machine and filled.

❺ Filled bottles are set on the corking table.

❻ Corks (that were previously stocked in a small bucket hanging from the labeling table, to the right of the corker, ready for insertion into the filled bottles) are moved from the corking table to the floor corker, and the corks are inserted.

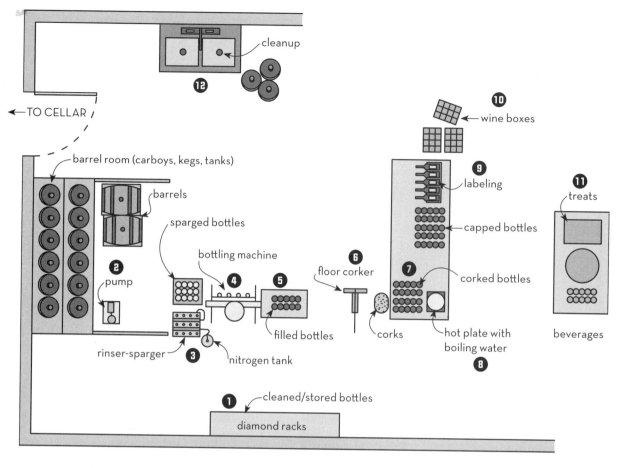

FIGURE 7.4 *Bottling Day Work Flow*

7 Corked bottles are placed on the finishing table and capsules slipped over the tops.

8 Bottles are dipped into boiling water to shrink the capsules and then placed in line for labeling.

9 Labels are applied, and finished bottles are placed in wine boxes.

10 Wine boxes are carried to the cellar, and the bottles are organized into the racks.

11 Crew members help themselves to a constantly replenished supply of treats, snacks, beer, wine, and sodas.

12 Empty containers are moved to the winery sink, cleaned, and returned to the barrel room.

As you can see, there's a lot of equipment being used on bottling day, and with several friends and family members taking turns at the different stations, keeping everything moving smoothly takes a fair amount of orchestration. Some of this equipment we haven't discussed yet, so let's walk through the line and describe (and build) much of it. We've already discussed stations 1 and 2 in detail, so we'll start with station 3, the rinser-sparger.

RINSER-SPARGER

THE RINSER-SPARGER WILL SANITIZE YOUR CLEAN BOTTLES with sanitizing solution and then replace much of the air in the bottles with nitrogen (or argon) to minimize the wine's exposure to air as the bottle is filling. If inert gas is not in the cards or budget for you, you can add it to the operation later, in which case the rinser-sparger becomes just a bottle sanitizer, with the gas valve left shut.

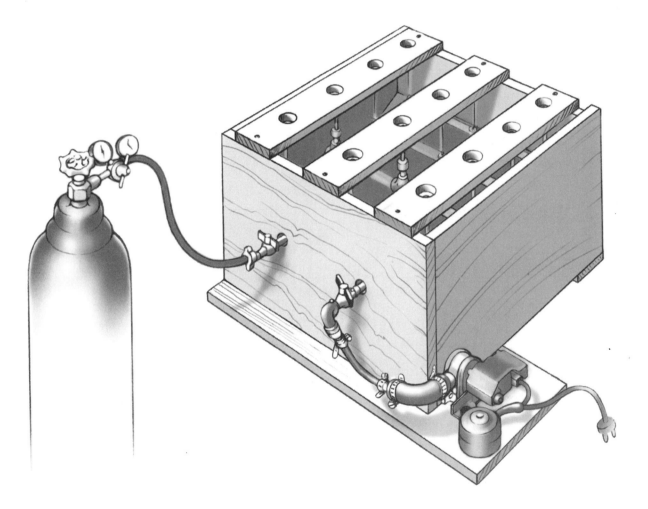

MATERIALS

- One 24" × 48" piece ½" ACX plywood
- Wood glue
- 1½" brads
- 1⅜" wood screws
- One 7-foot length ½" PVC pipe
- PVC adhesive
- Eight ½" PVC elbows
- Six ½" PVC tees
- Six ½" PVC crosses
- Twelve ½" PVC caps
- One 24" length ¼" copper tubing
- Silicone sealant
- Primer
- ½ quart acrylic enamel paint
- Three 18" lengths 1×4 lumber
- One washing machine pump
- Electrical plug
- Surface-mount electrical switch
- Electric "pigtail" (plug end of and extension cord)
- Construction adhesive
- One ¾" electrical conduit C clamp (one screw hole)
- One ⅜" wood screw
- Two ½" PVC ball valves
- One ½" PVC barb × slip elbow
- One ⅜" PVC barb × slip elbow
- One 3" × 24" piece ¾" plywood
- Plumber's tape (metal strapping, if the pump lacks a mounting plate)
- One 3" × 3" piece fine stainless steel mesh
- Stapler (with staples) or thumbtacks

BUILD IT!

1. Build the box.

Cut the pieces from the ½" plywood, as shown in the cutting diagram (see figure 7.5). Use wood glue and brads to fasten the sides (#1 and #2) to the front (#3) of the box. Then install the narrow flat bottom piece (#6), gluing and nailing it into place. On the inside face of each side piece, toward the back, draw a short horizontal line 5½" down from the top; this line marks the location of the top of the sloping bottom piece (#4). Then, measuring from the inside top corner of the narrow flat bottom piece, mark the point where a 15" diagonal line intersects (and terminates at) the horizontal line you just marked. Draw a line from the inside corner of the flat bottom piece to the mark you just made. Align the top of the sloping bottom piece on this line, and glue and nail it into place.

The last piece is the back (#5), which butts up against the sloping bottom piece and is sandwiched between the ends of the side pieces. Nail the back piece into place.

2. Assemble the manifold.

Cut the PVC pipe into 28 pieces at 2" long, six pieces at 3" long, and two pieces at 6" long.

Using PVC adhesive, glue a 2" piece of pipe into each end of the eight PVC elbows. Use the remaining 2" pieces to connect the elbows to the PVC tees and crosses in three rows, as shown in figure 7.7. Take care to keep the pieces perfectly parallel or perpendicular to each other, as shown in the illustration.

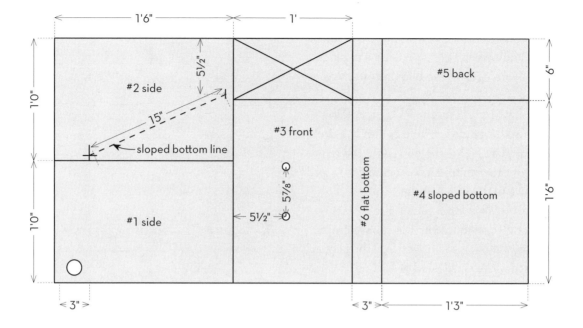

FIGURE 7.5 *Rinser-Sparger Cut Sheet*

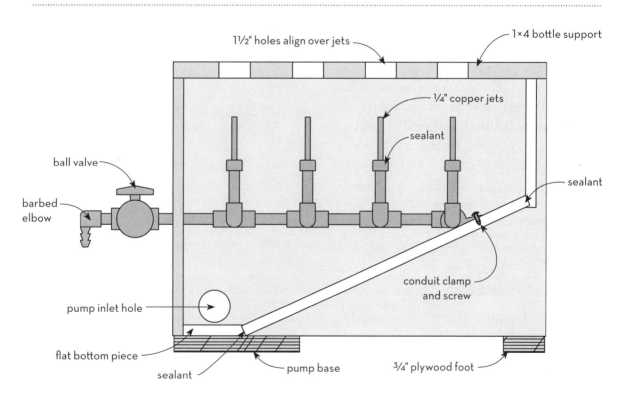

FIGURE 7.6 *Rinser-Sparger Cross Section*

Complete the manifold grid by connecting the three rows with the 3" pieces of pipe, as shown in figure 7.7. Glue a 6" piece of pipe into each of the two bottom cross fittings.

Drill ¼" holes into the PVC caps. (Drilling from the inside will help center the drill bit in the cap.) Glue the caps onto the riser pipes of the manifold, taking care not to get adhesive in the drilled holes.

Cut the ¼" copper tubing into 12 pieces at 2" long. Push these into the caps to create the jets of the rinser-sparger. Seal the joint at the caps with a small bead of silicone sealant.

On the front of the box, mark the vertical centerline. Measure up 5½" on this line, and draw a horizontal line here. Now measure the center-to-center distance between the 6" pipes at the front of the manifold. Divide this measurement by 2, and make a mark on the horizontal line at that distance on either side of the vertical line. These marks locate the centers of the holes through which the 6" manifold pipes will extend. At these marks, drill holes slightly larger (approximately ¼") than the diameter of the 6" pipes.

NOTE: *PVC adhesive sets up very quickly. When you're using it to connect two PVC pieces, glue both pieces to ensure a good seal and provide slightly more working time.*

3. Seal the box.

It's time to seal up the box so it will hold water. Apply one coat of primer to all surfaces of the wood. Apply one coat of acrylic enamel to the exterior and at least three coats to the interior. Paint the 1×4s (for the bottle supports) as well. Once the paint is thoroughly dry, apply a bead of

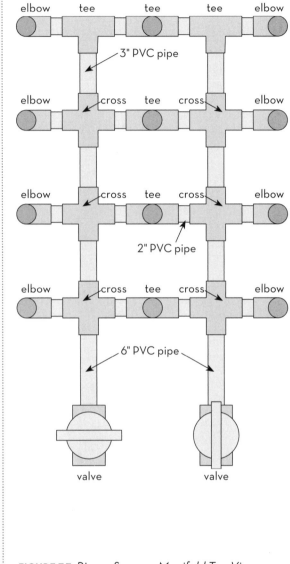

FIGURE 7.7 *Rinser-Sparger Manifold Top View*

silicone sealant in all the seams and joints on the interior of the box. Be sure to fill the V groove between the narrow flat bottom piece (#6) and the sloping bottom piece (#4) with sealant.

4. Drill the pump hole and install the pump.

The pump mounts just outside the box and is used to drive the sanitizing solution through the manifold jets. I was able to salvage a pump from a washing machine I found at an appliance recycling station. An appliance repair shop might also be a good source; perhaps they'd trade you for a bottle or two of your finest. Wherever you get it, take a good look at your washing machine pump to identify the infeed and outfeed ports. The outfeed may be identified by a rubber flapper, which prevents backflow into the pump. The two ports must be the same size, and they can be in line with each other or at 90° to each other. (Avoid pumps with both ports on the same side.) The pump may or may not have a mounting bracket, so we need to be a little flexible in getting it installed on the rinser-sparger.

Once you are confident about which port is the infeed, measure its outside diameter. Divide this measurement in half, and add 2⅝". Mark the centerpoint for the pump inlet hole on one side piece of the box (whichever will work better for your pump), measuring inward the distance you just calculated from both the front and the bottom. Drill a hole at this point, sizing it to match the outside diameter of the infeed port. Test-fit the pump to make sure it fits snugly.

5. Wire the pump switch.

The pump will be fitted with two electrical wires. Though there are other ways to do it, the easiest way to install a switch is to install a plug on those wires to use with a short, switched extension cord. Secure the switch to the side of the plywood box, near the motor, with some construction adhesive. Plug the pump into the switched extension cord, and then plug the switched extension cord into another extension cord long enough to reach a nearby GFCI-protected outlet.

Place a heavy bead of silicone sealant around the exterior of the infeed port of the pump and slip it into the hole in the side of the box.

NOTE: *Seal the wires coming from the pump in electrical heat-shrink tubing if they're not already, to protect them from being accidentally cut or shorted out.*

6. Install the manifold and make the pump connections.

Install the manifold in the box, extending the long 6" pipes through the two holes in the front piece. Set the back end of the manifold on the sloping bottom, parallel to the top of the box. Secure the manifold to the sloping bottom with the electrical clamp and a ⅜" wood screw. Cut off the 6" PVC pipe legs about 1" past the front of the box, and then glue a ball valve on each, followed by the ⅜" barbed elbow on the gas inlet and the ½" on the water port. One of these valves will be connected to your gas tank to feed gas into the manifold; the other will be connected to the pump to feed into the manifold whatever solution you put in the box.

Connecting the pump outfeed port to one of the valves on the front of the box via the barbed fitting may take a little transitioning. Start with the pump's outfeed hose: Clamp the hose to a PVC reducer with a threaded ½" hole. You may need to swap out the original pump hose with a piece of rubber radiator hose from an auto supply store to get all this to work together. The final connection is to connect the two barbed fittings with a short piece of ½" vinyl tubing, securing them with hose clamps.

The pump requires a mounting base secured to the plywood box. Build one from ¾" plywood, sizing it to accommodate your particular setup, and attach it to the bottom of the box. If the pump has a mounting plate, use it to secure the pump to the mounting base; if it doesn't, strap the pump down with some plumber's tape.

Install a small piece of fine-mesh screen over the pump's infeed port and secure it in place with staples or thumbtacks to keep small bits of things from clogging the jets.

7. Install the bottle supports.

Set the 1×4 bottle supports over the jets in the manifold, from front to back, and mark the centerpoints of the jets. Remove the 1×4s and drill 1½" holes at the centerpoints for the bottle necks. Screw the supports to the top of the box, centering the holes over the jets.

Connect your nitrogen tubing to the barbed fitting of the gas inlet valve on the front of the box, and you're ready to go.

USE IT!

To prepare the equipment, you must thoroughly clean it with some percarbonate (OxiClean), trisodium phosphate (TSP), or other low-foaming cleaning agent. Pour a gallon or so of this solution into the box, invert a dozen bottles into the holes in the bottle supports, turn on the pump, and open the pump valve. Let it run for several minutes, then shut the pump down and close the pump valve. Remove the bottles, dump out the cleaning solution, and run a couple of clean water rinses through the box.

Set your new rinser-sparger on a table near your (soon-to-be-built) bottling machine, and pour about a gallon of equipment sanitizing solution (see page 13) into the box. The liquid should fill the box to about 1" above the pump infeed port. Invert the clean bottles into the holes in the bottle supports. The bottles shouldn't touch the jets, but the jets will extend into the bottles 1" or so. Turn on the pump and open the pump valve. Sanitizing solution will spray up into the bottles and hit the punt, causing it to coat the interior of the bottles. Once the sanitizing solution is pumping vigorously, open the rinser-sparger's gas valve, and the combination of sanitizing solution and gas pressure will do a great job of getting the solution to coat the entire bottle. After a few seconds of having both valves open, close the pump valve and turn off the pump. Let the gas flow for about five more seconds, and then close the valves on the rinser-sparger and gas tank. Now the bottles are ready to be moved to station 4, where they'll be filled with wine.

FOUR-SPOUT BOTTLE FILLER

I USED TO GET A BIT IMPATIENT WAITING FOR BOTTLES TO FILL one at a time, and that frustration gave way to this four-spout bottling machine. It is sized to fit snugly between the uprights of the hydraulic press described in chapter 2 (see page 36). Alternatively, you could install a couple of feet on it so that it will sit on a table instead.

This machine is based on the Ferrari-brand bottle fillers sold by most local and online home winemaking supply stores. In addition to being extremely reasonably priced, they have an automatic shutoff and adjustable fill levels. They are gravity-fed, and they direct the wine to flow down the side of the bottles, and as such they are gentle on the wine. They fill a bottle in 20 to 25 seconds. Here's how to turn four of these bottle fillers into a machine that will rival those that cost thousands of dollars.

MATERIALS

- Two 19" lengths 2×4 lumber
- Two 30" lengths 2×4 lumber
- Eight 3" wood screws or nails
- Two 21⅞" lengths ½×4 hardwood board
- Two 3½" lengths 2×4 lumber
- Eight 1½" wood screws or nails
- Four Ferrari bottle fillers
- Four 1¼" U-shaped electrical conduit clamps
- Twelve ⅜" sheet metal screws
- Two ½" PVC slip x thread elbows
- Three ½" PVC slip x slip x thread tees
- One 2-foot length ½" PVC pipe
- PVC solvent glue
- Four ⅜" barbed × ½" male fittings
- One ½" barbed × ½" male fittings
- Two ½" U-shaped metal pipe clamps
- Four 6" lengths ½×2 hardwood board
- Eight 1½" pan-head wood screws
- One 4-foot length ⅜" ID (inside diameter) vinyl tubing
- Four ⅝" hose clamps
- One 5+-gallon plastic food-grade bucket
- One ½" PVC "bulkhead"
- One ½" plastic gate valve
- One ½" barbed × male thread PVC elbow
- One 6" length ½" I.D. vinyl tubing
- One 12" × 20" piece ½" plywood
- High-gloss acrylic paint (optional)

BUILD IT!

1. Construct the main frame.

Fasten one of the 19" 2×4s between the ends of the two 30" 2×4s, using 3" wood screws or nails. (See page 143 for notes on making a tabletop version.) On the other end of the assembly, fasten the other 19" piece between the 30" 2×4s, but on edge and flush with the side edges of the 30" pieces. The side on which this 19" 2×4 is flush will be the front of the filler, and this 2×4 will be at the top. You may want to paint all the wood pieces at this point, for looks and to make the equipment easier to clean.

2. Install the filler spout bar.

Draw a centerline along the length of one of the ½×4 hardwood pieces, and lightly mark the center point on it. Make a mark 2⅛" on either side of the centerpoint, on the centerline. From those points measure out and mark another 4¼," so you have four marks spaced 4¼" apart centered across this piece. Drill a ⅝" hole on a 45° angle at each marked location, angling the holes toward the same long side of the piece (this long side will be the top of the piece). These holes will receive the infeed spouts of the fillers.

Lay the main frame down on a bench or table with the front facing up. Place the 3½" 2×4s at the bottom of the frame, butted up against the inside of each side piece. Use 1½" wood screws or nails to fasten the drilled ½×4 to these two blocks, leaving just a bit of space (about 1⁄16") between the ½×4 piece and the sides of the main frame, so the assembly will slide up and down on the frame. Flip the whole frame with this sliding piece over, and fasten the other 1/2 × 4 piece to the blocks. Don't overtighten; the assembly must be able to slide on the frame.

3. Install the fillers.

Install the Ferrari fillers by placing the infeed ports into the holes on the sliding filler spout bar. Place a 1¼" electrical conduit clamp over each filler, aligning the clamp along the centerline you marked earlier. Predrill holes through the clamp's fastening holes, and fasten it into place with sheet metal screws. Take extreme care not to overtighten the clamp, which could crack the filler or cause its top to pop off, causing the filler to leak.

4. Assemble the manifold.

To assemble the filling manifold, cut pieces from the 1/2" PVC pipe to connect one PVC

elbow and the three PVC tees in a line, spacing them 4¼" apart, center to center. Use PVC adhesive to secure these pieces together, with their fittings all pointing in the same (downward) direction. Install an upturned elbow at the remaining end of the manifold. Screw 3/8" barbed fittings into the three tees and downturned elbow, and screw the 1/2" barbed fitting into the upturned elbow. Fasten the manifold to the back of the top piece of the frame with the 1/2" pipe clamps and sheet metal screws.

5. Add the bottle supports.

Mark up the underside of the bottom of the frame as you did the face of the filler spout bar, giving it four marks equally spaced at 4¼" along the centerline. Drill a hole in each 1/2 × 2, centered along its width and 1" in from one end, to receive a pan-head wood screw. Start the screw in the 1/2 × 2 and then screw it to the bottom of the frame at one of the marked points. You must be able

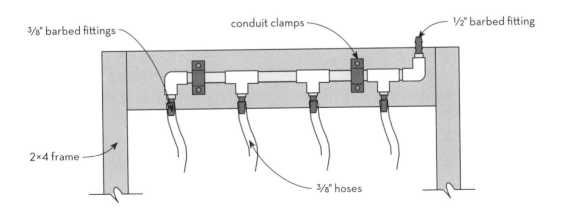

FIGURE 7.8 *Bottle Filler Manifold*

to rotate these pieces, which support the bottles, out of the way so that you can insert or remove the bottles, so keep the screws only modestly tight, allowing them to rotate with some minor resistance.

6. Fit the filler tubes.

Stand up the frame. Raise the filler bar and stand a bottle on each of the two outside bottle supports, then lower the bottle

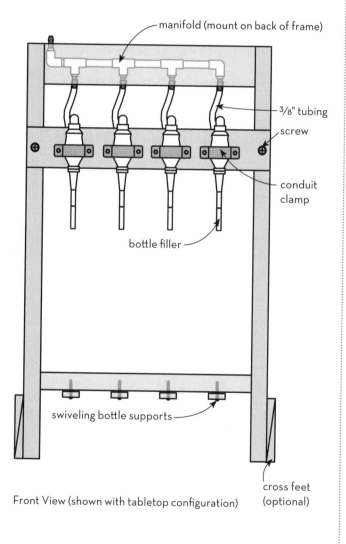

FIGURE 7.9 *Four-Spout Bottle Filler Assembly*

fillers into the bottles until the corks on the fillers sit in the bottles. Measure the distance between the barbed fittings on the manifold and the infeed ports on the fillers. Add an inch or two and cut a piece of the ³⁄₈" tubing to this length. Test-fit the tubing to make sure it does not kink when installed. Then install the tubing to connect the first filler and the first outlet port on the manifold, securing the tubing on the filler with a hose clamp. (A hose clamp isn't necessary on the barbed fitting of the manifold.) Repeat for the other three fillers.

7. Install the reservoir.

The bucket will become the reservoir for the filler. You can purchase a bucket with a spout or make a spout by drilling a hole, installing the bulkhead, and attaching the plastic gate valve and barbed elbow fitting to it.

Since the fillers are gravity fed, the reservoir needs to sit higher than the manifold. With the bottle filler set between the uprights of the press frame, you can temporarily screw a small piece of ¹⁄₂" plywood onto the top of the frame for the reservoir to sit on. Connect the barbed fitting on the bucket to the barbed fitting on the manifold with the ¹⁄₂" tubing and you're ready to bottle.

8. Prepare the filler.

Prior to using the filler, I rub some waxed paper over the sides of the frame to "slick up" the 2×4s so that the filler bar will slide smoothly up and down. Set up your press frame and fit the bottle filler frame between the two uprights. If needed, drive a screw through the filler frame into the press frame, or clamp them together.

NOTE: *If you're not using the press frame to support the bottle filler and would prefer to stand it on a table, there are a couple of adjustments you should make to the design:*

✳ *Use longer pieces for the sides of the frame, so that they extend about 6" beyond the bottom piece, to allow bottles to be inserted onto the filler spouts.*

✳ *Install a 12"-long 1×4 crosspiece at the bottom of each of these longer legs to act as a support stand. (See figure 7.9.)*

✳ *For the reservoir bucket, fashion a support stand (like a kitchen stool set on a counter behind the filler) so that it sits higher than the manifold.*

USE IT!

As with all winemaking equipment, start by cleaning and sanitizing the equipment well. Run sanitizing solution (see page 13) through the fillers, tubing, and manifold by putting about a gallon in the reservoir and hooking it all up.

This filler will fill four bottles at a time, but it is important to sort the bottles for height, because as is the case with most multispout bottle fillers, the support for all the bottles is fixed; you can't set it at one height for one bottle and a different height for the other three bottles. Set the height of the filler bar by installing two bottles in the outer positions, rotating the supports out to hold the bottles in place. Adjust the height of the bar so the bottles are sealed by the filler corks. Drill a hole in each end of the filler bar and put a screw through each hole into the frame. The screw doesn't

need to be driven in very far — just enough to hold the bar in place.

Check to be sure the gate valve is closed and all the tops of the Ferrari fillers are popped up by pinching the side buttons. Then pump or siphon your finished wine into the reservoir. Open the gate valve. Take a bottle off your rinser-sparger, insert it in the filler, and rotate the bottle support to hold the bottle in place. Tap the top of the Ferrari and filling will begin. Insert the next bottle and tap. Next bottle . . . tap. One more.

The bottles fill pretty quickly, and the fillers automatically shut off when the wine rises to the bottom of the spout. To adjust the fill level, change the location of the white cork on the Ferrari filler shafts. To adjust flow rate, tighten or loosen the top screw cap on the Ferrari fillers.

Once a bottle is full, pinch the two side buttons of the Ferrari filler, causing the top to pop back up, shutting the spout. If you remove the bottles before popping the top up, wine will start flowing from the spout as soon as you remove the bottle. I like to keep a cookie sheet below the bottling machine to catch these oopsies and other minor drips.

Next to the bottling machine I set up a small table to receive the filled bottles. It's big enough to hold up to a couple of cases worth of bottles in case the corker gets backed up (for example, if she takes a break to refill her wine glass). Then the filled bottles move to station 5, the corking queue. But first, a word about corks.

Corks

Much has been written about cork types and styles, and we won't rehash that information here. Just a few tips about preparing your corks for the bottling line:

1. Order your corks well in advance of bottling day.

2. Be sure your corks are "fresh." Old corks can be dried out, and potentially infected. Corks should come in a sealed plastic bag, which is filled with sulfur dioxide gas to maintain proper humidity and reduce the risk for cork taint.

3. Corks should be inserted directly from the bag into the bottles. Don't soak, rinse, or boil them. Not only will this increase the risk of infection, it can also remove some of the lubricant that the manufacturer puts on the cork and increase the potential for the cork being pushed back out of the bottle in cases of temperature increases or residual CO_2 in the wine.

4. If you're not buying your corks directly from the manufacturer, ask retailers how they package their corks. Some order bulk quantities and repackage them in smaller bags without the sulfur gas. If these repackaged corks are more than three months old, I recommend shying away from them.

On bottling day, open your bag of corks and place them in a clean, dry, wide-mouthed container, like a small plastic bucket, that will allow you to grab a cork without having to look or fiddle around trying to get it out of a clumsy container. Place this bucket at station 6, cork storage, on the opposite side of the corker from the table where the filled bottles are placed as shown in figure 7.4 on page 132.

Corkers

Inserting corks into bottles can be fun or frustrating, depending on the corker you use. You could use a mallet to bang them in; though this is the best option for plastic champagne corks, with any other type you'd become frustrated very quickly. As a first, and least expensive alternative, a double-handled lever corker will work for small batches. A corker of this type is frequently included in starter kits. To use it, raise the handles and place the cork in the corker, and set the bottle on the floor between your feet. Set the jaws of the corker on top of the bottle and quickly push down on the levers, inserting the cork. As you can tell, this machine requires a lot of work, and it is not always successful in completely inserting the corks.

A better option is a floor corker. You can find a couple types of floor corkers on the market. One is known as a Portuguese corker and the other as an Italian corker, the main difference between the two being that the Portuguese is slightly smaller and has plastic cork-compression jaws, while the Italian has metal jaws. Some complain that the Italian corker occasionally scores the corks during insertion. The Italian style, however, can be found in a model that will also insert large champagne corks and has an adaptor that can be fitted below the head to allow for installing metal crown caps (see figure 7.10). If you'll be making sparkling wines, the Italian corker would therefore have advantages over the Portuguese style.

Bench-style corkers are available as well, and they're nice in that they reduce the fatigue resulting from the frequent bending required by a floor corker. In fact, if you have a floor corker, you may want to experiment with setting it on benches of different heights to see what the ideal height is for you to allow for repetitive corking with minimal effort.

Floor corkers have a metal shaft with a spring below a round bottle platform. You place the bottle on the platform, compressing the spring, and then align the neck of the bottle with the head of the corker. You insert a cork into the hole in the head of the corker, and as you lower the lever, it locks the spring and shaft in place, compresses the cork, and presses it into the bottle. The pushing rod on the lever has a threaded adjustment that allows for precise insertion of the cork to a level slightly below the top of the bottle. This rod has a slight bend to it, so don't be alarmed when you get your floor corker home and find it bent. This is normal.

More advanced pneumatic corkers are available, but for most home winemakers they are prohibitively expensive. I highly recommend either the bench or floor corkers over other options, except for very small-volume winemakers. (And small volume winemakers usually become medium- to high-volume winemakers as the obsession grows!)

In our schematic bottling line, you can see the filled bottles are placed on the corking queue table. The volunteer operating station 7, the corker, takes a cork from the bucket with her right hand and a bottle from the table with her left hand, and she places both in the corker. Then with

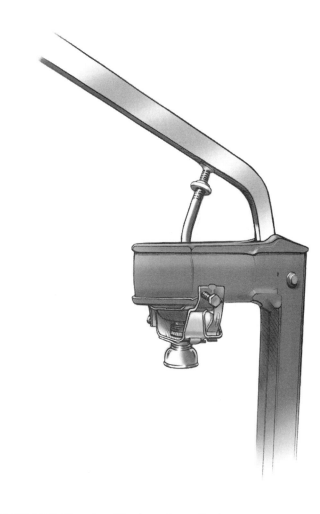

FIGURE 7.10 *Capping Attachment on a Portuguese Floor Corker*

both hands she lowers the lever, pushing the cork into the bottle. She removes the corked bottle and sets it on the finishing table, and we move on to station 8, the capsule queue. At station 9, the capsule master slips the shrink-wrap capsules over the necks of the bottles and finishes the tops of the bottles with the preselected neck wraps (see Bottle Capsules on page 146).

✻ Plastic and synthetic corks are usually much harder to insert into bottles than conventional corks, especially with a double-lever hand corker. To make the job of inserting synthetic corks easier, tie a short piece of fishing line to a wooden dowel. Insert the line into the neck of the bottle, and then insert the cork. The line creates an escape path for the remaining gas/air in the bottle, removing the back pressure. Once the cork is inserted, pull the line out of the bottle by the wooden dowel handle.

✻ If you're inserting champagne corks into sparkling wine bottles, be sure not to insert them too far, or you may never get them out.

Bottle Capsules

There are three basic types of bottle top capsules: foil, shrink, and wax. Whichever type of capsule you decide is best for your operation can be installed at this stage in the bottling line. To install foil capsules, you'll need a special piece of equipment called a spinner. In essence it spins some wheels around, and as the technician slowly pushes the bottle into it (or pulls the spinner onto the bottle), the foil takes the shape of the neck of the bottle.

Foils and spinners are, in my opinion, more expensive than can be justified for the home winemaker. They are also difficult for amateurs to operate, so they aren't a great method for capping bottles for inexperienced folks who come by to help out.

Shrink caps are a great alternative to foils. To the untrained eye they look almost identical to foils, yet unlike foils they can be installed by just about anyone after a couple of practice runs. In essence, the shrink cap is set in place over the bot-

FIGURE 7.11 *Heat-Shrink Capsule Installation*

tle and quickly heated with air or water. It almost immediately shrinks around the neck of the bottle. There are cap-shrinking air guns on the market; you insert the bottle into the gun and it shrinks the capsule. My preferred method is to use gently boiling water. Here's the technique my volunteers use:

Set a large pot of water (about 1 gallon) on a hot plate on a table next to the corker. Bring the water to a boil and adjust the heat to maintain a gentle rolling boil. Place the capsules over the bottles on the finishing table as they come off the corker. Hold the body of a bottle with one hand, and place the index finger of your other hand on the edge of the capsule, holding it in place while you invert the bottle. Slowly dip the neck of the bottle into the boiling water, and as soon as the capsule touches the water, remove your finger and continue lowering the bottle until the capsule is completely submerged. Then pull the bottle out and set it over and down the line. The capsule shrinks in only a second, so a moderately slow dip in and out will create a great-looking capsule. Obviously, take care not to stick your finger into the boiling water.

✳ *Foil stickers can be extra dressing for a monotone capsule. I found a little gold foil sticker that reflects a concept I can relate to our little winery, and I stick it on the capsules, adding just a touch of class for little expense. And since the stickers are placed on the capsule rather than the bottle, there's no scraping to get them off when you're recycling your bottle for the next year.*

A third capping alternative is to use wax. Melt the wax in a can placed in a pot of boiling water, and dip the corked bottle into the wax to the desired depth. You can dip on an angle or let the wax drip down the neck of the bottle to create interesting effects. I find the biggest downside of using wax is that when you open the bottle, bits of wax get everywhere.

FIGURE 7.12 *Foil Applied to Shrink Capsule*

Labeling

Moving down the line from the capsuling stations we arrive at station 10, labeling. Putting a label on your wine is a way to identify the goods in the bottle, remind yourself of how you made the wine, and make a statement about the winemaker. There are countless approaches to designing and printing labels, and here we can only scratch the surface of the available options. Some folks have their labels professionally designed and printed, and others use a piece of masking tape with an abbreviated indication as to what's in the bottle. Some embrace humor, have their kids' drawings on them, show a photo of their pet, or just use an attractive typeface.

As another of my hobbies I like to do watercolor painting, so many of my labels include my paintings. A given vintage might display several of my paintings on the labels, many of which have nothing to do with the wine inside. For instance, I put a painting of a killer whale on my Malbec, so now when I go down to the cellar looking for a Malbec, I can find the wine quickly.

Have fun making your labels and you will be rewarded every time you open a bottle, and your friends will be impressed with the professional appearance of your boutique wine.

In keeping with creating a professional appearance, take pains to install the labels straight, flat, and consistently in the same place on the bottles. To facilitate this, you can whip out a label alignment jig.

THIS LITTLE CONTRAPTION ALLOWS YOU TO SET UP a half dozen bottles at a time to have labels applied flat, straight, and aligned.

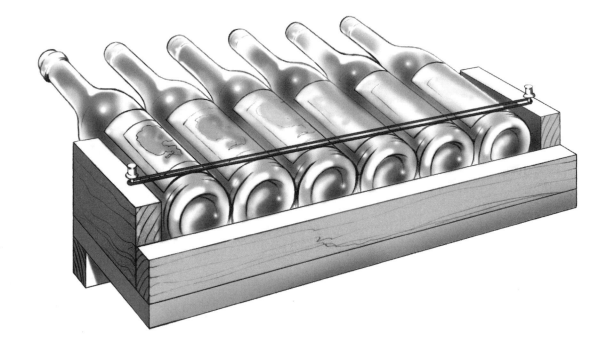

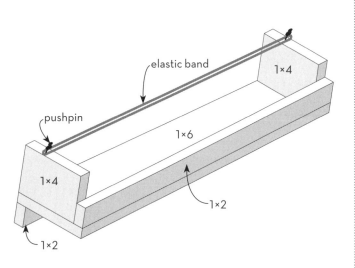

FIGURE 7.13 *Label Alignment Jig*

MATERIALS

- 1½" wood screws
- One 21" length 1×6 lumber
- Two 21" lengths 1×2 lumber
- Two 5½" lengths 1×4 lumber
- Two pushpins
- One long elastic band

BUILD IT!

Screw the 1×6 to the 1×2s, forming a Z shape. Then screw the 1×4s to the ends of the Z, as shown in figure 7.13.

USE IT!

Lay six bottles ready to be labeled, necks up, on the jig. Determine where you want the top or bottom of the labels and put a pushpin in the 1×4 side pieces at this location. Stretch the elastic band from pin to pin across the bottles and give it a little snap to straighten it.

Apply the adhesive of choice to the back of the labels (see below). Stick them to the bottles, aligning them with the elastic band, by pressing down first at the center of the label and then across each way. Remove the labeled bottles, tuck another six bottles under the elastic band, and label away!

LABEL ADHESIVES

As mentioned in the discussion of removing labels (page 123), it is wise to use an adhesive that allows you to remove labels easily but keeps them stuck in humid refrigerators or ice buckets. Some adhesives that I've found effective include:

» Glue sticks (nonpermanent)

» Elmer's glue

» Diluted wallpaper paste

» Milk

» Spray mount adhesive (very light coat)

» Self-adhesive label

To the Cellar

After the bottles are labeled, they're moved to station 10 — a cardboard wine box to be carried down to the cellar.

Oh, and be sure to include station 11, the refreshment center, to keep the party lively.

CHAPTER EIGHT

YOUR WINE CELLAR

WITH POTENTIALLY HUNDREDS or thousands of bottles of wine, every winemaker needs a place to store the bounty. The basic purpose of a cellar is to provide storage that is accessible, with controlled and relatively constant temperature and humidity. Ideal temperatures are around 55 to 60°F, and ideal humidity of around 65 percent. Your cellar can be part of your winery or totally separate from it. But because your winery will be a hub of activity, requiring various temperature changes for fermentation, for example, if you're able to allocate a separate space for your wine bottle storage, you'll have better cellaring success.

✳ *If your cellar area tends to have very low ambient humidity, you can install a small bubbling water fountain in your cellar. Set it on a bucket of water and cycle the water through the bucket so it does not dry up. Change the water in the bucket regularly to keep algae and other growth from occurring. And don't use chlorinated algae treatments, to avoid the potential of cork taint (TCA).*

✳ *If your cellar area tends to have high humidity, you may need to install a small dehumidifier to maintain the proper range.*

Selecting a Cellar Location

Every home has someplace that would be a good candidate to serve as a cellar. Think about the possibilities. Look through the clutter in a corner of a room and visualize stacks of wine bottles there. What about the area under the stairway? A broom closet? Some other places I've known winemakers to successfully convert or build into nice wine cellars include:

- » Basement room
- » Crawl space
- » One wall in the garage
- » Storage room
- » Unused bathroom
- » Outdoor storage shed
- » Cave
- » Root cellar
- » Oil-change pit in the garage floor
- » Swimming pool!

Once you've taken inventory of all the options, consider the pros and cons of each space. How hard will it be to convert it to a cellar? How much might the conversion cost? Will you be able to keep it at the proper temperature without expensive temperature-control units? And do you want this to be a purely functional wine storage room, or will it also serve as a tasting area, and for how many people at a time?

Once you settle on the best location and function for the cellar, then you can start laying out the plans. Start by sketching up the layout of the space on a piece of graph paper. Take careful measurements from wall to wall and of ceiling heights, and mark the locations of light fixtures, outlets, windows, doors, switches, posts, beams, pipes, wires, and any other features. Note whether the walls are interior or exterior walls, and whether there's air or backfill on the outside of exterior walls. If any of the walls or floor is in contact with earth, note whether it leaks.

Now that you've mapped out the space, you can decide whether you want to make

This cellar includes ladder racking, a curved corner rack, and double-sided waterfall racks with a display end cap. Low-voltage lighting highlights the bottles set on a slight angle.

it bigger or smaller by adding or removing walls. Before taking out any wall, however, it's very important to determine if it is load-bearing. If it is, can the load be transferred to a beam and posts or another wall without affecting the rest of the structure? This is obviously a question for a qualified building professional.

DRAWING CELLAR PLANS

WITH PRELIMINARY CONCEPTUALIZING DONE, it is time to draw up your final plans. If you're able to draw to scale on a computer, more power to you, but graph paper will work just fine.

1. Sketch out the final shape and configuration of the cellar to scale.

Most architects draw floor plans with a scale of ¼" equals 1 foot (1" equals 4 feet), and with that scale most cellar plans will fit on an 8½" × 11" sheet of paper. Plan on all walls being constructed from 2×6s, which will allow for plenty of insulation, unless your walls are backed up against a foundation that is backfilled with earth. In that case the wall can be left as concrete or block to let the earth act as a heat sink. More on that later.

2. Locate the door.

Once you've located all the walls, indicate the location of the door. Typical residential doors are sized in even increments from 28" to 36" wide (except 34") and 80" high. If possible, plan on a 36"-wide door or as close as possible to it, as the greater width will make moving wine into the cellar easier. And if possible, have the door swing out of the cellar, rather than into it, to maximize the storage space in your cellar.

3. Locate the wine storage racks.

Cut some strips of paper to scale to represent racks at 11" in width, and cut a circle to scale to represent the 30" in diameter you'll need for working space in the cellar. Play with laying out the strips on the plan. Don't limit yourself by considering placing racks only along the walls. Pulling racking into the center of the cellar will dramatically increase the amount of wine you can store. If you're considering a table or chairs or other pieces of furniture, cut out similar pieces of paper to simulate them.

4. Fine-tune the plans.

Once you have the layout configured, consider the work you might need to do to accommodate existing fixtures and features, and whether that work will be difficult or expensive. If any particular item seems like a real headache, revisit your plan to see what might be better tweaked to deal with that pipe, post, switch, or what have you. Having established work-arounds for these issues, you can draw your final plans and get busy with building the cellar.

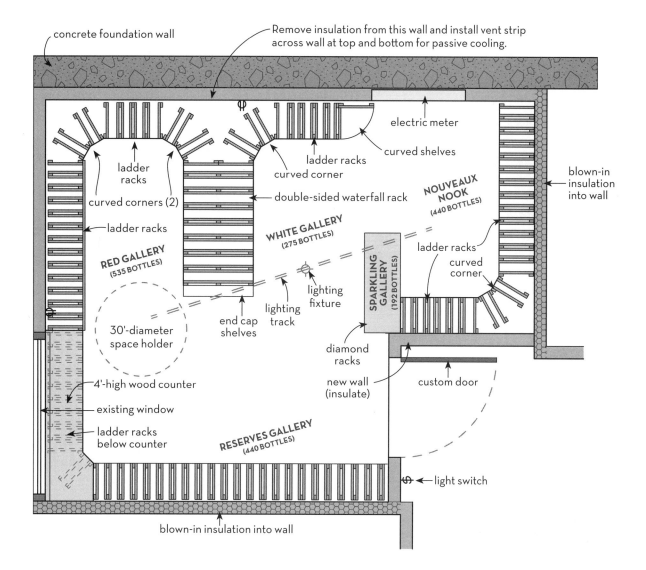

concrete foundation wall

Remove insulation from this wall and install vent strip across wall at top and bottom for passive cooling.

electric meter

curved shelves

ladder racks

curved corner

ladder racks

curved corners (2)

ladder racks

double-sided waterfall rack

NOUVEAUX NOOK (440 BOTTLES)

blown-in insulation into wall

WHITE GALLERY (275 BOTTLES)

RED GALLERY (535 BOTTLES)

SPARKLING GALLERY (192 BOTTLES)

ladder racks

curved corner

lighting fixture

30'-diameter space holder

lighting track

end cap shelves

lighting

diamond racks

new wall (insulate)

custom door

4'-high wood counter

existing window

ladder racks below counter

RESERVES GALLERY (440 BOTTLES)

light switch

blown-in insulation into wall

FIGURE 8.1 *Floor Plan*

AN INSPIRED PLAN

Play around with your ideas. Consider options that aren't obvious. Don't settle on your first design. Sketch one plan, then throw it away. Sketch another, and set it aside. Create a third, and you'll be ready to start fitting it into the space you've allocated. With yet another you'll be closer to perfect, and you can fix things that didn't work in the last design. Refine the plan. Try to visualize standing in the cellar when it's all done. Close your eyes. Reflect on all the great experiences you've had, and you'll end up with a remarkable plan and a cellar that you've already built before you ever start construction.

Building the Room

Following is an overview of how to build a large dedicated cellar space, along with considerations for framing and insulating the walls and ceilings and choosing flooring materials. These are general guidelines that can help you plan and create your own cellar, whether you're working with professionals or tackling the whole job yourself.

Layout and Framing

Lay out any new walls by marking their location on the floor. Again, walls should be constructed with 2×6s to allow for good insulation. If you're setting the walls on a concrete floor, the "plate" set on the concrete should be pressure-treated. Even on interior concrete (and other masonry) surfaces, untreated wood will eventually absorb enough moisture to rot and attract unwanted critters and mold. Frame the walls up with 2×6 studs set every 16". The door opening should have double studs and be framed 2" wider than the planned door; for example, if you're planning a 36"-wide door, the rough opening should be 38" wide. The door header can also be a double 2×6 and the height of the rough opening, from the floor to the bottom of header, should be 82¾" for a standard 80" door.

✱ *To square your new wall with an existing wall, use the 3-4-5 rule: From the point where the new wall and existing wall intersect, measure 3 feet along one wall and 4 feet along the other wall, and make a mark. Then measure diagonally between the two marks you just made. When the diagonal measurement equals 5 feet, the two walls are square to each other.*

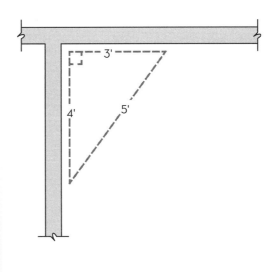

FIGURE 8.2 *The 3-4-5 Rule*

If one of your cellar walls is built against a foundation and you are planning on controlling the temperature with a cooling unit, you can save a few bucks by framing the wall with 2×4s instead of 2×6s, holding the back of the 2×4s an inch away from the foundation wall, which allows you to install R19 insulation in a wall framed with studs that would typically only handle R13 insulation. In any event, your studs should not be placed directly against the concrete foundation, to prevent decay.

For the ceiling, plan on a structure that will allow for R-30 or greater insulation. If you want to use batts for insulation (least expensive), then you need about 11" of clearance space above the ceiling.

Now is also a good time to plan for and install backing — blocks between the studs — for securing your racking. Rough out the racking layout on the floor, determine where the racks will need some support, and install the blocks. Note these locations on your drawings for future reference.

Wiring and Lighting

Next, install the necessary wiring for any power and lighting sources you might need, including overhead and accent lighting. Light switches should be placed on the doorknob side of the door if possible. Don't install the finished devices or fixtures at this time. If you have any doubts about your ability to wire correctly, consult or hire an electrician to do this work.

Insulation and Vapor Barriers

Considering that your cellar will be consistently 55 to 65°F, determine whether the average annual temperature outside the cellar will be higher or lower than the temperature inside the cellar. You will want to install a vapor barrier on the *warmer* side of the wall. For example, if you live in Arizona, the warmer side of an exterior wall will be the outside, so the vapor barrier should be installed on the exterior of the wall. On the other hand, if you live in Anchorage, you'd likely install the barrier on the inside of an exterior wall. For nearly all interior walls where the space outside the cellar will be heated or conditioned, the vapor barrier should be placed on the outside of the cellar wall.

A vapor barrier is not mandatory, particularly on exterior walls that are already finished. The cost of tearing out the siding or existing insulation does not warrant the benefit of the vapor barrier, so skip it. Wherever it is cost-effective and feasible, install 4-mil plastic sheeting (such as Visqueen) to the face of the studs prior to insulating in order to prevent convection currents of air from passing through the wall. Then install unfaced insulation batts — R-30 or R-38

in the ceiling, R-19 in the walls, and R-30 under the floor if the floor is framed wood. Apply a bead of caulking along the bottom plates to seal them to the floor, eliminating drafts and heat loss/gain.

Where you're building your cellar up against an already finished wall or ceiling, rather than tearing out the drywall to install batts, you can blow insulation into the wall with a rented insulation blower. Use a stud finder to locate each stud, and mark its location. Between the studs, drill a 2" hole about 9" down from the top of the wall. Blow the insulation into each stud bay following the insulation manufacturer's directions. Once the bay is full and you've cleaned up the mess, patch the drywall with expanding insulation foam, which comes in an aerosol can. Make a little space in the insulation behind the drywall and then fill the hole with just enough of the foam to create a mushroom-shaped cap coming out of the hole. After it is thoroughly dry, cut the foam button off with a serrated knife, and apply drywall tape and a few coats of joint compound over the hole. Finish as appropriate to match your wall's texture.

Passive Thermal Control

If your cellar is located in a garage or basement that has a concrete floor or an earth-backfilled foundation, you can take advantage of Mother Earth's natural temperature control. The earth acts as a heat sink, maintaining a constant temperature below what is commonly referred to as the frost line. For most of the country, this is a steady 55°F, an ideal temperature for your cellar. Concrete is a great conductor of heat, so as your cellar warms up, the earth on the other side of the concrete will draw in and absorb that heat. Conversely, if the cellar cools too much, the earth will stabilize the temperature.

To take advantage of this effect, do not insulate any foundation walls or concrete floors backed by earth. If you want to frame a wall up against the foundation, I suggest installing a vent strip near the top of the wall and another one near the floor. With these vents installed, the space between the drywall and the foundation will create convection currents. As warm air rises and contacts the cooler foundation, it will cool and sink, flowing against the wall and continuing to cool, only to be replaced at the top by the warmer air near the ceiling. Convection is very effective in maintaining a constant temperature in your cellar without expensive equipment and eliminating temperature stratification.

Active Temperature Control

In the event that passive thermal control is not your cup of tea and you elect to use a mechanical means to cool your cellar, there are a few options. Probably the best is to purchase and install a specially designed cellar cooler. These coolers are designed with a temperature setting commonly used for cellars and also control humidity. They are fairly expensive, however.

Some folks use air conditioners or "mini-split" systems that typically cool a space down to 60°F, but no lower, unless you trick them by putting an isolated heat source like a lightbulb next to their temperature sensor. In essence you warm only the space around the thermostat until the air conditioner cools the larger cellar space to the desired temperature, and then you dial back the temperature control until it clicks off the unit. You could rig up the heat source with a thermostatic control, similar to how we wired the controller in the fermentation chamber (see page 51).

One downside of an air conditioner is that in addition to cooling the space, it also reduces the humidity in the room, which can cause corks to dry out and leak. To remedy this, you can collect the AC's condensate, pipe it back into a bucket in the room, and install a bubbling fountain in the bucket, as described on page 150.

Drywall and Finishing

Install regular ½" drywall on walls and ceilings that have framing spaced at 16". Use ⅝" drywall for walls and ceilings with framing spaced at 24". Waterproof or water-resistant drywall is not necessary for a wine cellar. Tape and fill the joints, corners, and fasteners to the desired finish. Prime the new drywall with an acrylic drywall sealer prior to texturing (if you plan on texturing). Then paint with your favorite color and sheen of acrylic paint.

Flooring

The flooring material you choose for your cellar should help you achieve your heating/cooling goals, but keep in mind that hundreds of gallons of wine may be stored in there at any point in time. If you have a concrete slab floor that will passively help to achieve temperature stability, it is a good idea to help it out by using a hard surface like ceramic tile or other material with little thermal resistance. On the other hand, if you are putting your cellar on a wood floor with a crawl space or heated room below, besides making sure the floor framing is well insulated, use a material that will complement the insulating properties of the floor system, such as wood, cork, or other soft, thick material that resists heat transfer.

You might consider a combination of flooring materials. In my cellar, which was built in a basement with a slab-on-grade floor, I really liked the idea of using cork, but to encourage the passive cooling provided by the bare concrete, I painted the concrete floor under the wine racking in a cork color and installed cork flooring only on the walking surfaces. Bottles in the racks cover up the concrete. This enables me to benefit from the passive cooling and minimize flooring costs at the same time.

For decorative purposes, flooring can add a lot to the ambience of the room, so think about borders, medallions, or other motifs that could enhance the look and function of your floor. Be sure to follow the manufacturer's recommendations when selecting and installing any floor covering, with particular attention to how the flooring might respond to the ambient conditions.

Furniture and Decor

Many winemakers like to include a tasting table and chairs or other interesting pieces of furniture or racking in their cellars. Before designing a lot of space to be consumed for a tasting room, keep in mind that the temperature in the cellar is going to be pretty low and not terribly comfortable for lengthy stays. I had an old oak antique roll-top desk that I worked into the design for my cellar. Sentimental value for the desk won out over the additional bottle storage I would have gained by not keeping it, so it sits majestically in the cellar and is the centerpiece of my Reserves Library. Friends and family continue to contribute to the cellar with wrought-iron racks, glasses, banners, and so on.

> Before designing a lot of space to be consumed for a tasting room, keep in mind that the temperature in the cellar is going to be pretty low and not terribly comfortable for lengthy stays.

My wife made little ceramic placards with numbers and letters. We installed the numbered placards above the angled bottle display for each column, identifying the stacks 1, 2, 3, and so on, and we placed the letters alongside each row, giving us an easy reference as to where each bottle is stored when consulting our cellar log.

Racking

There are lots of different styles of racking you can use in your cellar, so it's worth considering the advantages and disadvantages of each as you work out the details of your design. They include flat shelves, display shelves, ladder racking, waterfall racking, diamond bins, radiused ladders, curved end shelves, end caps, and others. You've laid out the locations of the racking in your plans. Now you need to decide what type of racking would be best for your cellar. Here we'll explore some of the different options.

Ladder Racks

Ladder racks are made from a pair of floor-to-ceiling uprights with small crosspieces nailed to them. When the two racks with crosspieces are stood next to each other and tied together, they support a column of bottles. The bottles are individually supported, meaning each one is independent of the others and can be removed without moving any other bottles. The crosspieces, or ladder "rungs," can be installed on opposite faces of the uprights, so that the racks can be lined up side by side to create a row of bottle stacks. At each end of the row, the paired uprights will have crosspieces installed on only one side.

Any number of materials will work for ladder racks, from walnut to oak, redwood, cedar, or pine. The cost of each varies widely, so some research and budget consideration should take place before you decide on any one species. I was very fortunate to find a cedar mill that was closing out its inventory of rough-sawn materials, which I was able to mill into finished pieces. The cedar smells wonderful! (I would, however, avoid aromatic or "Tennessee" cedar, which can have an overwhelming aroma.)

Depending on your cellar configuration, you might have use for a variety of ladder racking styles, including straight racks, curved corner racks, and waterfall racks. All of these use the same basic ladder construction. If you'd like to build more than a few stacks of racks, it's well worth your time to create a simple jig that makes the assembly fast and accurate. The jig described here works for one- and two-sided ladder racks, corner racks, and waterfall racks.

LADDER RACKING JIG

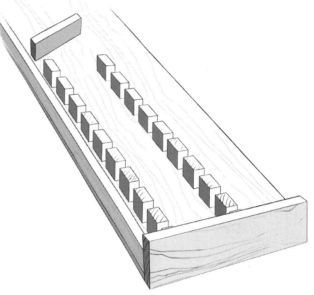

THIS LADDER DESIGN assumes a ceiling height of at least 97" for your cellar. If your ceiling height is lower, adjust the top of your jig and material lengths accordingly. The total height of the racks should be at least 1" less than the finished ceiling height to allow you to assemble the racks on the floor and then clear the ceiling as you stand them up for installation.

MATERIALS

- One 16" × 96" piece ¾" CDX plywood
- Three 8-foot lengths 2×4 lumber, each ripped into 2"-wide strips
- 2½" wood screws
- One 16" length 1×4 lumber

BUILD IT!

1. Install the guides.

Lay the sheet of plywood across a pair of sawhorses or a bench. Lay one of the 8-foot-long, 2"-wide strips ripped from a 2×4 along one edge of the plywood, with its 2" side set vertical. Screw the strip to the plywood, keeping it as straight as possible. Screw the 1×4 into the edge of the plywood on one short side, forming a stop for the bottom of the uprights. In the finished jig, the 2" piece ripped from the 2×4 is the front edge guide, and the 1×4 is the bottom guide.

2. Mark the rung layout.

Lay out the locations of the rungs by measuring up from the 1×4 bottom guide and marking the plywood at the following points (see figure 8.3):

» 3½"	» 38¼"	» 74"
» 7¾"	» 42½"	» 79"
» 12"	» 47½"	» 83¼"
» 16¼"	» 49⅞"	» 87½"
» 20½"	» 57"	» 91¾"
» 25½"	» 61¼"	
» 29¾"	» 65½"	
» 34"	» 69¾"	

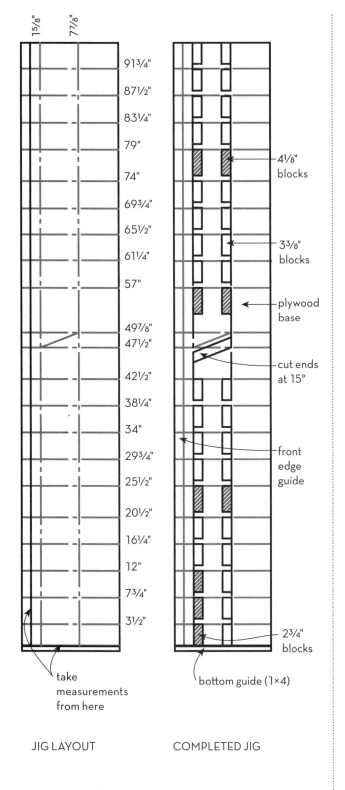

FIGURE 8.3 *Ladder Racking Jig*

Using a square, mark a line across the plywood at each of these marks, square to the front edge guide. Measuring from the inside edge of the front edge guide, make a mark at 1⅝" at the top and bottom of the plywood, and draw a straight line or snap a chalk line lengthwise between the marks. Make another line 7⅞" from the front edge guide in the same manner.

3. Install the blocks.

Cut the other strips ripped from 2×4s into 32 blocks at 3⅜" and 8 blocks at 4⅛". With the 1½" dimension of these blocks against the plywood, you'll screw the blocks through predrilled holes to the plywood, aligning them on the inside corners of the short horizontal lines and the long vertical lines (see figure 8.3). Be sure to predrill the blocks to keep them from splitting. The blocks will form a negative skeleton of the racking. Beginning at the 3½" mark and working up, install five pairs of 3⅜" blocks, then one pair of 4⅛" blocks, and then four pairs of 3⅜" blocks.

Next, lay out the display shelf guide by marking a diagonal line between the long vertical lines, from the 47½" mark on the 1⅝" line to the 49⅞" mark on the 7⅞" line (see figure 8.3). Cut the ends of two pieces of ripped 2×4 at 15°, cutting across the 1½" dimension; screw these ¾" below the display shelf line.

Starting at the 57" mark, install one pair of 4⅛" blocks, then four more pairs of 3⅜" blocks, then one pair of 4⅛" blocks, and finally four pairs of 3⅜" blocks.

LADDER RACKING

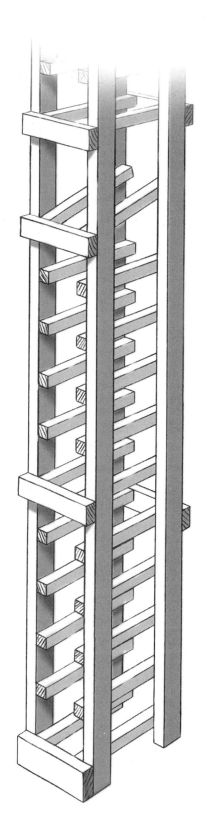

A LADDER RACK IS MUCH LIKE IT SOUNDS — a pair of "ladders" that face each other, with each opposing set of "rungs" supporting one bottle. The rungs are positioned to allow a bit of space between bottles. These racks are versatile in that they allow you to access any bottle in the racking at any time, unlike other stacking types of racks. This project shows you how to build straight ladder racking using the jig described on page 159.

MATERIALS

See step 1 on page 162 for calculating lumber quantities.

- 8-foot lengths 1×2 lumber (for uprights, cross ties, and nailing strips)
- 10½" lengths 1×1 lumber (for ladder rungs)
- 8-foot lengths 1×4 lumber (for baseboard and ceiling trim)
- 1¼" brads
- 2" brads
- 2½" wood screws

BUILD IT!

1. Calculate quantities.

For each ladder, you'll need two 8-foot lengths of 1×2. For rungs, the ladders use 10½" lengths of 1×1; each single-sided (end) ladder needs 20 rungs, and each double-sided ladder requires 40 rungs.

To calculate the total number of ladders you'll need, measure the total length of racking in inches and divide by 4.25 (the on-center spacing of the ladders). Multiply this number by 2 (the number of uprights per ladder) and add 2 (the uprights for the end racking) to get the total number of uprights you'll need. For the rungs, count the total number of ladders, subtract 1, then multiply that number by 40.

For the horizontal 1×2 cross ties and nailing strips, you'll need seven pieces to span the length of the racking. Four will be cross ties, and three will be nailing strips.

Similarly, the 1×4 baseboard will span the length of the racking, as will the ceiling trim, if you want it.

2. Construct the ladders.

Keep in mind that you'll have a left end ladder and a right end ladder. For the left one, place a straight 8-foot 1×2 upright into the jig, tight against the front edge guide and the bottom guide. Place another 1×2 upright opposite, tightly against the blocking and the bottom guide. Lay 1×1 rungs in the slots between the blocks, tight against the front edge guide. Nail the rungs and uprights together with a single 1¼" brad

at each intersection. Carefully remove the finished ladder.

For the right end ladder, lay down the rungs first, followed by the uprights. Nail the pieces together, and remove the completed ladder from the jig.

For each double-sided ladder, lay in a course of 1×1s, then the uprights, then another course of rungs. Nail these together with 2" brads.

3. Cut the ties, nailing strips, and trim.

Count the number of ladders you will be standing up. Multiply this number by 4.25 and add ¾". This will be the length of your four 1×2 cross ties, three 1×2 nailing strips, and 1×4 baseboard and ceiling trim. Cut the pieces and set them aside.

4. Mark the supporting wall.

Mark the locations of the studs and/or backing you will screw the nailing strips to. You'll install screws at about every other stud (approximately 32" apart) and at 91" and 20" above the finished floor. Note that these are the screw locations; make your marks slightly above or below these points so you can see them when you stand up the racks, and the nailing strips won't cover them up.

5. Assemble the ladders.

Lay the ladders facedown on the cellar floor, with their bottom ends against the supporting wall. Stack them all tightly together in the order they'll be assembled. Then position the end ladder approximately where it will be stood up. Install the bottom nailing strip as shown in figure 8.4, flush with the outside of the upright, nailing it into the upright with a 2" brad. Install the other two nailing strips in the same manner.

Position the first double-sided ladder next to the end ladder, spacing it 3½" from the end ladder's upright. (You can use a 2×4 block to set this spacing, but every fifth upright or so, measure the overall dimension to make sure you're maintaining the 4¼" on-center spacing, to prevent compounded errors.) Nail the three nailing strips into it at the nailing strip locations. Repeat to install the remaining ladders.

6. Mount the racking.

Once you have assembled all the ladders into a single rack, stand the racking up against the wall. Use a level to make sure the uprights are plumb in both directions, then screw the top and bottom nailing strips to the wall. (It's easier to do this before installing the front cross ties, as the fronts of the ladders will spread apart to allow you to get your drill and hand between them.) Install the front ties, baseboard, and ceiling trim as shown in figure 8.5.

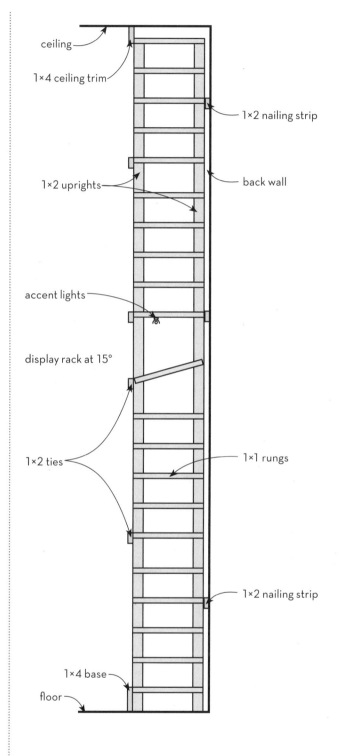

FIGURE 8.4 *Ladder Racking Cross Section*

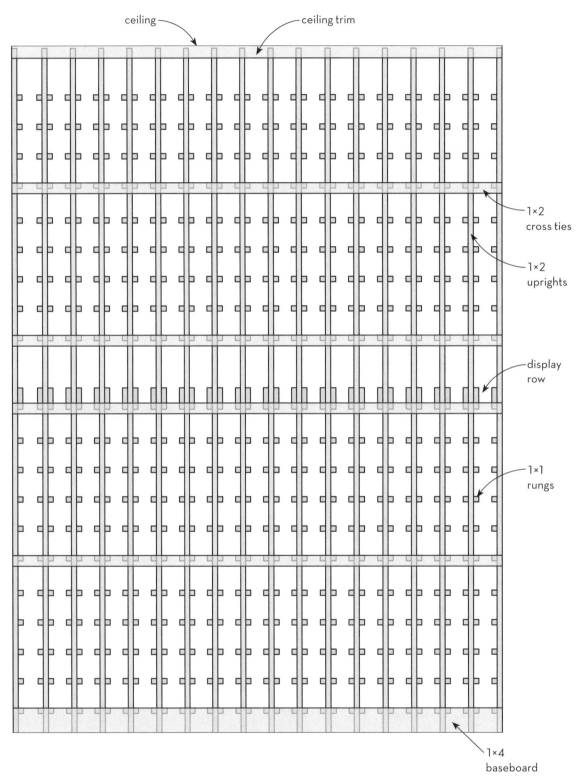

FIGURE 8.5 *Full-Height Ladder Racks*

CURVED CORNER RACKING

INSIDE CORNERS CAN BE A BIG WASTE OF SPACE for a racking system.
Filling the corners with these curved ladders allows for maximum use
of the space while creating a really elegant look.

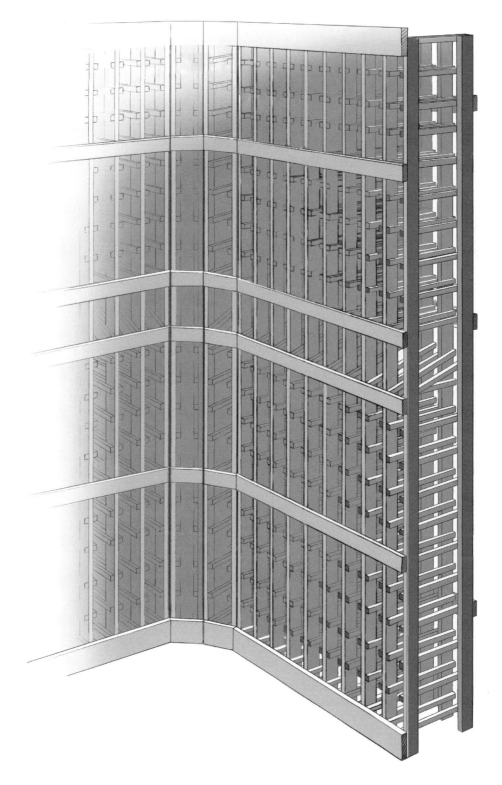

MATERIALS

- Four 5⅛" lengths 1×2s (for front cross ties)
- Two 5⅛" lengths 1×4 (baseboard ties)
- Two right end ladder racks (as described in ladder racking project, page 161)
- Two left end ladder racks (as described in ladder racking project, page 161)
- 2" brads
- Six 5" lengths 1×2 lumber (for back nailing strips)
- Scrap 1×4

BUILD IT!

1. Build the corner unit.

Cut each end of the 5⅛" front cross ties at a 15° angle so the angles are opposed (not parallel to each other). Nail a cross tie to the front of a pair of left and right ladders at the same height as each of the horizontal crosspieces on the regular ladder racks. Flip the ladders over and install the back nailing strips so you have two sets of ladder racks.

Create a few 30° triangle guides from some 1×4 scraps by cutting two sides at opposing 15° angles meeting at the top of the triangle. Use these guides as spacers between the uprights of the ladders to position each set together at the proper angle. Align the front crosspieces, and nail the two ladder racks together.

2. Install the corner unit.

It's a good practice to set any corner units in place prior to mounting the straight runs of racking. To do this, mark a line on the floor 11¾" out from each wall that forms the corner. Stand the corner unit up on the floor so the bottom front corners of its outer uprights sit on these lines. Use a square on the floor to transfer these locations to the supporting wall of the straight racking, to mark where the ends of the straight racking will terminate. Draw a plumb line up the wall at the termination point to guide the straight racking installation. Once the corner and straight sections are in place, nail the two units together.

WATERFALL RACKING

WATERFALL RACKING CAN PROVIDE SOME REAL DRAMA in the appearance of your cellar, and if it's set up as a peninsula extending into the room, it can add a lot of useful bottle storage without obstructing the view across the cellar. Transitioning into the waterfall from curved corners is quite spectacular.

If your cellar has the room, you can use longer ladder rungs to build a double-sided rack.

MATERIALS

See ladder racking project (page 161) and instructions on page 168 for guidance on calculating material quantities.

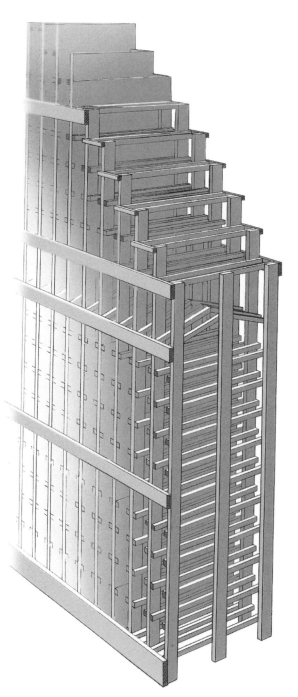

BUILD IT!

Calculate your materials as described for the ladder racking project (see page 161), except here your uprights will start at one height and become incrementally shorter (by 4¼" or 5", depending on the row). For single-sided waterfall racking, you'll need two uprights per stack and 10½" ladder rungs. For double-sided waterfall racking, you'll need three uprights per stack and 23" ladder rungs.

Check your plans to see how far into the room the waterfall can extend and how high you want its lowest "step." I like to set the shortest column so the angled display row is itself the lowest step. I install concealed lighting above the display row and an end cap shelf (see page 169) to terminate the waterfall. Once again, figure you need 4¼" on-center spacing between uprights.

Start construction at the lowest height, beginning with the end ladder and followed by double-rung ladders, until you reach the top of the waterfall at a wall or other rack. Each consecutive ladder increases in height either 4¼" or 5", depending on whether there is a continuous front tie in that location. Note that each double-rung ladder does not get a rung on its upper outside end (see figure 8.6).

Cut a 5"-long 1×1 for each step in the waterfall. Use it to cap each step, nailing it to the top of the outer upright and to the top rung position of the inner upright.

For a double-sided peninsula, build the ladder in the jig as described in the ladder racking project, but let the rungs extend out past the jig. Once the front and center uprights are nailed in place, flip the whole ladder over, install another upright in the jig, and nail the other ends of the rungs to the back upright.

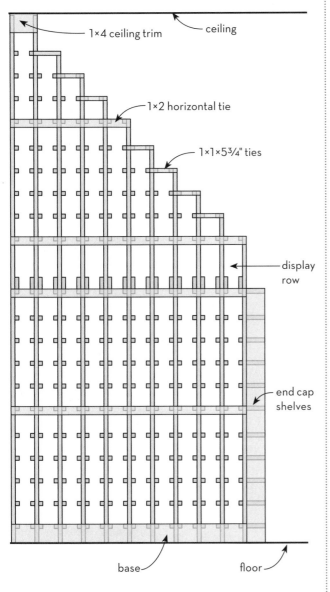

FIGURE 8.6 *Waterfall Ladder Racks*

END CAP SHELVES

END CAP SHELVES PUT A NICE FINISHING TOUCH at the bottom of waterfall racking. They're great for placing wines on display, highlighting them and reminding the cellar master of his special-occasion wines.

MATERIALS

- Two 1×4s approximately the height of the lowest column of the waterfall racking
- Five 21½" lengths 1×4 lumber (for double-sided racks)
- One 23" length 1×4 lumber (for double-sided racks)
- Five 21½" lengths small molding
- 2¼" screws
- Finish nails

BUILD IT!

Cut the two 1x4 uprights ¾" shorter than the final height of the shelving. Lay them together and mark the edges of the uprights at the desired spacing for four 21½" shelves. The bottom shelf should be set about 3½" above the floor to allow for the fifth 21½" piece to be installed as a toe-kick. The remaining shelves can be equally spaced between the top and the toe-kick.

Install the 1×4 toe-kick at the bottom, using finish nails, then add the 23" 1×4 at the top, nailed down into the uprights. Place the shelves on the marks and nail them in place.

At the front edge of each shelf, install the small moldings, which will keep the bottles from rolling off.

Stand the end cap shelves up against the end of the waterfall racking and toenail or screw the unit to the uprights of the waterfall racks.

DIAMOND BINS

DIAMOND BINS ARE GREAT FOR STORING A CASE OR MORE of the same wine in a very compact space. They don't allow for sorting through to find a particular bottle, because only the bottles on top of the bin are easily accessible. Another thing to keep in mind is that some bottle shapes are better suited to diamond bins than others. Bordeaux-style bottles, with long straight sides, work well, but if you stack Burgundy- or Hock-style bottles in a diamond bin, it is best to store them with their necks to the wall or you may have wine bottles cascading onto the floor.

This design for diamond bins will hold about 100 bottles in 11 compartments and works with the heights of the previously described ladder racking.

MATERIALS

- Four 8-foot lengths 1×6 lumber
- Three 32" lengths 1×4 lumber
- Finish nails
- Four 30½" lengths 1×4 lumber
- Thirty-six 20⅞" lengths 1×2 lumber
- Ten 11" lengths 1×1 lumber
- Scrap 1×2 (for nailers; optional)
- 2¼" wood screws
- 2¼" trim head screws

BUILD IT!

1. Build the carcase.

For the uprights, set two 1×6 boards side by side. Temporarily tack two 1×2 ties across them, making an 11"-wide board, to make installing the tops and bottoms a bit easier. Remove them when the carcase of the rack is formed. Repeat with the other two 1×6 boards to make two sets of uprights.

Across the top of the uprights, fasten a 32" 1×4 over the center, where the 1×6 boards meet, driving a finish nail into both pieces to tie them. Nail a 32" 1×4 to either side of the center piece, leaving about a ¼" gap between the boards, to form the top of the unit.

In a similar fashion, install three 30½" 1×4s for the floor of the carcase, nailing through the uprights and into the floor-boards. The tops of these floorboards should be 4¼" above the bottom of the uprights. Install the last 1×4 as a toe-kick below the floorboards, setting it vertically and recessed slightly.

2. Assemble the diamonds.

Stand up one 1×2 and nail a second one into the top of the first. Rotate the 1×2s so the second one is vertical, and nail on a third. Repeat in this "pinwheel" fashion to make a square measuring 21⅝" on each side. Now make eight more of these squares.

Connect three squares by standing them up on edge and nailing a 1×1 in opposite inside corners (installing two 1×1s per triple square). On the outside of these squares, install a 1×1 on the corners that do not have an interior 1×1. Repeat to make three triple-square boxes.

3. Square up the carcase.

Lay the carcase down and measure and mark the midpoint between the top of the floor and the bottom of the top piece on each upright. Square up the carcase frame by measuring diagonally between opposing corners and adjusting the frame as needed (by racking — applying inward pressure to both opposing corners with the longer measurement) until the measurements are equal. If the frame doesn't stay in place in a square position, tack a temporary diagonal brace from the top to an upright to keep it that way.

4. Install the diamonds.

Place one diamond into the frame with the corners that have interior 1×1s on the center marks you made on the uprights. Screw or nail through the 1×1s into the uprights to secure the diamond in place. Install the other diamonds above and below the center one, aligning the top and bottom points of the diamonds. After fastening the diamonds to the carcase frame, fasten them to each other with the 1×1s installed on the exterior of the diamonds.

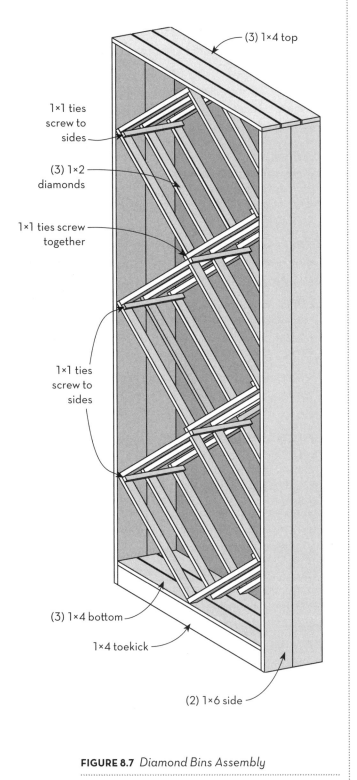

1×1 ties screw to sides

(3) 1×4 top

(3) 1×2 diamonds

1×1 ties screw together

1×1 ties screw to sides

(3) 1×4 bottom

1×4 toekick

(2) 1×6 side

FIGURE 8.7 *Diamond Bins Assembly*

5. Mount the unit.

If the unit is to be stood up against a wall, screw a couple of 1×2 crosspiece nailers to the back of the unit, one near the top and the other near the midpoint. Stand up the unit and anchor it to the wall by screwing it into the studs or lumber backing and fastening it to any adjacent racks.

VARIATION

This diamond bin assembly is easily modified to shorter heights; simply reduce the height and width proportionally. Or you can lay it on its side to serve as a counter-height rack.

Corner Shelves

At the ends of straight runs of ladder racking, you can transition from a harsh square corner to curved shelves that visually return the system back to the wall. Four or five shelves cut at an 11" radius and installed at the last ladder rack will give you a great place to display interesting winemaking devices and gifts to adorn the cellar, helping to create a soothing and artistic space.

Cellar Lighting

When planning lights for your cellar, keep in mind the three general types of lighting: ambient, task, and accent. Ambient lighting will provide general space illumination, allowing you to move through safely and reflecting the colors of the room. Task lighting will put more focused light on an area where you will need to look more closely at a specific object or function. And accent lighting will highlight something in the room to draw your eye to it or create a special effect.

As with any good lighting planning, consider all three lighting methods for your cellar. How do you want the ambience of the cellar to feel when you and your guests walk in? Big and bright? Subtle and warm? Glowing? For a big and bright feel, fill the room with fluorescent lights. For subtle and warm, use halogens or incandescents and control them with a dimmer. For a glowing feeling, consider using a lighting source that lights up the ceilings and walls without the light fixture being seen.

Task lighting will come into play if you have a table, counter, or other stand that you'll use for keeping a cellar log or any other activity for which you might need

Low-voltage accent lighting helps spot a special wine, and the custom tile placards above provide row identification to note the location of your wines in your cellar log.

extra light without affecting the ambient light effects. Recessed cans and track spotlights are good for this kind of lighting. Again, dimmers can help create the perfect level of light needed.

A good example of accent lighting in a cellar would be a strip of low-voltage or LED lights installed directly over the row of display bottles in your ladder racking. A flip of a switch turns your dark bottles into shimmering greens, ambers, rubies, and browns. And your labels are there for all to see, so you can select the perfect bottle for the moment.

CHAPTER NINE

BUILDING THE BACKYARD VINEYARD

THE ONLY THING BETTER THAN MAKING GREAT WINE is making great wine from fruit you grow yourself. The transformation that grapevines make during a season's growth can be exciting, excruciating, exuberant, and exulting. You'll feel the glee of bud break and the trepidation of powdery mildew and pests; you'll mark your calendar on the first day of *véraison* (color change of the grapes) like it's your child's birthday, and you'll scream at the birds for their pecks on your precious ones.

Growing your own grapes is quite possible on most parts of the continent, but selecting the right grape and rootstock is important and takes diligent research. Once you decide on the varietal, hybrid, or other kind of grape you feel is best suited to your backyard, there are several factors to consider, including:

» Location of the sun and amount of direct exposure on your planting site

» Air/breeze circulation

» Soil composition (have a soil analysis done at your local agricultural extension)

» Neighbors' use of herbicides and how they apply them

» How many vines you want to plant and how much wine you want to make; are you overplanting for your capacity?

» Vine and row spacing

Pick the best available site in your yard for your vineyard. Assuming you will plant more than one row, you should space your rows far enough apart that they don't cast shadows on one another. If you plan to mow or use an ATV to run between the rows, try to keep them spaced approximately 6 feet apart; on the other hand, if you are going to be doing your work manually, you could space them as closely as 5 feet apart. Spacing of the vines in the row is normally dependent on the varietal and pruning method you choose. More vigorous vines will be spaced farther apart than less vigorous vines. Consult other local grape growers to find out what is working for them. They might even give you some prunings in the late winter that you can root.

Rooting Cuttings

Obtaining cuttings from local growers is a great way to get your backyard vineyard started for very little expense. Some growers will let you pick up their cuttings after they're done pruning, while others will go out and cut fresh ones for you (possibly for a small fee). Cuttings should be ¼" to ¾" in diameter and about 12" to 18" long, and they should have at least three buds (the more the better). When taking a cutting, I like to cut the bottom of the stick square and the top at an angle, to make it easier to determine which end should be planted. Cut the top about 1" above a bud and the bottom only about ¼" below a bud.

Store cuttings wrapped in a wet paper towel in a plastic bag in a refrigerator until you're ready to start them. The basic method for starting cuttings is simply to plant them in a mixture of peat moss and perlite. Once they're planted, keep them in

Yours truly enjoying a moment among my vines at the entrance to my backyard vineyard.

a cool, dark place on a warm heating pad. If you plant them all close together, the roots could grow together, and when you pull them apart to transplant them into your vineyard they could break. Planting them in paper cups, as described in the following project, takes care of this problem.

CUTTING PROPAGATION BED

HERE'S HOW I SET UP my propagation bed to root up to 50 cuttings.

MATERIALS

- Peat moss
- Perlite
- One 18-gallon (more or less) plastic bin
- 5-ounce paper cups
- Heating pad (be sure it doesn't have an automatic shutoff)
- Rooting hormone

BUILD IT!

Mix up a planting medium of equal parts peat moss and perlite, and spread it in a 6" layer over the bottom of the Roughneck bin. Wet it all down to the point that it forms a clump in your hand when squeezed.

Trim the bottoms of your cuttings with sharp shears so they are fresh. Count the number of cuttings you're starting, and fill that number of paper cups with the peat/perlite mixture from the bin. Leaving the rest of the planting medium in the bottom of the bin, nestle the cups into the bin, making sure they still have a bit of medium beneath them. Water the bin again to create a very moist base, but not a saturated one. The point is to have the moisture conduct heat throughout the medium.

For each cutting, if it is still not moist from the damp paper towel, dip it in some water and shake it off, and then dip it into the rooting hormone. Poke a hole into the peat/perlite medium in one of the paper cups with a pencil, and push the cutting into the hole. Press the peat around the cutting.

Once all your cuttings are set into their cups, place the bin on the heating pad, and set it for medium heat. Insert a thermometer into the peat/perlite in the bin, and keep an eye on it. You want to maintain a constant temperature around 75°F while keeping the ambient air temperature in the range of 50° and the light minimal. Keep the medium in both the cups and the bin moist but not saturated. You're working on growing roots now, and even though you'll be excited when the buds start growing leaves, keep the light low, air cool, and bottom warm. If you plant these cuttings with little roots and lots of leaves, the leaves will demand more water than the new roots can conduct, and the plants may wilt and die.

Once the cuttings have grown some nice roots and a few little leaves, and all chance of frost has passed, it is time to plant them out in the vineyard.

VINEYARD TRELLIS

IN COMMERCIAL VINEYARDS, trellises typically consist of sturdy end posts installed vertically or on an angle, with smaller intermediate posts spaced 20 to 30 feet apart in a row. One wire is strung from post to post to support a drip irrigation system off the ground. A second wire supports main branches off the grapevine trunk, called canes or cordons, and the upper wires support branches that grow up from the canes and cordons. The posts are usually made from rough-cut poles and are not very finished looking.

The trellis system described here follows the commonly used vertical shoot positioning (VSP) system, which consists of four wires. A number of other wire configurations are available and may be preferable for different varietals and climates. Check with other grape growers and agricultural extensions in your area for their recommendations.

While you can certainly build a trellis matching the look of a commercial vineyard, many home winemakers have yards that are nicely landscaped and want their vineyard to have a more finished appearance, embellishing the rest of the softscape and hardscape surrounding their homes. Your vineyard can be a truly relaxing place to walk through with a glass of wine after a long day at the office. Here's an easy-to-build trellis system that works great for a backyard and will support your grapevines for years of trouble-free grape growing. I'll describe one 70-foot-long row. Your row length and numbers of rows may vary.

MATERIALS

- Two 9-foot lengths pressure-treated 4×4 lumber
- Wood end-cut preservative (optional; for treating cut ends of pressure-treated wood)
- Three 8-foot lengths pressure-treated 4×4 lumber
- Two 8-foot lengths pressure-treated 3" × 4" landscape timbers (with two rounded sides) or 4×4s
- Two 2" × 6" metal straps
- 80 lineal feet 12-gauge galvanized high-tensile wire
- 300 lineal feet 14-gauge galvanized high-tensile wire
- Twenty galvanized fence wire staples
- 16d galvanized nails

BUILD IT!

1. Dig the post holes.

Lay out the locations of your 9-foot 4×4 end posts, giving yourself adequate room to walk, wheel, or drive past them on each end. Unlike in a commercial vineyard, no wires will extend past the end posts, so you can set them within 3 to 6 feet of fences, your house, or other obstructions. Using a manual or powered post hole digger, dig a 3-foot-deep hole for each end post. If you have a number of post holes to dig and you're using a manual clamshell-type digger, you can mark the wood handles at 3 feet with a felt-tip marker to indicate the full depth.

2. Set the posts.

If your 9-foot posts were cut from a longer piece, paint the cut ends with the end-cut solution (as directed by the manufacturer) to forestall rot. Working with one post at a time, stand up the post in the hole, and backfill with some of the soil you dug out to hold the post in place. Use a level to plumb it up in both directions, and secure it by backfilling with the rest of the soil. Compact the dirt as you backfill; you can use the end of one of the other 4×4s or a sledgehammer to effectively compact it. Don't set these posts in concrete, as doing so will make replacing the posts in the future (if necessary) very difficult.

3. Install the intermediate posts.

Measure the distance between the two end posts and divide by 4; in the case of a 70-foot row, you would have 17.5 feet. Mark the ground between the posts at three equidistant locations. (If you're working with a different row length, my rule of thumb is to keep the spacing between posts as close to 20 feet as possible, so if you have a row length of 100 feet, you should add one additional intermediate post.)

Run a string line from the top of one end post to the top of the other end post. Dig holes for the 8-foot 4×4 intermediate posts at the locations you marked, making them about 2 feet deep. Drop each post into its hole and adjust the depth so the top of the

post is at the same height as the string line. Plumb, backfill, and tamp the soil around the posts, as before.

4. Brace the end posts.

Cut one end of each 8-foot landscape timber on a 45° angle, across the flat face. Measure along the row to a point 54" from one end post, and here dig a hole 18" deep on a 45° angle. Insert the flat end of the brace into the hole and use it to compact the soil at the base of the hole; the brace needs to go in about 2" farther than you've dug. Place the 45° angle cut of the timber against the end post so the angle cut sits flat against the inside face of the end post. Tack the timber to the end post with

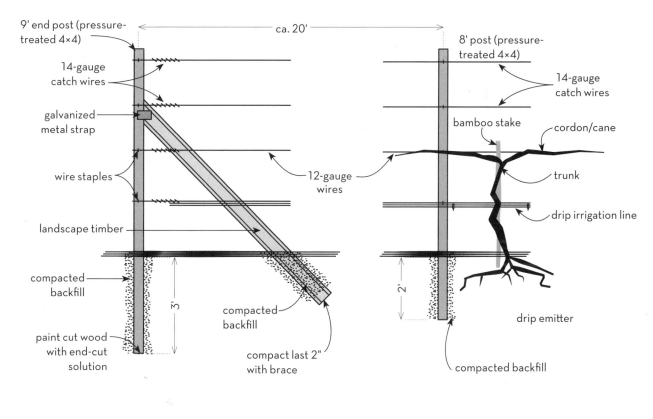

FIGURE 9.1 *Vineyard Trellis*

a galvanized nail, then reinforce the joint with the 6" metal strap and galvanized nails. Have a helper hold a heavy mallet or sledgehammer to support the post on the opposite side as you nail so that the impact of nailing doesn't loosen the posts. Brace the other end post in the same manner.

5. String the wires.

Mark the inside face of the end posts at 15", 36", 48", and 70" above the ground, then start a wire staple at each location. You'll install 14-gauge wire for the bottom and two top rows and 12-gauge wire for the row at 36". For each wire, slip one end of the wire through one of the wire staples, letting it extend about 3 feet, and then roll the wire down the length of the row to the opposite end post (take care not to let the wire uncoil on its own or you'll have a giant spaghetti mess of wire to untangle). Cut the wire off the roll about 3 feet past the opposite end post.

Wrap the wire tightly around the first end post (where it's slipped under the staple) two times; using a hammer to bend it around a corner helps shape it to the square wood posts. You should have about 12" of wire remaining, and you should wrap that several times around the running section of wire. To make twisting the short wire around the long wire easy, you can make a simple wire twister as shown in figure 9.2.

Tighten the wire staple on the wire, then add another staple on the back side of the post, over the two lengths of wire. At the other end of the row, slip the wire

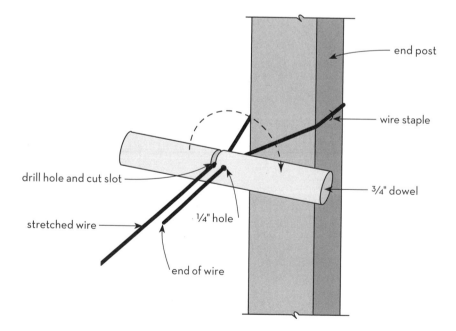

end post

wire staple

drill hole and cut slot

³/₄" dowel

stretched wire

¼" hole

end of wire

FIGURE 9.2 *Wire Twister*

through the staple and pull the wire taut, using two claw hammers or a cat's paw: Grab the wire with one hammer claw and pry against the post to really tighten it up, and use the other hammer to tighten the staple on the wire to hold it tight. Then wrap the loose wire end around the post twice and twist it around the running wire, as before, and add a staple on the back side of the post.

Because wire tends to expand and contract with temperature changes, you might get some slack in the summer and extra tightness in the winter. This is fine for the 14-gauge wires, but the cordon or "fruiting" 12-gauge wire needs to remain fairly taut for vine support. To give you a bit more flexibility and tightening capability, you might want to buy in-line trellis wire tighteners from an orchard supply store. These allow you to ratchet down the wires in the summer and loosen them in winter.

After the wires are strung to the end posts, fasten them in a straight line to the intermediate posts with partially driven wire staples.

ADDING DRIP IRRIGATION

There are a number of options for watering your grapevines. As with roses, keeping water off the leaves will help reduce the incidence of mildew, which can destroy a crop in very short order. Many vineyards use drip irrigation, which offers precise control over the location of the water. To prevent damage to drip irrigation lines during cultivating, weeding, and cover crop control, you can suspend the drip system on your trellis system, on a wire strung about halfway between the ground and the fruiting wire.

Because vineyard sizes and water supply systems vary widely, consult your local suppliers for recommendations on system sizing, water pressure, and other details specific to your situation. As a general example, the basic materials needed to add an irrigation line to the trellis shown here include:

» 80 lineal feet of ½" irrigation drip system tubing

» Two drip emitters per vine

» 20 electrical zip ties

Vine Stakes

You'll train each vine to a stake until its trunk reaches the desired height and can support its own weight. These stakes should be about 4 feet in length — long enough to be driven into the ground and then tied to the 36"-high (12-gauge) cordon wire. You can use any number of types of stakes for this purpose, from steel reinforcing bar (rebar) to bamboo stakes. It's easiest to install the stakes just after you plant your vines or cuttings, so they don't interfere with preparing the planting hole.

Grow Tubes

Grow tubes are narrow paper or plastic tubes set over the vines in their first year of growth to protect them from animals, frost, and damage from tools like string trimmers and cultivators. There are many options available; choose the material that best meets your needs. Some vintners use cardboard 1-quart milk cartons, and others use rigid plastic tubes that snap together. My vineyard is steep and impossible to work with anything other than hand tools, and I have access to many different construction materials, so I use some 12"-long pieces of black plastic corrugated drain pipe. Not only are they effective in keeping the tiny vines safe from errant string trimmers, but the black color also warms the ground around the vines. I have kept them in place for several years just to keep the trunks protected.

Vineyard Art

That extra little personal touch you add to your vineyard could spark conversations, be a source of entertainment, and possibly even be good for the environment and your vineyard. Trellis posts provide the perfect location for any number of crafty pieces. My wife is a pottery sculptor and has hand-built some "critters" depicting caricatures of the many different types of wildlife we see around our home winery. Birds, a fox, a coyote, raptors, a bunny, and a squirrel adorn our posts. Up near our street, our house numbers are displayed on posts, with hand-carved grapevines winding around the numerals. It's interesting that the birds avoid the parts of the vineyard where the critters are. Maybe having 22 sets of eyes looking every which way scares them off.

Whirligigs, windsocks, and wind chimes could be interesting post toppers, and their constant movement offers some protection against birds. Topped with flags on national holidays, they host a patriotic display.

You can make some interesting row markers that designate the kind of grape growing in each row. Owl and bat houses could help keep the vermin and insect populations down. Birdhouses and feeders mounted in the spring can provide a source of refuge and propagation for a number of desirable species of our feathered friends. (But take them down at *véraison!*)

Again, have fun with it. The vines will be dormant for five or six months a year, so the extra little pizzazz will certainly be an interesting and fun way to dress up your backyard vineyard.

CHAPTER TEN

BARREL FUN

W INERIES GET RID OF A NUMBER OF BARRELS EACH YEAR, when they have given up their oakiness. You can obtain these neutral barrels for next to nothing (at least relative to the hefty cost of new barrels), and a crafty home winemaker can do any of a number of things with them, besides just cutting them in half to make planters or fountains. This chapter gets you started with a few fun projects for accessorizing your winery with this perfectly fitting raw material.

Anatomy of a Wine Barrel

Let's begin with a brief lesson on barrel terminology and how to break down a barrel like a pro.

» *Bilge* — the widest circumference of a barrel, around the bunghole

» *Chime* — the angle cut at the ends of the staves

» *Croze* — the groove cut near the ends of a stave that keep the heads in place

» *Head* — the flat circular part that forms either end of the barrel

» *Hoop* — one of the metal circular straps that hold the barrel together

» *Stave* — one of the curved and beveled wood pieces that form the sides of the barrel

To break down your newly acquired barrel, remove the little nails that hold the hoops in place. Remove the hoops, and the barrel will just fall apart.

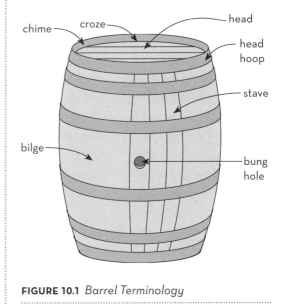

FIGURE 10.1 *Barrel Terminology*

THE "WINEDIRONDACK" CHAIR

NOW THAT YOUR WINERY IS BUILT AND OPERATING at peak efficiency, and your vineyard is a lively, interesting place to visit and a source of some great raw materials for your wines, it's time to sit back, relax, and enjoy the fruits of your efforts. But wait! In order to "sit back," of course, you're going to need a nice, comfortable, wine-themed chair or two.

MATERIALS

- One wine barrel (225 liter/59 gallon)
- 2" galvanized wood screws
- 1" galvanized wood screws
- Wood plugs (sized to match the counterbores you use for the screws)
- Finish materials (as desired; see step 9)

BUILD IT!

1. Break down the barrel and sort the staves.

Remove any tacks or nails that hold the hoops in place. Step back and the barrel will fall apart like a rose blooming in a time-lapse video. (But if it doesn't, give it a little help with a hammer.) Sort the staves by width. Set aside the six widest staves for the back of the chair. The next four widest staves will become the legs. The next widest stave will become the front leg brace.

Because we're working with pieces that are neither straight nor square, it is important to think about symmetry rather than "square and plumb," as you would with other projects. Also, since the width varies among staves and along the length of individual staves, some fitting and customizing will be required to achieve a nice piece of furniture.

2. Prepare the back and front legs.

On two of the staves you have determined to be the legs, measuring from the croze (the notch) toward the chime (the angle-cut end), make a mark at 3/4". Cut the tips off the staves at this mark. These staves will become the back legs.

On the remaining two leg staves, which will become the front legs, cut off one end square to remove the entire portion from the croze to the end. This end will be the bottom of the front legs. (Tip: Since the edges of staves aren't exactly straight, a square cut means that the cut end is perpendicular to the centerline of the stave, not necessarily to the side edges.) Measure up from this end 20½", and cut each leg square at this point; this end will be the top of the front legs. Measuring up from the bottom, mark each leg at 14½"; these marks denote the location of the top of the front leg brace. At these marks, measure the width of the wide (outer) sides of each leg. Add these widths together, plus another 24"; the sum should be around 30". This will be the length of the front leg brace.

3. Shape the front leg brace.

On the stave designated as the front leg brace, mark the centerpoint along its length (at the bilge). Divide the sum you calculated in the preceding step by 2, and measure and mark that length in either direction from this centerpoint. Cut the brace off square at this point. (Alternatively, you could make these cuts at a 7° angle toward the inside of the stave to match up with the angle of the leg.)

Measure the width and thickness of each rear leg at the end you trimmed off. Lay the brace on a bench, and on its top edge, mark the width and thickness of each rear leg, measuring in from each end.

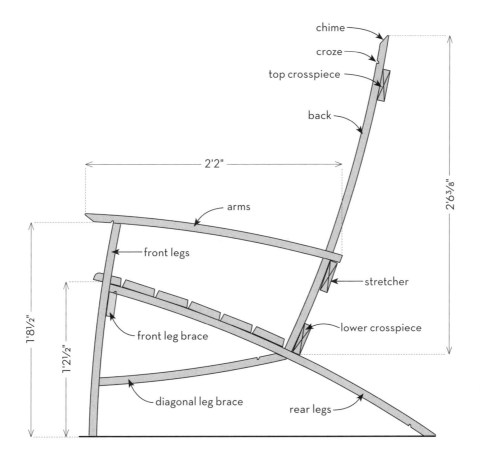

FIGURE 10.2 *"Winedirondack" Chair Side View*

Using these marks as guides, cut a notch into the top edge of the front brace at each end; when installed, the rear legs should fit down into the notches with their tops flush with the top of the brace.

Next, set another stave on edge on the brace, so that it forms a concave curve from the top of one notch to the top of the other. Trace the curve onto the brace and then cut the brace to match, to shape the seat of the chair (the seat dips in the center, as shown in figure 10.3).

4. Cut the rest of the main pieces.

Cut the six back staves at 32", and cut two arm staves at 26", leaving the chime and croze on all of these pieces. Rough-cut the three back crosspieces and six seat staves at about 30", cutting from the center portion of the staves.

Now is a good time to mill the cut pieces to the finish you desire. Since the insides of barrels are usually not planed or sanded, and the exteriors are typically sanded with a very coarse grit across the grain, achieving a smooth finish can require a fair amount of sanding. You might also want to round over the edges of the seat staves with a router, especially the front edge of what will be the leading seat piece.

5. Assemble the legs and braces.

Fasten the rear legs to the front leg brace by screwing down through the top of the legs into the notches of the brace, using 2" screws. Clamp the front legs to the front face of the brace so that the tops of the rear legs are 14½" up from the bottoms of the front legs. Drill counterbored pilot holes through the back of the brace. Screw through the back of the brace and into the front legs with 1" screws, taking care not to drive them through the front of the legs. Keep these screws a bit loose for now.

The back will be fastened to the rear legs 22" from the front legs. Mark this spot, and then measure the distance from the bottom of the rear legs at this spot to the approximate center of the front legs. Cut a diagonal leg brace to span this distance, as shown in figure 10.2 (approximately 27" long), and screw it into place using 2" countersunk screws driven through the front legs and the 1" screws to fasten the thinner tapered end to the rear legs.

6. Assemble the chair back.

To build the chair back assembly, mark the centerpoint on the inside of one of the back crosspieces; this will be the lower crosspiece. Add up the widths of the chair back pieces, measured across their bottom ends; the sum should be roughly 21". If the sum is less than 21", measure 10½" in each direction from the centerpoint of the lower crosspiece, and at these two points make a ¾" notch in the bottom edge of the lower crosspiece (similar to the notches in the top of the front leg brace). These notches will set down over the rear legs where the back assembly is installed. (If the sum of the widths of the back pieces is greater than 21", measure out half of that sum plus ¼" instead.)

Lay two of the back pieces together at the centerpoint of the lower crosspiece, with their cut ends on the crosspiece and the ends with the croze extending up. Push the cut ends tightly together, allowing the tops to splay out. Screw these back pieces to the lower crosspiece with one 1" wood screw driven through a countersunk pilot hole (don't tighten the screw all the way yet). Repeat with the other back pieces. When all the back pieces are installed, their cut ends should form a slight arc, with all the corners lining up and touching.

Adjust the tops of the back pieces so they are all equally spaced. To maintain this equal spacing, you may at this point want to cut a piece of the bilge hoop and clamp it to the tops of the back pieces. Then flip the back assembly over and put a couple of 1" screws through the lower crosspiece and into each of the back pieces.

The middle crosspiece, called the "stretcher," will receive the back ends of the arms. Measuring up from the bottom, mark the back face of the two outside back pieces at 9½". Measure the total width of the back assembly at this point. Add the width of the cut ends of the arms to this measurement, and cut the stretcher piece to this length (by marking the center point and from there measuring half this length in either direction). Cut a ¾" notch in each end of the top of the stretcher to receive the ends of the arms. Position the stretcher so its top edge is on the 9½" marks, and fasten the stretcher to each back piece with two 1" screws.

Finally, position the top crosspiece so its top edge is 28" above the bottoms of the outside back pieces. Trace along the outside edges of the outside back pieces to mark the end cuts for the crosspiece. Cut the top crosspiece to size, and fasten it to each back piece with two 1" screws.

7. Install the seat slats.

Lay the six seat pieces side by side on the floor or a bench, and measure across the bilge line (widest point) of these staves. This dimension should be about 18". If it's only about 16", add another stave to increase the seat depth.

Measuring from the front of the front legs, mark the top face of the rear legs at 18". At this spot, position the rear legs so the span between their outside edges matches the width of the unnotched bottom edge of the lower crosspiece. Clamp a temporary tie across the back legs to hold them at this spacing while you install the seat slats.

Set a seat slat in place at the 18" marks, and mark the outside edges of the rear legs on the slat. Add ½" to these marks so the seat will overhang the rear legs, and cut the slat to size. Install the slat with a couple of 1" countersunk screws driven up through the bottom of the rear legs. Repeat this process to install the next four (or five) seat slats.

Notch the front seat slat to fit between the front legs. You also might have to rip it down its width so it doesn't overhang the front leg brace by more than about 1". Install the front slat to complete the seat.

8. Install the back and arms.

Position the back assembly on top of the rear legs, up against the rear seat slat. Fasten the rear legs to the lower crosspiece with two 2" screws driven up through the legs.

If necessary, add a temporary support behind the back to hold it up while you install the arms. Set the arm pieces on the top of the front legs so the croze lines up with the front of the legs, and the chime forms the front of the arm. Predrill and countersink two 2" screws down through the arms and into the front legs. Adjust the angle of the back so the ends of the arms rest on the stretcher and are flush with the back of the stretcher. Clamp the arms firmly in place and test out the chair; adjust as necessary to find the most comfortable angle for the back. Drill and countersink two 2" screws through the arms and into the stretcher. If necessary, trim off any overhanging portion of the stretcher that extends past the arms.

9. Finish the chair.

Set the chair on a level, flat surface. Press the chair down so that all four legs sit squarely on the floor to eliminate any teetering, then tighten down all the partially driven screws.

To put the finishing touches on the chair, glue wood plugs in the counterbores to hide the exposed screw heads, and sand the plugs flush. Sand any cuts made after the preliminary milling and finishing. Apply your choice of exterior-grade stains and/or varnish or polyurethane to bring out the character of the old oak barrel.

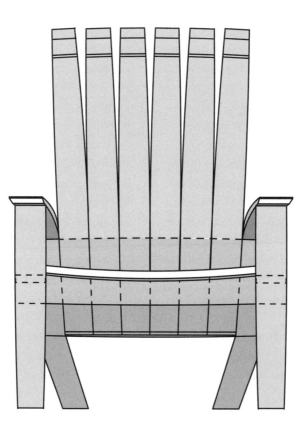

FIGURE 10.3 *"Winedirondack" Chair Front View*

DECORATIVE BARREL STAND

IF YOU HAVE A NEW, SMALL-FORMAT BARREL just filled with wine and want to show it off in style, here's a cool little stand to set it up off the floor and cradle that new baby.

MATERIALS

- Four equal-width barrel staves
- One 4-foot length 1×6 oak board
- 2" #8 wood screws
- Finish materials (as desired; see step 4)

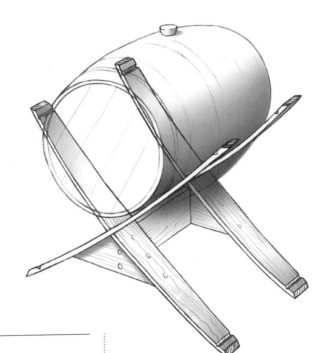

BUILD IT!

1. Form the *X* legs.

Stand your barrel on the floor or a bench. Position two of the staves to make an *X* over the second-to-last metal hoop of the barrel. The former inside of the staves should be against the barrel. Mark the edges of the two staves where they intersect.

At the marks you made, cut halfway through each stave, and use a chisel to remove the material between the cuts, forming a notch. Test-fit the two staves to make sure that they will interlock, and sand or chisel the notches as necessary. Using these two staves as templates, mark and cut the other two staves to match.

2. Create the triangle braces.

Set one pair of interlocked legs on the floor around the barrel. Lay the oak 1×6 across the supports, with its top edge at the very bottom of the point where the two staves intersect, and trace the outside edges of the legs onto the 1×6. Cut the board along these lines to create a triangular brace. Use the cut brace as a template to trace another piece just like it, and cut it from the board. Lay the two leg pairs down and glue and screw the braces across the staves, with three evenly spaced 2" wood screws driven through the braces and into the legs.

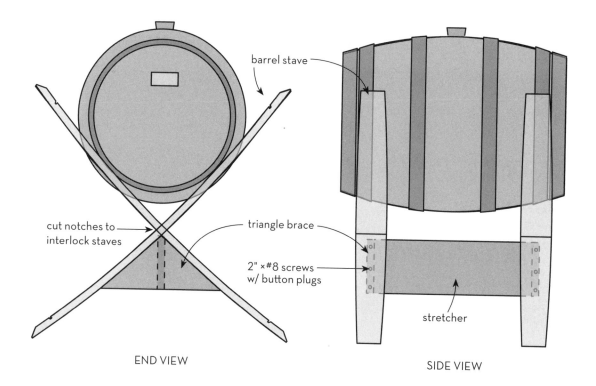

FIGURE 10.4 *Decorative Barrel Stand*

3. Add the stretcher.

Cut the remaining piece of 1×6 approximately the length from the second hoop to the opposite second hoop on your barrel; this will become the stretcher. Install this piece between the two triangle braces, screwing the parts together.

4. Finish.

Sand the piece to the desired smoothness and apply a finish of your choosing.

USE IT!

Set the barrel in the stand, fill it, and admire your baby and handiwork!

And what will you do with all those leftover oak scraps? Cut them up and toast them, as described on page 193.

WINERY STOOL

BARREL STAVES, HEADS, AND HOOPS CAN BE FITTED TOGETHER to make a great stool for sitting on as you perform all those lab tests or just contemplate your bubbling air locks over a glass of wine.

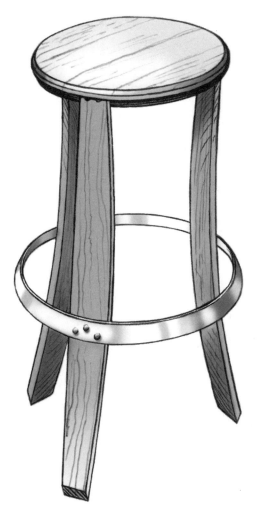

MATERIALS

- Three barrel staves
- One 12"-diameter disk cut from ¾" plywood
- Six 2" wood screws
- One barrel head hoop
- Nine ¾" round-head wood screws
- One barrel head
- Four 1¼" wood screws
- Finish materials (as desired)

BUILD IT!

Cut the three staves at 23" in length, or as desired. Screw the 12" plywood disk over the cut ends of the staves, using two 2" wood screws per stave, and spacing the staves equally around the disk. Make a mark 6" up from the bottom end of each stave, and loosely clamp the hoop to the three legs at these points to hold them in place (while still allowing for some minor movement). Set the stool on a level floor and check the plywood subseat for level in a number of directions. Adjust the legs as necessary until the subseat is level, then tighten the clamps securely to the hoop.

Predrill three holes through the hoop into each leg, and secure the hoop with a round-head wood screw driven through the hoop and into a leg at each hole.

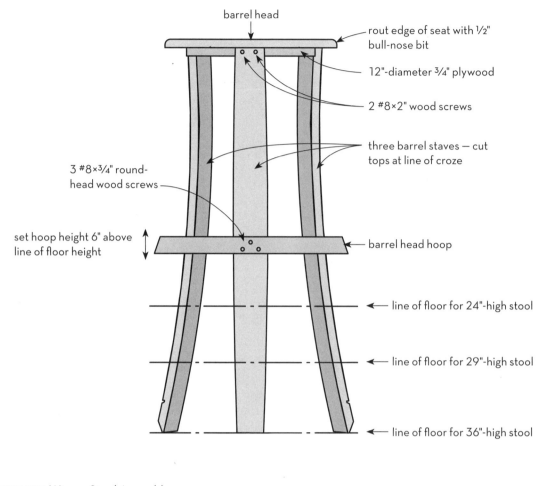

barrel head

rout edge of seat with ½" bull-nose bit

12"-diameter ¾" plywood

2 #8×2" wood screws

three barrel staves — cut tops at line of croze

3 #8×¾" round-head wood screws

set hoop height 6" above line of floor height

barrel head hoop

line of floor for 24"-high stool

line of floor for 29"-high stool

line of floor for 36"-high stool

FIGURE 10.5 *Winery Stool Assembly*

Cut the head of the barrel to the desired diameter, typically 14" to 16". If desired, rout a bull-nose or chamfer edge around this seat. Place the seat on the floor or a bench, with its finished top facedown, and flip the stool over onto it, centering the stool on the seat. Predrill and screw the subseat plywood to the seat, using 1¼" wood screws.

Sand and finish the stool as desired, or just leave unfinished to reflect your barrel's history.

USE IT!

I don't think a lot of explanation is needed here. Relax and enjoy!

MAKING YOUR OWN TOASTED OAK

HOME WINEMAKERS TYPICALLY MAKE WINE IN BATCHES that are much smaller than what would fill a standard wine barrel, so we tend to use small glass or stainless containers instead of barrels. This means that in order to get the benefits of oak in our wines, we have to put the oak in the wine rather than putting the wine in the oak. Oak is commercially available in a number of forms, including dust, chips, cubes, sticks, slats, and staves. I've been successfully making my own very high-quality toasted French oak from a neutral barrel a winemaker gave me several years ago, and now you can too!

When a barrel is declared "neutral" by a commercial winemaker, the wine has penetrated the barrel somewhere between ⅛" to ¼" and will no longer impart much of the oak characteristics, so they will sell them (or give them to a grateful winemaking friend like you) for a small fraction of their original price. This is a great opportunity for us home winemakers who would otherwise have to pay a lot for toasted oak chips and the like. For our purposes, there is a bounty of perfectly good oak left in one of these barrels. All we have to do is knock it down (see page 184), cut it up, toast the pieces to the desired level, and voilà! A lifetime supply of oak for a tiny price and little effort.

NOTE: *An important word of caution: Be sure to get your barrel from a reputable, trustworthy winery. Do not use barrels from hardware stores or garden supply stores, due to the potential presence of infectious critters and toxic chemicals used to treat the wood.*

MATERIALS

- Staves from an oak barrel

BUILD IT!

1. Cut the staves to size.

Rip your staves (freehand) down the middle on a table saw to create a straight edge to run along the saw fence for further rip cuts. Set the fence at ¼" and rip the half-width pieces into ¼"-thick strips. Then, cut each of the strips into three pieces crosswise. Cut as many of these as you'll need — I usually use three or four of these pieces in a 5- or 6-gallon carboy. Note: as a way to add tannins to their wines, winemakers often add oak dust to their fermenting wine. So don't throw away that sawdust under your saw when you're finished with the cutting!

2. Toast the stave pieces.

If you've ever successfully roasted marshmallows, you can easily toast these oak pieces. It is helpful to have some idea of what commercially available oak cubes or the insides of toasted barrels look like, so you have a good idea of the desired color for various toast levels. Start by firing up your barbecue, and when it's hot, lay the pieces on the grill. If you're using a charcoal grill, I suggest using oak instead of charcoal for the fire, just like the old-time coopers used. I typically get the temperature inside the barbecue up to about 425°F and control it by opening and closing the lid as necessary to keep the staves from catching fire. Like marshmallows, the stave pieces will start to smoke as they toast; when they start smoking, flip them over and repeat until they are at the perfect toast. A full grill of staves typically takes about 10 to 15 minutes to get to a medium toast.

Don't walk away from the barbecue while you're toasting your oak. You basically have tinder-dry kindling over a fire, so careful monitoring is required. Once the staves are done, they will look and smell fantastic.

USE IT!

Having been over a flame for 10 to 15 minutes, the staves are sterilized, so just let them cool down and they should be ready to insert into your containers. The staves are good for one batch of wine but can be transferred from vessel to vessel at rackings, with a rinse-off to remove sediment and any tartrate crystals.

✳ *You may be tempted to try toasting oak under a broiler in your oven, but putting kindling in your stove is not something I recommend, having learned the hard way.*

INDEX

Page references in *italics* indicate illustrations.

Other Storey Titles You Will Enjoy

Brew Ware: How to Find, Adapt & Build Homebrewing Equipment,
by Karl F. Lutzen & Mark Stevens.
Step-by-step instructions to build tools to make brewing safer and easier.
272 pages. Paper. ISBN 978-0-88266-926-7.

Cellaring Wine, by Jeff Cox.
A sourcebook to create a system for selecting wines to age, storing them properly, and
drinking them when they are just right.
272 pages. Paper. ISBN 978-1-58017-474-9.

Cider, by Annie Proulx and Lew Nichols.
Thorough coverage of every step of cider making, from choosing and planting the best
apple varieties to making sweet and hard ciders, sparkling cider blends, and cider-
based foods.
224 pages. Paper. ISBN 978-1-58017-520-3.

From Vines to Wines, by Jeff Cox.
A complete home winemaking education in one book — from planting vines to pulling
the cork.
256 pages. Paper. ISBN 978-1-58017-105-2.

The Home Winemaker's Companion, by Gene Spaziani and Ed Halloran.
A guide for all levels, starting with your first batch of kit wine to mastering advanced
techniques for making wine from fresh grapes.
272 pages. Paper. ISBN 978-1-58017-209-7.

The Vegetable Gardener's Book of Building Projects.
Simple-to-make projects include cold frames, compost bins, planters, rasied beds,
outdoor furniture, and more.
152 pages. Paper. ISBN 978-1-60342-526-1.

The Winemaker's Answer Book, by Alison Crowe.
A reassuring reference that offers proven solutions to every winemaking mishap,
written by *WineMaker* magazine's Wine Wizard.
384 pages. Flexibind. ISBN 978-1-58017-656-9.

These and other books from Storey Publishing are available
wherever quality books are sold or by calling 1-800-441-5700.
Visit us at *www.storey.com*.